JOURNAL · OF
M · O · R · A L
THEOLOGY

VOLUME 11, NUMBER 2
JULY 2022

TEACHING CATHOLIC SOCIAL THOUGHT

EDITED BY
JON KARA SHIELDS

JOURNAL · OF
M · O · R · A · L
THEOLOGY

Journal of Moral Theology is published semiannually, with regular issues in January and June. Our mission is to publish scholarly articles in the field of Catholic moral theology, as well as theological treatments of related topics in philosophy, economics, political philosophy, and psychology.

Articles published in the *Journal of Moral Theology* undergo at least two double blind peer reviews. To submit an article for the journal, please visit the "For Authors" page on our website at jmt.scholasticahq.com/for-authors.

Journal of Moral Theology is available full text in the *ATLA Religion Database with ATLASerials®* (RDB®), a product of the American Theological Library Association.
Email: atla@atla.com, www.atla.com.
ISSN 2166-2851 (print)
ISSN 2166-2118 (online)

Journal of Moral Theology is published by The Journal of Moral Theology, Inc.

Copyright© 2022 individual authors and The Journal of Moral Theology, Inc. All rights reserved.

Pickwick Publications, An Imprint of Wipf and Stock Publishers, 199 W. 8th Ave., Suite 3, Eugene, OR 97401
www.wipfandstock.com. ISBN: 978-1-6667-5409-4

JOURNAL OF MORAL THEOLOGY

EDITOR EMERITUS
Jason King, *Saint Vincent College*

EDITOR
M. Therese Lysaught, *Loyola University Chicago Stritch School of Medicine*

SENIOR EDITOR
William J. Collinge, *Mount St. Mary's University*

ASSOCIATE EDITORS
Jean-Pierre Fortin, *St. Michael's College, University of Toronto*
Alexandre A. Martins, *Marquette University*
Christopher McMahon, *Saint Vincent College*
Mary Doyle Roche, *College of the Holy Cross*

MANAGING EDITOR
Kathy Criasia, *Mount St. Mary's University*

BOOK REVIEW EDITORS
Mari Rapela Heidt, *Notre Dame of Maryland University*
Kate Ward, *Marquette University*

EDITORIAL BOARD
Christine Astorga, *University of Portland*
Jana M. Bennett, *University of Dayton*
Mara Brecht, *St. Norbert College*
Jim Caccamo, *St. Joseph's University*
Carolyn A. Chau, *King's University College at Western University, Ontario Canada*
Meghan Clark, *St. John's University*
David Cloutier, *The Catholic University of America*
Christopher Denny, *St. John's University*
Julia Fleming, *Creighton University*
Joseph Flipper, *Bellarmine College*
Nichole M. Flores, *University of Virginia*
Craig Ford, *St. Norbert College*
Matthew J. Gaudet, *Santa Clara University*
Natalia Imperatori-Lee, *Manhattan College*
Kelly Johnson, *University of Dayton*
Andrew Kim, *Marquette University*
Warren Kinghorn, *Duke University*
Leocadie Lushombo, *Santa Clara University*

Ramon Luzarraga, *St. Martin's University, Lacey, Washington*
William C. Mattison III, *University of Notre Dame*
Christina McRorie, *Creighton University*
Cory D. Mitchell, *Mercy Health Muskegon*
Suzanne Mulligan, *Liaison with
Catholic Theological Ethics in the World Church
Pontifical University, Maynooth, Co. Kildare, Ireland*
Sheryl Overmyer, *DePaul University*
Anna Perkins, *University of the West Indies*
Matthew Shadle, *Marymount University*
Joel Shuman, *Kings College*
Christopher P. Vogt, *St. John's University*
Paul Wadell, *St. Norbert College*

JOURNAL OF MORAL THEOLOGY
VOLUME 11, NUMBER 2
JULY 2022

CONTENTS

Resistances to *Amoris Laetitia*: A Critical Approach
   Antonio Autiero 1

The Border, Brexit, and the Church: US Roman Catholic and Church of England Bishops' Teaching on Migration 2015–2019
   Victor Carmona and Robert W. Heimburger 15

A Synodal Alternative for Ecclesial Conflict: Marshall Rosenberg's Nonviolent Communication
   Mary Lilian Akhere Ehidiamhen 45

Review Essay:
Theological Ethics of Life: A New Volume by the Pontifical Academy for Life
   Roberto Dell'Oro and M. Therese Lysaught 65

Teaching Catholic Social Thought Symposium:
Teaching Catholic Social Thought: A Symposium Introduction
   Jon Kara Shields 78

Catholic Social Living: Teaching Students to "Live Wisely, Think Deeply, and Love Generously"
   Bernard Brady 87

Resisting Gnostic Spiritualism in the Catholic Social Teaching Classroom
   Joyce A. Bautch 98

Teaching Catholic Social Thought Online in the Philippines: From a Challenge to an Opportunity
   Teofilo Giovan S. Pugeda III 105

Formative Figures for Catholic Social Witness
   Daniel Cosacchi 117

Solidarity, Praxis, and Discernment: Formation at the Catholic Worker
   Casey Mullaney 127

"Are We Theologians?": A Practical Theology Approach to Catholic Social Teaching with Women Religious in East Africa
  Sarah C. DeMarais 136

Pedagogical Reflections by East African Women Religious Alumnae of the Loyola Institute for Ministry
  Srs. Charity Bbalo, Lucy Kimaro, and Jane Frances Mulongo 146

Book Reviews
Peter Cajka, *Follow Your Conscience: The Catholic Church and the Spirit of the Sixties* .... Maria C. Morrow 166

Charles C. Camosy, *Losing Our Dignity: How Secularized Medicine Is Undermining Fundamental Human Equality*
  .... Ramon Luzarraga 168

Ki Joo Choi, *Disciplined by Race: Theological Ethics and the Problem of Asian American Identity* .... David Kwon 169

Daniel K. Finn, *Faithful Economics: 25 Short Insights*
  .... Chris Gooding 171

Najeeb T. Haddad, *Paul, Politics, and New Creation: Reconsidering Paul and Empire* .... Jeffrey L. Morrow 173

Conor M. Kelly, *The Fullness of Free Time: A Theological Account of Leisure and Recreation in the Moral Life* ...... G. D. Jones 174

Matthew Levering, *The Abuse of Conscience: A Century of Catholic Moral Theology* .... Kathryn Lilla Cox 176

Marc LiVecche, *The Good Kill: Just War and Moral Injury*
  .... Darren Cronshaw 178

Angela McKay Knobel, *Aquinas and the Infused Moral Virtues*
  .... Nicholas Ogle 180

Joel Oesch, *Crossing Wires: Making Sense of Technology, Transhumanism, and Christian Identity* .... Simeiqi He 182

Robert Chao Romero, *Brown Church: Five Centuries of Latina/o Social Justice, Theology, and Identity* .... Jens Mueller 183

Resistances to *Amoris Laetitia*: A Critical Approach

Antonio Autiero

WHEN POPE FRANCIS PROMULGATED THE apostolic exhortation *Amoris Laetitia* on March 19, 2016, a thrill of exultation went through many people, both within and outside the church. The work of the two Synods on the family and the hopes of renewal which had animated the synodal dynamic came together in the papal document. However, not only positive feelings and new certainties emerged. Doubts, questions, and cyphers for opposing positions found expression. These reactions of a different tenor mirrored the discussions during the two sessions of the Synod on the family.[1] Nothing would be as it had been; a turning point had been reached, and a new page in the ecclesial consciousness had been opened—a page not to be turned back.

The picture has not changed in the intervening years. *Amoris Laetitia* elicits both sincere adherence and cautious reactions, broadens the horizon both of theological culture and of pastoral praxis, but also continues to evoke resistances of varying intensity and significance.

---

* This paper was presented at the 44th Brazilian Congress of Moral Theology in September 2021. The conference was dedicated to Pope Francis's apostolic exhortation *Amoris Laetitia*, on the fifth anniversary of its publication. Due to the COVID-19 pandemic, this conference was held online.

[1] The letter of the four cardinals (Brandmüller, Burke, Caffarra, and Meisner) to Pope Francis, dated September 19, 2016, is well known. They set out four questions on points in *Amoris Laetitia* they saw as a source of confusion: "Letter from Four Cardinals to the Holy Father: The Full Text and the Dubia," *Tiscali News*, November 16, 2016, notizie.tiscali.it/esteri/articoli/divorziati-4-cardinali-contro-papa-lettera-testo/. For a thorough study of its contents, see Antonio Autiero and Stephan Goertz, "A proposito di dubbi, errori, e distinzioni. Una postfazione," in Stephan Goertz and Caroline Witting, eds., Italian ed. by Antonio Autiero, *Amoris Laetitia. Un punto di svolto per la teologia morale?* (San Paolo: Cisinello Balsamo, 2017), 257–69. For a broader picture of the critical positions, see Robert Dodaro, ed., *Permanere nella verità di Cristo: Matrimonio e comunione nella Chiesa cattolica* (Siena: Cantagalli, 2015), with contributions by five cardinals of the Catholic Church (Brandmüller, Müller, Caffara, De Paolis, and Burke) and four other scholars (Mankowski, Rist, Vasil', and the editor); Livio Melina, ed., *Conversione pastorale per la famiglia: sì, ma quale? Contributo del Pontificio Istituto Giovanni Paolo II al Sinodo* (Siena: Cantagalli, 2015).

To study this panorama of "yes's," "no's," and "perhaps's"—with particular attention to the resistances—is a task we take up here, after offering some preliminary remarks.

First, we restrict the field of our reflections. The resistances or negative reactions to *Amoris Laetitia* may be practical or theoretical. The first type refers to a scanty consideration of the papal document and the entire synodal process for the initiation and development of new pastoral praxis in the local churches. In a recent, well-documented article on the reception of *Amoris Laetitia*,[2] James Keenan, SJ, draws our attention to the vocabulary that the document employs, which can and ought to be the basis for a renewed theological-pastoral approach to marriage and the family. He also supplies highly relevant information about the situation in many dioceses. He investigates, by way of paradigm, dioceses in the USA, in which both the bishops and diocesan structures have displayed resistance toward *Amoris Laetitia*, mostly in terms of indifference and lack of attention. This type of practical resistance erodes *Amoris Laetitia* in its foundations and threatens to reduce it to irrelevance. While this kind of attitude ought to be investigated, in order better to grasp its implications and extent, it is not explicitly at the center of my reflections here. I wish rather to look at the "theoretical" resistance.

Second, examining the resistance to *Amoris Laetitia* can have various goals and be carried out with a variety of intentions and styles. One can be swept away by a *vis polemica* that seeks to obey an apologetic impetus from the papal document and regards the emerging resistances as easily recognizable, thanks to their level of incompetence or incompleteness. One could thus easily be led to distance oneself from them in the name of a perfunctory judgment that automatically sees what is new as best. Such an ideological position impairs our understanding of the meaning of the questions involved. I shall endeavor here to escape this ideological perspective and polemical intention to approach the question of the resistance to *Amoris Laetitia* in dialogue with both the visible and hidden levels on which the arguments play out. In this regard, tackling the question of the resistances with heuristic and hermeneutic sensitivity allows us to see a much more composite picture that does justice to the complex character of the questions. This circular critical attitude and its results depend on the capacity for self-criticism. Looking at the resistances also means looking at the potential contained in *Amoris Laetitia* that demands further development. This study can serve to display *Amoris Laetitia*'s vitality and demonstrate its generative energy for a new framework of theological thinking and ecclesial praxis.

---

[2] James Keenan, "Regarding *Amoris Laetitia*: Its Language, Its Reception, Some Challenges, and Agnosticism of Some of the Hierarchy," in *Perspectiva Teológica Belo Horizonte* 53, no. 1 (2021): 41–60.

DOCTRINE AND TRUTH

A recurrent sign can be noted at the beginning of every new pontificate, namely, the will to renew the life of the church. With John XXIII, it was a matter of "aggiornamento," of which Vatican II was only the dawn; with Paul VI, it was the will to confront in a spirit of dialogue the challenge of the modern world in its progress; with John Paul II, it involved beating the new path of the human being as "the path of the church." All these inspirations show the irrepressible newness of the Gospel, which demands landslides and reshuffles, renewal and new beginnings. While all this certainly generates new inspirations, awakens new adherences, and kindles enthusiasms that otherwise would have slumbered, it nevertheless brings us back to the question of the protection of the doctrines connected to the faith, and to the safekeeping of the truth, as something absolutely essential, if we are to be faithful to the Gospel.

It is against this background that we must understand the beginning of Francis's pontificate and his decision to convoke a Synod on the family, first in an extraordinary and then in an ordinary session, preceded by a wide movement of consultation of the community of believers with regard to their experience, with an eye to the times that lay ahead. This already disturbs anyone who has a functional and limited understanding of the value of life-experience and does not recognize the genetic value of the experience on which a person reflects as a significant factor in the elaboration of practical truths linked to the sphere of morality. The synodal event and the apostolic exhortation connected to it expressed a change of route in the genesis of moral consciousness in relation to marriage and the family. There is a will to listen to people's experience and accompany them on the way; there is a will to draw near the fragility of the family's existence and affective relationships, not primarily with a codex of truth to be defended or with norms to be imposed but with the awareness of the need to put questions to these practical truths in order to grasp their basis, comprehend their content, and verify their effectiveness. The turning point for the genesis of the ethical visions proposed in today's world is irritating and upsetting (I use the word in a rather negative sense) for those not acquainted with an inductive approach to practical knowledge and who consider this approach inadequate. The deductive habit, on which the tradition of Catholic moral theology is largely based, was put to a hard test by this conspicuous change of pace.

In the years prior to *Amoris Laetitia*, there was certainly no lack of elements calling into question the traditional solutions to moral problems, including especially problems linked to the sphere of sexuality and the family. The prevalence of the deductive approach, reinforced by its anchoring in an anthropological vision with a clear metaphysical foundation and only scant consideration of the scientific knowledge produced by the biological sciences,[3] had however maintained the scheme of reference basically unaltered. The decades of the moral magisterium of John Paul II are emblematic in this regard. They signal a consolidation of the main axis of a deductive moral theology and the primacy of truth. The most striking expression of this consolidation is the encyclical *Veritatis Splendor* (VS).[4] The Synod and *Amoris Laetitia*, thanks to their will to take an incarnate look at the real conditions under which conjugal relationships and the family exist, dislodged what had been regarded as already clarified and defined once and for all by the moral teaching of the preceding decades. This overturning brought forth a new language. Above all, the relationship between doctrine and praxis, truth and freedom was balanced differently.

The resistances to *Amoris Laetitia* on this front are considerable. Although expressed in different ways, these resistances all form branches of one and the same vine, namely, the value of doctrine for church life. The latter does not immediately involve dogmatic levels of doctrine, but in some respects, we are not very far from these. *Amoris Laetitia* does not deconstruct the system of doctrine about marriage and the family; indeed, it solidifies the meaning and value of this doctrine on the basis of reading Scripture and recalling the Gospel of love. *Amoris Laetitia* does not take the easy turn of a superficial shortcut of a generically pastoral kind, discounting truth and invoking merciful understanding of difficult situations. What *Amoris Laetitia* does is to allow the call of the Gospel to the authenticity of life and relationships to live in creative osmosis with the *conditio humana* that the same Gospel addresses. One who laments that *Amoris Laetitia* distorts doctrine in favor of *de facto* adaptations of a pastoral type bases his argument on a dichotomy between doctrine and praxis where the primacy of the former determines the subordination of the latter. Critics of *Amoris Laetitia* stylize the relationship between orthodoxy and orthopraxis in an emphatic manner, thus producing an altered dialectic that is not circular and dynamic but linear and descending from the second term to the first.

Something more is at stake—something that those who express their resistance to *Amoris Laetitia* fail to see with adequate clarity,

---

[3] For a good historical reconstruction of a sexual moral theology of this kind, see the recent book by Eberhard Schockenhoff, *Die Kunst zu lieben. Unterwegs zu einer neuen Sexualethik* (Freiburg: Herder, 2021).

[4] See Magnus Striet, "Johannes Paul II. und das Ende einer Lehramtsepoche," in Stephan Goertz and Magnus Striet, eds., *Johannes Paul II.—Vermächtnis und Hypothek eines Pontifikats* (Freiburg: Herder, 2020), 61–84. The reference to *Veritatis Splendor* occupies an important place in the *dubia* of the four cardinals, posing the problem of the continuity or discontinuity between *Veritatis Splendor* and *Amoris Laetitia*. On this, see Angel Pere-Lopez, "*Veritatis Splendor* and *Amoris Laetitia*: Neither Lamented nor Celebrated Discontinuity," *Nova et Vetera* 16, no. 4 (2018): 1183–214.

something that takes their argument back into a closed vision. They ignore the fact that the very idea of doctrine has been undergoing a striking evolution for some time now. In the mid-1980s, the American theologian George A. Lindbeck gave rise to a broad debate with his book *The Nature of Doctrine*.[5] He sees a threefold ideal-typical model for the understanding of the concept of doctrine. The first is the cognitive-propositional model widespread in the Western rationalist tradition. The focus is placed on propositional utterances that function as transporters of doctrinal truths. These are perceived and organized in a system of knowledge and belief to be received and transmitted, thus creating the nucleus of tradition binding for the present and the future. The static character of this model is obvious. It is moderated and overcome in the second model, which Lindbeck calls experiential-expressive, close to the liberal theology of the post-Enlightenment epoch and harmonizing well with the theological approaches of writers such as Paul Tillich, Karl Rahner, and Bernard Lonergan. A renewed attention to the subject and his or her history led to an attempt to bind together truths to be believed, doctrinal pronouncements, and expressions of an existence open to salvation. Even in this model, however, the links that can explain permanence and change in the doctrinal structure of religious knowledge remain to some extent unresolved. This is why Lindbeck proposes, in an attempt at a synthesis, a third model he calls cultural-linguistic and sees as "equipped to account more fully than can the first two types for both variable and invariable aspects of the religious traditions."[6] The horizon of understanding of this cultural-linguistic model of understanding the nature of doctrine draws on references to other branches of knowledge (anthropology, philosophy, and sociology)[7] and regards the system of what we define as culture and language as the paradigmatic structure for understanding the doctrine of religious traditions. A doctrine of this kind,

> Like a culture or a language ... is a communal phenomenon that shapes the subjectivities of the individuals rather than being primarily a manifestation of those subjectivities. It comprises a vocabulary of discursive and non-discursive symbols together with a distinctive logic or grammar in terms of which this vocabulary can be meaningfully deployed. Lastly, just as a language (or "language game," to use

---

[5] George Lindbeck, *The Nature of Doctrine: Religion and Theology in a Postliberal Age* (London: SPCK, 1984).
[6] Lindbeck, *The Nature of Doctrine*, 17.
[7] Sociology draws our attention to the intertwining of persistence and change as a necessary pendulum swing; we cannot think of one without the other (and vice versa). See Orlando Patterson, "The Mechanisms of Cultural Reproduction: Explaining the Puzzle of Persistence," in Laura Grindstaff, Miriam Ming-Cheng Lo, and John R. Hall, eds., *Handbook of Cultural Sociology,* 2nd ed. (London: Routledge, 2020), 122–32.

Wittgenstein's phrase) is correlated with a form of life, and just as a culture has both cognitive and behavioral dimensions, so it is also in the case of a religious tradition.[8]

The reference to Lindbeck, quite apart from the provocative value of his approach,[9] functions as a hermeneutical instrument to grasp the tensions that critics of *Amoris Laetitia* emphasize. They see the doctrine in a kind of immutability and change as a betrayal of the doctrine. This tension, however, is a definitive impoverishment of the doctrine itself. The systematic theologian Michael Seewald, whose thinking is close to that of Walter Kasper, places an accent precisely on the relationship between Gospel and dogma, in order to assert the dynamic nature of doctrinal propositions as historical expressions of the Gospel: "The dogma is therefore a means in view of an end, not an end in itself. As a means, it is absolutely necessary, but at the same time, it must ask whether, as times change, it is capable of corresponding to its own proper end, that is to say, to the exposition of the Gospel in propositional form."[10] Doctrinal formulations express the richness of the Gospel, but never contain it in an exhaustive manner. They constitute a second-order level of truths, what we might call (with Lindbeck) a grammar of the rules of expression, while first-order truths place the emphasis on the "performatory conformity of the self to God."[11]

Amoris Laetitia restores an equilibrium that recognizes the primacy of the Gospel vis-à-vis the expressions of doctrine and rules. The tradition had understood and preserved these, but they must continuously be rethought in light of the Gospel. In this sense, *Amoris Laetitia* does not downgrade doctrine, but gives it validity; it does not subject it to the "dictatorship of relativism" denounced but frees it from the temptation of stagnation. Doctrine is an open word generated by the Gospel for the human being of today, while at the same time being prompted continuously to give an account of its closeness to the Gospel in the time that lies ahead.

---

[8] Lindbeck, *The Nature of Doctrine*, 33.
[9] See D. F. Ford, "The Nature of Doctrine: Religion and Theology in a Postliberal Age by George A. Lindbeck," *Journal of Theological Studies* 37, no. 1 (1986): 277–82. For a careful presentation of the genesis and significance of Lindbeck's thought, see Hans-Joachim Tambour, *Theologischer Pragmatismus. Semiotische Überlegungen zu George A. Lindbecks kulturell-sprachlichem Ansatz* (Münster: LIT, 2002).
[10] Michael Seewald, *Il dogma in divenire. Equilibrio dinamico di continuità e discontinuità* (Brescia: Queriniana, 2002), 12.
[11] Lindbeck, *The Nature of Doctrine*, 66.

GREATNESS AND FRAGILITY OF LOVE

The tensions that have come to light in the reactions to *Amoris Laetitia*—including accusations of heresy[12]—regarding the mutability or immutability of doctrine are closely linked to a second theme. This theme mostly moves in the direction of the anthropological-moral sphere and encompasses a broad spectrum from basic affirmations to concrete implications. The church's attention to marriage and the family is not new. Its teaching in this area has been constant and incisive.[13] *Amoris Laetitia* takes a critical look at two signals accompanying the understanding of marriage and the family, consolidated in the tradition,[14] with the intention of renewing them.

The first factor we must mention is that the tradition has for a long time given priority to an institutional-juridical understanding of marriage and the family. In the interplay between civil and canon law, the foundational act and conjugal conduct have been regulated by the juridical framework. The form of marriage and its connection with the reality of the sacrament, as well as the duties of the spouses in relation to the ends of the conjugal bond, have long been seen from the juridical perspective, where the consideration of the subjects involved has not been particularly relevant. Up to the turning point reached with *Gaudium et Spes*, the primacy of the juridical over the anthropological certainly is the determining sign of the traditional vision that influenced the conjugal institution. The endeavors generated by the complex process of the definition and recognition of marriage as a sacrament—despite all the possible sources of meaning (from the nuptial symbolism in the Bible to the semantics of the theology of the sacraments and the elaboration of a conjugal spirituality)—have not succeeded in shifting attention to the subjects of the conjugal relationship. They have basically retained, without any change, the primacy of marriage as a juridical institution. One epiphenomenon of this picture is the way in which the woman, in markedly patriarchal cultures, enters into the conjugal dynamic and lives its various modulations. The predominant goal connected to the institution of the family, namely that of "multiplying" (we recall here the image of "the family as the basic cell of society"), has also conditioned the perception of the woman,

---

[12] See *Correctio filialis de haeresibus propagatis*, July 16, 2017, www.correctiofilialis.org/wp-content/uploads/2017/08/Correctio-filialis_English_1.pdf.

[13] This is well documented in Pontificio Consiglio per la Famiglia, ed.,, *Enchiridion della famiglia e della vita. Documenti magisteriali e pastorali dal Concilio di Firenze (1439) a Papa Francesco* (Rome: Libreria Vaticana, 2014); Gilfredo Marengo, *Generare nell'amore. La missione della famiglia cristiana nell'insegnamento ecclesiale dal Vaticano II a oggi* (Assisi: Cittadella, 2014).

[14] I have sketched this in Antonio Autiero, "Rapporti, legami, famiglie. Forme di vita in transizione," in Gianni Picenardi, ed., *Persona, psiche e società. Sulle tracce dell'uomo. Atti del XVI corso dei Simposi rosminiani 24–27 agosto 2015* (Stressa: Edizioni Rosminiane, 2016), 45–64.

wife, and mother, as natural *locus* of the generative process and of the educational task. This has also led to ascribing to the man the characteristics of guide and guardian of the family, which have not always been kept separate from deviations such as domination and the desire to possess the other. These functions and roles have taken precedence over the identities of persons and their relationships.

For those who see in *Amoris Laetitia* the attempt to bypass this order of things, resistance is not a secondary matter. Nor is it incomprehensible. Interpreted in its rarefied and abstract quality, the juridical-institutional order produced an ideal picture of marriage and the family. The loss of this picture is seen as the effect of a shift towards the universe of the persons and their relationships, itself perceived as a deviation for which *Amoris Laetitia* bears responsibility. One must ask whether such a resistance is not paying a disproportionate debt to the presumed guarantees of the stability of the institution of marriage promised by the law—with the result that one demeans the anthropological values of the life-project of persons and the concrete decisions they take in order to make this project possible. One must ask whether the resistances to *Amoris Laetitia* on this point are not in fact signals of the erosion of trust in the ability of persons to take on responsibility with regard to their own life-projects in a relationship. One who has recourse to the certainty of law, understanding this not only as positive law but above all as natural law, is reducing the reality of the love between persons to the law and exposing marriage and the family to the rhetoric of a stability that encounters not life itself, but merely the regulatory structures of legal systems. For *Amoris Laetitia*, what is involved rather is a journey of the incarnation of conjugal experience that, while not ignoring juridical instances, passes them through the crucible of the anthropological values expressed via the intentions, will, and responsibility of persons. The primacy of love, strongly confirmed in *Amoris Laetitia*, maintains the observance of the juridical system but accompanies this with the interior spring of the life choices taken by persons able to open themselves to the *de facto* and challenging horizon of love.

A second factor is the strong accent on the natural-law dimension of the traditional way of looking at marriage. This factor led to an ever-stronger emphasis, of an ontological type, on the being of the person, with the result that marriage and the family were seen in an idealized manner. A moral theology of marriage constructed around this kind of ontological backbone is not able to draw near the existential conditions and lived histories of individuals and their relationships. *Amoris Laetitia* takes a very different line. Its structure manifests all the richness of the ideals inspired by the Creator's plan and the salvific grace of the sacrament, while at the same time taking account of the life stories in which the conjugal relationships unfold. Reading people's lives and taking seriously the concrete experiences of what happens in marriage turns out to be a powerful source of understanding of the family and the affective relationships that take place in it. *Amoris Laetitia* looks at the *de facto* condition of family life with an eye that is disenchanted but not resigned, while paying critical attention to those factors that have acquired their own specific weight in contemporary culture, such as gender sensitivity and the dynamic understanding of the construction of identities and roles.[15] This promotes an awareness of the centrality of persons rather than institutions and the concreteness of experience rather than the abstraction of an idealized frame of reference. *Amoris Laetitia* makes a good attempt at understanding marriage and the family in a more calibrated equilibrium between nature and culture, ontology and history, and ideals and the lived life.

The resistances to *Amoris Laetitia* are also due to this difficult metabolization of the change of pace and paradigm. The assumption of the category of fragility, so central to *Amoris Laetitia*, irritates those who prefer to deduce from the idea of human nature an idealized and abstract picture of marriage and the family and consider the failures that may occur as either a hostile fate to be resisted or a moral disorder to repent for. The vocabulary of mercy, gesture of welcome, care for the fragility of love—is perceived by those who resist the novelty of *Amoris Laetitia* as a loss of the ontological consistency of the conjugal bond and a misplacement of the moral sense in favor of a comprehension making unjustifiable concessions.

CONSCIENCE AND MORAL ACTS

From the two factors indicated above follow at least two consequences. Their function is to make explicit the reference to topics that always emerge when resistance to *Amoris Laetitia* finds expression. The first consequence is recurrent reference to *Veritatis Splendor* in the critical reflection on *Amoris Laetitia*, especially with a view to reinforcing a correct idea of moral conscience that—it is alleged—*Amoris Laetitia* has blatantly altered. In particular, there is a repeated refusal to accept what *Veritatis Splendor* no. 54 calls "a 'creative' understanding of the moral conscience," seen as a contrast to the correct teaching of the tradition. To distance oneself from creative conscience would mean affirming that conscience has the character of the executive organ of morality, whose substance is decided on the basis of the

---

[15] The very brief but rather severe verdict of *Amoris Laetitia* on "the various forms of an ideology of gender" (56) is well known. This has led to criticisms of *Amoris Laetitia* from other quarters, such as the IG Feministische Theologinnen, "Kein Grund zur Freude: Das päpstliche Schreiben 'Amoris Laetitia,'" April 15, 2016, feministische-theologinnen.ch/wp-content/uploads/2016/04/IG_Stellungnahme_AmorisLaetitia.pdf. However, this verdict must be understood in the context of the approach of *Amoris Laetitia* to the condition of the person as a sexed being. On the positive values and critical aspects of this approach, see Lisa Sowle Cahill, "*Amoris Laetitia*: A New Approach to Sex and Gender Ethics," *Asian Horizons* 12, no. 2 (2018): 296–314.

nature of the acts themselves. The knot is resolved in an antithesis positing as alternatives the objective level of morality established on the basis of the acts carried out and the subjective level affirming the primacy of the person and his or her moral substance, expressed in intentionality and responsibility for the choice of the right actions in relation to the concrete situation in which the subject is called to act.

Conscience and acts are two corresponding sides of one and the same dynamic of moral action: the quality of the acting person as subject and the concrete result of the actions the subject carries out. The objective tenor of moral judgment, which proceeds via the deontological line of the foundation of norms, makes the actions independent of the world of the subject, definitively isolates these actions and crystallizes them in a closed consideration of their very nature, finalities, and modalities. The sign of their moral value would be inscribed upon such actions *per se,* and the subject would be obliged to comply with this value via the applicative *locus* that is his or her conscience. *Veritatis Splendor* considers this path of foundation of moral norms to be the only path, in fidelity to the church's tradition, that can guarantee the moral order.[16]

Amoris Laetitia's position on conscience and moral acts surprises its critics, who immediately denounce its breach with the tradition—by which they explicitly mean *Veritatis Splendor*.[17] Such critics find little relevance in the hermeneutical horizon in which *Amoris Laetitia* is located, which makes conscience the gravitational center of the subject's encounter with God, as no. 16 of *Gaudium et Spes* reminds us. This is where the moral dimension is verified: the subject is not the judge of morality, in the (scarcely critical) sense of a badly understood autonomy; moral authority rather is constituted in the dialogical relationship with God who summons him or her to the good. From this fontal point of the moral character of the subject flow the actions that he or she carries out, actions having a moral dimension because they are the expression of the moral substance of the subject and, in a definitive manner, of his or her relationship to God.[18]

---

[16] In this respect, *Veritatis Splendor* takes up and enshrines a line of thinking in moral theology presented by authors such as John Finnis and Germain Grisez in the preceding decades. Their positions are well analyzed by Wolfgang Mommsen, *Christliche Ethik und Teleologie. Eine Untersuchung der ethischen Normierungstheorien von Germain Grisez, John Finnis und Alan Donagan* (Altenberge: Oros, 1993).

[17] See Nadia Delicata, "*Amoris Laetitia* and *Veritatis Splendor* on the Object of the Act," *Melita Theologica* 67 (2017): 237–65.

[18] See Delicata, "*Amoris Laetitia* and *Veritatis Splendor*," 241–42: "Questions surrounding the meaning of the object of the act are not merely a matter of philosophical preference, but ultimately, as *Amoris Laetitia* shows, of evangelical truth and therefore of the authenticity of the church herself as witnessed in her pastoral practice. But this attestation is true only insofar as we also understand what, in our contemporary cultural context, is at stake for the evangelizing mission of the church."

The non-atomization (and autonomization) of moral acts and the refusal to disconnect them from the source of the subject who carries them out provide a new and different perspective on the question of intrinsically evil actions. This last node has been taken up with vehemence in order to intensify the hostility toward *Amoris Laetitia*, which allegedly employed approaches neither univocal nor resolutive to the question of the *intrinsice malum*. Critics of *Amoris Laetitia* (and of no. 304 in particular) have made no effort to understand the horizon of meaning of the apostolic exhortation, nor to contextualize the teaching of *Veritatis Splendor* (no. 79) against the background of the elaboration of this set of problems, which has seen considerable developments in recent years, especially in the attempt to bring together the world of the subject and weight of his or her actions.[19]

FROM JUDGING TO CARING

The second consequence is linked to the nature and importance of the experience of the couple. In more restrictive terms, one could speak here of the weight of circumstances in the definition of the moral quality of the state of marriage. One who looks at the circumstances from the perspective of a moral theology subordinate to the primacy of the juridical dimension considers them as a sort of accidental periphery, coordinates with a marginal character forming a framework for the moral action that do not touch its substance. However, the history of moral theology from the Middle Ages onwards clearly attests the consolidation of a much broader awareness.[20] Circumstances are a substantial factor that speaks the language of the context because they express the historical condition of the subject and the incarnate character of his or her moral choices. From this perspective, experience takes on a value that far exceeds strict conformity to an already defined juridical-ethical order, a value that demands to be recognized in the uniqueness characterizing life stories and their moral tensions.

The resistances to *Amoris Laetitia* with regard to "irregular situations" belong to the dynamics of this intersection between theory and praxis. The starting point is the emphatic way of defining these concrete expressions of life (the term "situations" has negative connotations) as inconsistent with the given rule ("irregular," in fact). They then insist on a verdict of conformity, whose inexistence leaves no room for more flexible considerations. This reflects the rigid canon of an irremediably negative evaluation. In the decisive paragraph no.

---

[19] See Nenad Polgar and Joseph A. Selling, eds., *The Concept of Intrinsic Evil and Catholic Theological Ethics* (London: Lexington, 2019), with interesting historical reconstructions and semantic developments of this category which, unfortunately, *Veritatis Splendor* presents in a static manner.

[20] The voluminous study by Johannes Gründel, *Die Lehre von den Umständen der menschlichen Handlung im Mittelalter* (Münster: Aschendorff, 1963) is a classic work on this matter.

305, *Amoris Laetitia* tackles this complex nexus in a different way. It attributes a different weight to circumstances in recognition of the value of people's life stories.[21] This also shows the importance—by no means rhetorical or merely cosmetic—of an attitude that cares for the life stories of persons and their relationships.

The transition from the tribunal of judgment to the will to exercise care draws attention to the substantial image of accompaniment typical of *Amoris Laetitia* unfortunately ignored or denigrated by those who barricade themselves in utter rigidity behind positions of resistance. The implications on the value level of conjugal conditions that take shape after a first breakdown have a significance and substance so broad that they can be recognized as "signs of love which in some way reflect God's own love" (*Amoris Laetitia*, no. 294) without depriving them of the intimacy and closeness that find expression in the sphere of sexuality. If *Amoris Laetitia* thus overcomes the rigid way of looking at things in no. 84 of *Familiaris Consortio* (living together like brother and sister!), this is done precisely on the basis of a paradigmatic structure with a more balanced and constructive anthropology. The failure to recognize this ultimately means neglecting the historical dimension of persons and their life choices; it means absolutizing the objective truth of moral acts while ignoring the "*veritas vitae*"[22] in which conscience and history, subject and acts encounter and balance each other. In this truth of or for life, the pastoral dimension of moral theology, as intended and demanded by *Amoris Laetitia*, finds its definitive expression.[23]

CONCLUSION

Our critical examination of the resistances to *Amoris Laetitia* has shown that, apart from the substance of the individual questions that come to light in the criticism of the apostolic exhortation, the understanding of the typological approach and hermeneutical structure to which they refer is highly relevant. With this as our starting point, we can derive points of reflection that help us keep our attention on the

---

[21] The recognition of levels of authenticity in the quality of relationships built up after the breakdown of an earlier matrimonial bond paves the way to forms of welcoming and accompanying that can also involve access to the sacraments, as *Amoris Laetitia* n. 351 suggests.

[22] This expression goes back to Pope Adrian VI. See Rudolf Hein, "Gewissen im Spannungsfeld von Autonomie und Wahrheit. Denkanstöße durch das Konzept der veritas vitae bei Adrian von Utrecht," *Studia Moralia* 55, no. 2 (2017): 243–69.

[23] On the meaning and substance of this pastoral dimension, see Ronaldo Zaccharias, "Amoritas laetitia: um'sim radical à pastoralidade da teologia moral," *Perspectiva Teológica Belo Horizonte* 53, no. 1 (2021): 17–39. On the relationship between pastoral and moral theology, see Antonio Autiero, "Amoris laetitia tra teologia pastorale e teologia morale," in Antonio Autiero, ed., *Per una nuova cultura pastorale. Il contributo di* Amoris Laetitia (Milan: San Paolo, 2019), 23–39.

topic of the family and affective relationships, to comprehend the development of the models, and accommodate their fragilities.

Faithfulness to the tradition is not simply the gesture of repeating its provenance. Faithfulness to the tradition also involves a creative approach to a vision always open to new perspectives. This generates a sensitivity that, in epistemological terms, retrieves the historical-cultural context of the way in which doctrines were and continue to be formed. The investigation of this historical-cultural context liberates it from rigid visions and entrusts it to the creativity that provides inspiration for the future.[24]

Forgetfulness of this doctrinal dynamic accentuates the tendency of doctrines to stagnate. Even more seriously, it relies on a "locking device" that ultimately reduces the space of vitality and action of the Spirit.[25] Those who defend the truth of doctrines very frequently do so through an exclusive and binding reference to teachings of the magisterium, understood in a strict sense. What Karl Rahner called *Lehrauthorität der Gläubigen*, "the teaching authority of the faithful," counts for little in their eyes.[26] In this dismissal, they neglect the *sensus fidelium* and thus its indispensable importance for practical truths and moral theology.[27]

The resistances to *Amoris Laetitia* are definitely the product of disturbing deficits in the realms of anthropology, theology, and ecclesiology. When we look carefully at these deficits, it helps not only to grasp better the significance of these resistances but also to take up a (self-)critical spirit and see the important points. *Amoris Laetitia* must be received not as a self-contained document but as one element in a process open to marriage and the family as realities in movement. And this takes place against the constructive background of a passion for

---

[24] Pope Francis spoke some very incisive words on this subject at the General Audience of June 23, 2021, press.vatican.va/content/salastampa/it/bollettino/ pubblico/2021/06/23/0404/00886.html, commenting on the Letter to the Galatians: "There is no lack even today, in fact, of preachers ... who take their places not primarily in order to announce the Gospel of the God who loves human beings in Jesus, crucified and risen, but in order to repeat insistently, as true and genuine 'guardians of the truth'—that is what they call themselves—what is the best way to be Christians. And they declare in strong words that this is what true Christianity is ... often identified with particular forms of the past. ... Even today ... there is the temptation to shut oneself up in some certainties acquired in past traditions .... One of the traces of this way of proceeding is rigidity. ... What the apostle points to is the liberating and ever new path of Jesus crucified and risen; it is the path of the proclamation that is realized through humility and fraternity ... And this gentle and obedient path goes ahead in the certainty that the Holy Spirit operates in every epoch of the Church."

[25] I refer here to the reflections by Andrea Grillo, *Da museo a giardino. La tradizione della Chiesa oltre il "dispositivo di blocco"* (Assisi: Cittadella, 2019).

[26] Karl Rahner, "Zum Verhältnis von Theologie und Volksreligion," in *Schriften zur Theologie*, vol. 16 (Einsiedeln: Benziger, 1984), 185–95.

[27] See Charles Curran and Lisa Fullam, eds., *The Sensus Fidelium and Moral Theology* (New York: Paulist, 2017).

human beings and their relational capacities in service to a church faithful to the newness of the Gospel. ■

Antonio Autiero (born in Naples, Italy, 1948) received his doctoral degree in moral theology at the Accademia Alfonsiana in Rome and in philosophy at the University of Naples. In 1991, he became professor of moral theology at the University of Münster (Germany), where he taught until his retirement in 2013. Antonio Autiero has authored or edited books and articles on fundamental moral theology and applied ethics. He is a member of the Stem Cell Research governmental commission in Berlin and the Planning Committee of Catholic Theological Ethics in the World Church (CTEWC).

The Border, Brexit, and the Church: US Roman Catholic and Church of England Bishops' Teaching on Migration, 2015–2019

Victor Carmona and Robert W. Heimburger

IN EARLY 2022, UKRAINIAN REFUGEES BEGAN making their way to the borders of the United Kingdom and the United States. As they seek refuge from war, on arrival they and those providing them with assistance face the effects of migration policies that reflect the influence of right-wing populism. The June 2016 "Leave" vote for Brexit and the November 2016 election of Donald Trump left their marks, both made possible by anti-immigration sentiment among voters. Additionally, in the US, political parties are preparing for midterm elections in November 2022. Soon after, parties in both countries will turn their attention to their 2024 national electoral contests: general elections in May for the UK and presidential elections in November for the US. Migration will likely once again be front and center. How, then, will Church of England bishops and Roman Catholic bishops in the US respond? How will their churches' teaching address the influence of right-wing populism in the migration debate?

The need to discern what challenges the coming years might bring to Christians in both churches and countries (including immigrants and non-immigrants) is evident, and more so for those providing humanitarian assistance and working towards immigration reform. This article analyzes and assesses the teaching of US Roman Catholic and Church of England bishops regarding refugees and asylum seekers, the undocumented, and other migrants from 2015 to 2019—in the aftermath of Donald Trump's presidential campaign with its focus on the US-Mexico border and the Brexit referendum. That four-year span is sufficient to offer an initial response to the questions we raised above.

Our analysis carries forward an ongoing discussion on each side of the Atlantic about how Christians, immigrants and non-immigrants alike, should respond to immigration law and policy in our time. In the US, Gregory L. Cuéllar furthers a "borderland hermeneutic" to resacralize the borderlands and its people in the wake of immigration and detention policies aimed at controlling and dehumanizing persons with black and brown bodies.¹ Turning our attention to the power of a rhetoric shaped by xenophobia and racism, Matthew A. Shadle interrogates the legal/illegal frame that informs the Trump Administration's policies and demonstrates that its purpose is to distinguish "good" immigrants who assert existing racial, social, and gender hierarchies from "bad" ones who do not.² Statements by the Catholic church in the US, he concludes, have failed to recognize that this rhetorical strategy has little to do with affirming the rule of law. Additionally, Miguel De La Torre offers a collection of essays that speaks to the many concerns the Trump Administration's policies raised among Christians, including John Fife, who highlights the broad coalition of immigrant allies that organized resistance in response.³ In the UK, Anthony Reddie provides a theological critique of the understandings of what it means to be "Great Britain" that led to Brexit in *Theologising Brexit*.⁴ Susanna Snyder, Pia Joliffe, Samuel Burke, OP, Ben Ryan, Adrian Pabst, and Anna Rowlands respond to post-Brexit British immigration policies with Christian ethics from varying perspectives within the Anglican and Roman Catholic church traditions in *Fortress Britain*?⁵ Another edited volume features Anglican voices on *The Future of Brexit Britain*, with attention to questions of nationalism, race, and migration from Sam Norton, R. David Muir, Doug Gay, and Anthony Reddie.⁶ In *What Does God Think About Brexit?*

---

*Victor Carmona thanks Daniel Flores, Roman Catholic bishop of Brownsville, Texas, for wisdom and support during early research that led to this article, and the Hope Border Institute, for their insights and analysis on the effects of migration policy in the El Paso-Ciudad Juarez border region. Robert Heimburger thanks Sarah Etheridge at the Lambeth Palace Library; Josh Harris at Refugee, Asylum, and Migration Policy (RAMP); and Ben Ryan and Rhiannon Monk-Winstanley at the Mission and Public Affairs Division of the Church of England for helping him find sources and understand the landscape of Church of England political involvement. Both co-authors thank Anne Blankenship, Malcolm Brown, M. Daniel Carroll R., Katie Cross, Aaron Gross, Susanna Snyder, and Casey Strine for reading drafts, and those at the American Academy of Religion who responded to the earliest draft. We are also grateful for comments from anonymous reviewers. Mistakes and oversights are ours.

¹ Gregory L. Cuéllar, *Resacralizing the Other at the US-Mexico Border: A Borderland Hermeneutic* (New York: Routledge, 2020), chapters 1 and 4.

² Matthew Allen Shadle, "Interrogating the Legal/Illegal Frame: Trump Administration Immigration Policy and the Christian Response," *Journal of Ecumenical Studies* 55, no. 1 (2020): 91–103.

³ John Fife, "Enough of Us Came Together to Carry All of Us Forward," in *Faith and Reckoning after Trump*, ed. Miguel A. De La Torre (Maryknoll, NY: Orbis Books, 2021), 247–55.

⁴ Anthony G. Reddie, *Theologising Brexit: A Liberationist and Postcolonial Critique* (London: Routledge, 2019).

⁵ Ben Ryan, ed., *Fortress Britain? Ethical Approaches to Immigration Policy for a Post-Brexit Britain* (London: Jessica Kingsley, 2018).

⁶ Jonathan Chaplin and Andrew Bradstock, eds., *The Future of Brexit Britain: Anglican Reflections on National Identity and European Solidarity* (London: SPCK, 2020).

David Nixon assesses populism and the possibility for reconciliation.[7] Justin Welby, Archbishop of Canterbury, also wrote in response to Brexit in a book we deal with in this article.[8] Our article furthers and bridges both discussions by focusing on teaching on migration by the bishops who oversee the Church of England and the Roman Catholic Church in the US and assessing its ability to address the populism that underlies our societies' and governments' response to forced migrations at the US-Mexico border and Brexit.

Our argument proceeds in three sections. In the first, we offer brief accounts of the Trump presidential campaign and the Brexit referendum and then turn to the work of sociologists and political scientists to understand how right-wing populism shaped both outcomes. This research highlights concerns with our political systems' ability to acknowledge the human dignity of immigrants and refugees and the solidarity necessary to sustain our democracies. In the second section, we highlight cases where the Catholic and Anglican churches engaged in public communication to confront populist immigration policies, informed by Scripture to different degrees, using a wealth of genres in various settings. Books, pastoral letters, joint statements, and press releases have been used to communicate in public settings from migrant shelters at the US-Mexico border to the House of Lords in the UK Parliament. In the third and final section, we assess our churches' responses to a claim that stems from right-wing populism, the claim that migrants represent an inherent threat in a world where scarcity reigns. We conclude that our churches' responses must more clearly attend to the dual function of their teaching: not only shaping just immigration policies, but also forming communities of faith that acknowledge the human dignity of migrants and act accordingly. While the discernment of legal and policy goals is desirable, it is only part of the picture. Anglican Bishop Paul Butler and Catholic Bishop Mark Seitz embody a more integral approach that pursues those goals while first inhabiting the world of Scripture alongside migrants who "read" Scripture with their lives. By following their example, our churches may offer a more faithful response to the influence of right-wing populism on both sides of the Atlantic.

MIGRATION AND OUR SOCIAL LOCATIONS

Our social locations influence our critical analysis of our churches' teaching, part of an ongoing dialogue on the ability of moral theology to speak to and from the complex multi-layered realities of immigrant

---

[7] David Nixon, *What Does God Think about Brexit? A Theological Reflection*, Palgrave Pivot (Cham: Palgrave Macmillan, 2019).
[8] Justin Welby, *Reimagining Britain: Foundations for Hope* (London: Bloomsbury Continuum, 2018).

and minority communities, their churches, and their cross-border communities. Both of us are lay theologians with interests in Christian ethics and migration shaped by our experiences with the US and the UK immigration systems and ministry within two distinct Christian traditions.

I, Victor Carmona, was born in California and grew up in Baja California, Mexico. My experience with the US immigration system came early in life. As a child who crossed the border at least weekly, I learned of the privilege that US citizenship entails. While in graduate school in Indiana, I married a Mexican citizen. At our interview for her permanent residency visa, the officer informed us that she would be deported. Apparently, we had submitted the wrong paperwork in an incorrect sequence. We lived under the threat of deportation for nearly a year. This experience, normal for mixed-status families, cut deep.[9] Leaving home each morning was hard, because we did not know if we would be together by the end of the day. Although I had ministered with migrants and researched migration for years when I worked with the Mexican Conference of Catholic Bishops and the Missionary Oblates of Mary Immaculate, I had not experienced firsthand the fear and pain they and their loved ones live through every day of their lives. The process was confusing, expensive, and highly uncertain. While we were ultimately able to stay together, we had never *known* such powerlessness nor thirst for hope.

I, Robert Heimburger, am originally from Alabama and have lived in the UK for more than a decade. I emigrated to pursue studies and held student visas until I met and married a British citizen. While this path makes me a privileged sort of migrant, I experienced difficulties in the migration process. In a year when I finished my doctorate and made the transition to work, my family and I barely met the financial standard to renew my visa. Had we not met that standard, I would have had to leave my wife and our son to return to the United States alone. After navigating the fees, paperwork, and ceremonies of the naturalization process, I eventually became a dual US-UK citizen. During this period, I also moved churches, from Presbyterian and Episcopal in the United States and Canada to the Church of England and finally the Scottish Episcopal Church. With an Anglican chaplaincy, I ministered to students who were mostly from outside Britain, and I have served as lay preacher in parishes in England and Scotland.

---

[9] Mixed-status families include citizens and non-citizens (whether they be permanent residents and/or undocumented immigrants). We had joined the nearly two million married couples whose marriages suffer under the strain of a broken US immigration system. See "Profile of the Unauthorized Population: United States" (Washington, DC: Migration Policy Institute, 2019), www.migrationpolicy.org/data/unauthorized-immigrant-population/state/US.

THE US-MEXICO BORDER, BREXIT, POPULISM, AND MIGRATION

Brief accounts of the Trump presidential campaign and Brexit referendum against the backdrop of the Syrian exodus are necessary to contextualize the content and influence of Roman Catholic and Anglican teaching on migration amid rising populism in the US and UK.

The 2016 Trump Campaign and Migrants

Donald Trump announced his successful campaign for the presidency on June 16, 2015. He framed his speech that day, and his presidential run, using a clear narrative: America is failing, and he will make it great again. "The US has become a dumping ground for everybody else's problems," Trump said. Immigrants from Mexico, the rest of Latin America, and the Middle East, were exhibit number one. He continued: "When Mexico sends its people, they're not sending their best. They're not sending you …. They're sending people that have lots of problems, and they're bringing those problems with us. They're bringing drugs. They're bringing crime. They're rapists. And some, I assume, are good people."[10] While striking, Trump's simplistic use of moral categories to explain the complexities of migration across the US-Mexico border or its relationship to other facets of American life proved to be politically effective.

The moral character of immigrants (and by extension of their US-born descendants) alongside the broader question of their impact on the country was front and center in Trump's narrative. While members of the Republican establishment hoped he and other candidates would eventually tone down the rhetoric against immigrants, refugees, and minority communities, it only hardened once he took office.[11] For example, then-candidate Trump reacted to the San Bernardino mass shootings of December 2, 2015, by calling for an all-out ban on Muslim immigrants. The shooting, perpetrated by a Pakistani permanent resident and a US citizen of Pakistani descent, nicely fit his narrative. The US is at war, he (and other candidates) claimed, and the government must react accordingly.[12] Barely a week after his inauguration on January 20, 2017, President Trump signed an executive order titled

---

[10] Washington Post Staff, "Full Text: Donald Trump Announces a Presidential Bid," *Washington Post*, June 16, 2015, www.washingtonpost.com/news/post-politics/wp/2015/06/16/full-text-donald-trump-announces-a-presidential-bid/.

[11] That sense was grounded on the results of the 2012 presidential election post-mortem report by the Republican National Committee. One of the recommendations states: "When it comes to social issues, the Party must in fact and deed be inclusive and welcoming. If we are not, we will limit our ability to attract young people and others, including many women, who agree with us on some but not all issues," "Growth & Opportunity Project" (Washington, DC: Republican National Committee, 2013), 8.

[12] James Oliphant and John Whitesides, "For Republican Presidential Candidates, War Rolls Easily off the Tongue," *Reuters*, December 9, 2015, www.reuters.com/article/us-usa-election-war-idUSKBN0TS16420151209.

"Protecting the Nation from Foreign Terrorist Entry into the United States."[13] The order, which critics called a Muslim ban, suspended refugee admissions from Syria and other mainly Muslim countries for 120 days. With a five to four vote, the Supreme Court upheld a third version of the ban (which by then the Trump Administration had reframed as a travel ban) on June 26, 2018.[14]

In order to address the negative effect that, according to Trump, Mexican and other Latin American immigrants were having on the US, the Trump Administration took less than ten weeks in office to acknowledge it had enacted a policy of family separation at the US-Mexico border.[15] Its aim was to deter the immigration of refugees and asylum-seekers from Central America who were crossing the border with their children. Until then, the policy under the Obama Administration had been to detain mothers with their children (under eighteen) in detention centers as their petitions played out in the US immigration system. Over a year later, after mass opposition at home and abroad, President Trump signed an executive order ending family separation on June 20, 2018.[16] Six days later, a US District Judge in the Southern District of California issued a nationwide preliminary injunction ordering the government to reunite children with their parents within thirty days.[17] Miriam Jordan reports that as of 2021, over 1,000 children "likely remain separated from their parents, and another 500 or more were taken from their parents who have yet to be located."[18]

The Brexit Referendum, Syrian Exodus, and Migrants

In the same year that Trump was elected, British voters elected to exit the European Union. On June 23, 2016, a slight majority indicated their desire for "Brexit," reversing decades of cooperation with European states in a move that surprised many. Prime Minister Theresa

---

[13] Donald J. Trump, "Executive Order: Protecting the Nation from Foreign Terrorist Entry into the United States," January 27, 2017, www.whitehouse.gov/the-press-office/2017/01/27/executive-order-protecting-nation-foreign-terrorist-entry-united-states.
[14] Trump v. Hawaii, 138 U.S. 2392 (2018).
[15] Justin Barajas, "How Trump's Family Separation Policy Became What It Is Today," *PBS NewsHour*, June 14, 2018, sec. Nation, www.pbs.org/newshour/nation/how-trumps-family-separation-policy-has-become-what-it-is-today.
[16] Richard Gonzales, "Trump's Executive Order on Family Separation: What It Does and Doesn't Do," *NPR*, June 20, 2018, www.npr.org/2018/06/20/622095441/trump-executive-order-on-family-separation-what-it-does-and-doesnt-do.
[17] Kristina Davis and Alene Tchekmedyian, "San Diego Federal Judge Orders Separated Children Reunited with Parents within 30 Days," *San Diego Union-Tribune*, June 27, 2018, www.sandiegouniontribune.com/news/courts/sd-me-judge-ruling-20180626-story.html.
[18] Miriam Jordan, "Separated Families: A Legacy Biden Has Inherited from Trump," *The New York Times*, February 1, 2021, www.nytimes.com/2021/02/01/us/immigration-family-separations-biden.html.

May negotiated with the European Union during years of Parliamentary and public debate over Brexit, and a strong victory for "Leave" proponent Boris Johnson's Conservative Party in the December 2019 elections ensured that Britain would leave the European Union.

An essential factor in why many British voters opted to leave the European Union was the perception of immigration as a threat. Other factors entered into the debate: the UK economy, taxes paid to the European Union, the extent to which the European Union was democratic, and the trustworthiness of politicians. The campaigns to "Leave" highlighted fears about immigration,[19] like in a Vote Leave poster that announced, "Turkey (population 76 million) is joining the EU." Below footsteps moving through an open UK passport, it added: "Vote Leave, take back control."[20] This poster played on racist and anti-Muslim prejudices as it turned past discussion about Turkey joining the European Union into the false claim that Turkey *was* joining. Voting followed the lead of the campaign: intentions to vote "Leave" correlated with beliefs that immigration levels were too high.[21]

A vote for Brexit, a vote for Britain to exit the European Union, was a vote to leave the zone of free movement around the European Union. Polish and other Eastern European migrant communities in Britain had grown since being allowed free movement in 2004, with comparatively lower-income countries Romania and Bulgaria entering the free movement zone in 2014.[22] An example of growing opposition to these EU migrants comes from a study describing Northern English teenagers' discourse about "the Polish," ascribing to them strange physical features and clothing, and speculating that as they spoke Polish, they might be planning a rape.[23] Whether voters saw immigration to the UK as an economic, linguistic, cultural, or sexual threat, fears about immigration and the desire to "take back control" resonated with many but not all of the more than 17 million people who ultimately voted to "Leave."

---

[19] Stuart Gietel-Basten, "Why Brexit? The Toxic Mix of Immigration and Austerity," *Population and Development Review* 42, no. 4 (December 2016): 674, doi.org/10.1111/padr.12007.
[20] Simon Goodman, "'Take Back Control of Our Borders': The Role of Arguments about Controlling Immigration in the Brexit Debate," *Yearbook of the Institute of East-Central Europe (Rocznik Instytutu Europy Środkowo-Wschodniej)* 15, no. 3 (2017): 41.
[21] Dominic Abrams and Giovanni A. Travaglino, "Immigration, Political Trust, and Brexit: Testing an Aversion Amplification Hypothesis," *British Journal of Social Psychology* 57, no. 2 (2018): 310, 324, doi.org/10.1111/bjso.12233.
[22] "Freedom of Movement in the EU," Citizens Information, April 9, 2021, www.citizensinformation.ie/en/moving_country/moving_abroad/freedom_of_movement_within_the_eu/freedom_of_movement_in_the_eu.html.
[23] Stephen Gibson, "Constructions of 'the Polish' in Northern England: Findings from a Qualitative Interview Study," *Journal of Social and Political Psychology* 3, no. 2 (October 1, 2015): 47–48, 50–51, 54, doi.org/10.5964/jspp.v3i2.414.

As a backdrop to the Trump election and the Brexit vote, civil conflict in Syria sent large numbers of Syrians along with Afghans, Iraqis, and others into Europe to apply for asylum. A photograph publicized on September 2, 2015, of three-year-old Alan Kurdi, a Syrian boy found dead on a Greek beach, formed a diptych with images of groups of migrants walking across Europe, the one image eliciting compassion and the other fear.[24] Widely called "the migrant crisis" or the "Syrian refugee crisis" in terms implying that migrants bring crisis rather than respond to crisis,[25] we prefer to call this phenomenon the "Syrian exodus."

Anti-Immigrant Populism in the US and UK

While the Trump Administration took other ethically questionable actions to deter immigration, its early policies towards immigrants from Central America and majority-Muslim countries reflect the campaign narrative that helped Mr. Trump gain the necessary political support to be elected. In that narrative, immigrants and refugees are among the main reasons for America's woes. Real and figurative walls are the solution. An analogous narrative seems to have taken hold of UK voters who lent their support to leave the European Union (albeit to a lesser extent). Why?

The literature in political science and sociology suggests an emerging consensus among scholars that both outcomes speak to a rise in populism depending on *and* furthering the perception of immigrants as a threat. Political scientist Graham Wilson identifies six parallels in rhetoric and strategy on both sides of the Atlantic. Three stand out. First, the Trump and "Leave" campaigns used populism, "a language whose speakers conceive of ordinary people as a noble assemblage not bounded narrowly by class; [who] view their elite opponents as self-serving and undemocratic; and seek to mobilize the former against the latter."[26] That language disparages expert knowledge as elitist, including—if not more so—on the topic of immigration policy. Second, both campaigns "promised to reduce immigration" in ways that conform to John B. Judis's description of right-wing populism as "the mobilization of the people against an elite that allegedly coddles 'an out group,'

---

[24] Helena Smith, "Shocking Images of Drowned Syrian Boy Show Tragic Plight of Refugees," *The Guardian*, September 2, 2015, www.theguardian.com/world/2015/sep/02/shocking-image-of-drowned-syrian-boy-shows-tragic-plight-of-refugees.

[25] Lesley J. Pruitt, "Closed Due to 'Flooding'? UK Media Representations of Refugees and Migrants in 2015–2016 – Creating a Crisis of Borders," *British Journal of Politics and International Relations* 21, no. 2 (2019): 391, doi.org/10.1177/1369148119830592.

[26] Graham K. Wilson, "Brexit, Trump, and the Special Relationship," *British Journal of Politics and International Relations* 19, no. 3 (2017): 544, doi.org/10.1177/1369148117713719.

or an unpopular minority."[27] Both campaigns had access to research suggesting that opposition to immigration, legal and undocumented, was a powerful sentiment that could be weaponized in their favor. Finally, both campaigns invoked xenophobia and racism to underpin support from potential voters: in the case of the UK, through fear of migration from Eastern European and majority Muslim countries (including via false rumors that Turkish membership in the European Union was imminent);[28] in the case of the United States, through the President's promise to build a wall that, as policy experts have indicated, will not deter immigrants from entering the country illegally or petitioning for asylum at ports of entry.

Sociologists have produced research offering helpful distinctions between right and left-wing populist movements, more so when it comes to their interaction with immigrants, refugees, and minority communities. On the one hand, this research suggests that contemporary populist movements on both ideological ends are reacting to the global financial crisis that hit non-elites particularly hard during the first decade of the millennium. As Silke Roth demonstrates, they share a critique of neoliberalism, international elites in finance and the economy, and appeals to the people to correct the current state of affairs. On the other hand, "How they conceptualize 'the people' varies considerably."[29] Roth argues that while left-wing populist movements attempt to be inclusionary to build broad coalitions to pursue such correction, right-wing movements engage in othering to do so. Thus, "What far-right and populist movements from the right in Europe and the United States share is the fact that they are anti-feminist, anti-immigrant, homophobic movements which seek to 'take back' the country in the name of native (White) populations."[30]

From a theological perspective, these findings ground an implicit concern with the ability of the US and UK political systems and their societies to respect the human dignity of immigrants and refugees. Additionally, Judis and Roth voice an explicit concern around solidarity that deserves consideration. Judis calls attention to an impoverished underclass that he believes is threatening the "social solidarity" that sustained social democracy in the US and the UK.[31] His thinking suggests that immigration by low-skilled workers contributed to the growth of that underclass and weakened the ability to protect labor

---

[27] Wilson, "Brexit, Trump, and the Special Relationship," 545.
[28] Wilson, "Brexit, Trump, and the Special Relationship," 546.
[29] Silke Roth, "Introduction: Contemporary Counter-Movements in the Age of Brexit and Trump," *Sociological Research Online* 23, no. 2 (June 1, 2018): 497, doi.org/10.1177/1360780418768828.
[30] Roth, "Introduction," 498.
[31] John Judis, "The Two Sides of Immigration Policy," *The American Prospect*, Winter 2018, prospect.org/api/content/44d1fa7d-4b69-584b-b0f8-a41f415f6926/.

rights within both countries' political systems—another reason to "defend the labor rights of all residents in the United States, even those without papers, and to resist wholesale raids."[32] From a sociological perspective, it is evident that the solidarity required is not easily attained. As Roth reports, counter-movements like the Women's March on Washington face difficulties when "crafting solidarities across differences."[33]

THE TEACHING OF TWO CHURCHES' BISHOPS ON MIGRATION: AN ANALYSIS

During the Brexit-Trump era, the Roman Catholic Church in the United States and Mexico and the Church of England made claims about the meaning and implications of migration in light of their shared Christian faith. As such, their interventions in the public square through multiple kinds of texts along with direct and indirect lobbying are representative of their teachings on migration. Here, we have chosen to use a broad definition of teaching to accommodate how each church conceives of its teaching function in the lives of their communities of faith and wider society. We understand our churches' teaching to mean their expressions of the content of the Christian faith, as rooted in both Testaments. Their teaching has implications for each church and each country's actions toward migrants today. To facilitate our analysis, we focus below on expressions of that teaching by our communities' bishops. That narrow focus does not intend to deny the teaching function possessed by other clerics, religious, or laypersons (including through preaching), nor does it intend to diminish the vital function their praxis plays in shaping our churches' teaching on migration. Indeed, their praxis is an expression of that teaching. That is particularly the case with migrants themselves and those who serve them in shelters, parishes, and beyond.

With regard to sources, in the US, Roman Catholic bishops have written multiple texts that state, apply, and develop their church's teaching on migration. Here, we focus on texts they wrote between January 20, 2017, when the Trump Administration began, and the end of 2019, prioritizing those texts that address the Muslim ban and family separation. To narrow the focus further, we primarily analyze two kinds of documents—statements written collectively by border bishops and pastoral letters. We also do not substantially engage papal teaching on migration unless border bishops do so. We also consider, though in a secondary manner, press releases by ecclesial organizations in which a Catholic bishop is quoted.[34]

---

[32] Judis."Two Sides of Immigration Policy."
[33] Roth, "Introduction," 501.
[34] Individual dioceses, state conferences of Catholic bishops, and the United States Conference of Catholic Bishops also offered multiple press releases on immigration

Unlike the Roman Catholic Church in the US and Mexico, Church of England bishops made no collective statements about migration in the era of Brexit, limiting the sources we can examine. Still, they made claims about the Syrian exodus and other migrations which, in a broad sense, provide teaching on migration. Their teaching was expressed in many genres, from speeches and documents presented to the Church's General Synod, to speeches in the UK Parliament's House of Lords, editorials, press releases, a book, and a statement with an ecumenical body. To present those multiple genres, we focus our analysis on the teaching of the two bishops—Paul Butler, the Bishop of Durham, and Justin Welby, the Archbishop of Canterbury—who spoke and wrote most regularly on migration between September 2, 2015, when a Syrian migrant child's body prompted the bishops to act, and the end of 2019, when British withdrawal from the European Union was assured.[35]

The following section analyzes how our churches' teaching engages the politics of populism while remaining grounded in Scripture. To that end, we first examine how their teaching engages in public debate and then analyze how bishops provide biblical grounds for it. The two subsections are not mutually exclusive. Instead, each foregrounds an aspect of our analysis while leaving the other in the background. Each subsection focuses on the Church of England's teaching first and then moves to the Roman Catholic Church's teaching.

ENGAGING THE POLITICS OF ANTI-MIGRANT POPULISM
Church of England: The Case of Paul Butler, Bishop of Durham

The Syrian exodus moved the Church of England to action in its General Synod, the UK Parliament, and the international community. Soon after the 2015 publication of the photograph of three-year-old

---

during this time span. While these do not carry the same pastoral and theological weight as joint collegial statements or individual pastoral letters, they do represent a mechanism that quickly connects the church's teaching to the US immigration debate and the administration of the country's immigration system. The Archdiocese of Los Angeles, the California Conference of Catholic Bishops, and the USCCB are notable on this point, with active communications offices that sent out press releases with bishops' reaction to the Muslim ban, the Supreme Court's ruling upholding the third version of the ban, and family separations at the border. For a collection of reactions, see "Trump's Action Banning Refugees Brings Outcry from U.S. Church Leaders," *Catholic News Service*, January 30, 2017, cnstopstories.com/2017/01/30/trumps-action-banning-refugees-brings-outcry-from-u-s-church-leaders/.

[35] There appear to be no prior publications surveying Church of England teaching or action on migration besides treatments of historical periods that ended at least a century ago. For Butler, the Syrian exodus of 2015 prompted him to lead not only churches but civil society and government in resettling refugees from Syria to Britain. Welby spoke and wrote at key junctures in response to Syrian migrants and the EU referendum. Their stories stand alongside those of many other bishops and priests who have contributed voices on migration from within the Church of England during the period considered here.

Syrian migrant Alan Kurdi's dead body on the Greek island of Kos, Paul Butler, the Anglican Bishop of Durham, wrote his fellow bishops to say that something must be done. As many in the Church of England and other churches in the UK responded, Butler was among the leaders of the response, championing community sponsorship, where community groups like parish churches could work with the UK Home Office to host Syrians resettled directly from refugee camps in and around Syria.[36] Butler was able to promote this answer to the Syrian exodus not only by participating in charitable and cooperative efforts—first chairing the National Refugee Welcome Board and then serving as a trustee of Reset Communities and Refugees[37]—but also through speaking and writing in his unique role between church and state as a Lord Spiritual in the House of Lords, UK Parliament's upper house.

Butler directly and indirectly responded to the politics of populism in three episodes worthy of our attention because they offer a robust example of the Anglican Church's teaching on migration amidst Brexit.[38] In the first episode, Butler presented a document he wrote with Philip Fletcher on "The Migration Crisis" to the Church of England's General Synod, a governing body consisting of bishops, priests, and elected laypeople.[39] Describing the challenges faced by those fleeing Syria and commending responses from the UK government, charities, and church actors, the document includes one obvious moral claim: "There is a vigorous tradition of British hospitality to refugees." In the debate that followed, Butler again mentions hospitality as a British value that "stands close to the heart of the Gospel."[40] His comments become more theological when, after describing the large numbers of forcibly displaced persons, he says that "God knows every one of them by name" and "each one [is] made in God's image and someone for whom Jesus Christ died." Upon cataloguing a list of places of suffering, he adds: "All of this suffering is the cry of my neighbor."[41] The Synod went on to approve a motion, calling on parishes, dioceses, and local and national government to work together to resettle refugees

---

[36] "Syrian Vulnerable Persons Resettlement Scheme (VPRS): Guidance for Local Authorities and Partners" (Home Office, July 21, 2017), www.gov.uk/government/publications/syrian-vulnerable-person-resettlement-programme-fact-sheet.
[37] "About Reset," Reset Communities and Refugees UK, accessed March 18, 2022, resetuk.org/about/about-reset.
[38] Alongside these three episodes were many others, recorded and unrecorded: pastoral conversations, committee meetings, and private meetings and correspondence with the UK Home Office.
[39] Paul Butler and Philip Fletcher, "The Migration Crisis" (Church of England General Synod, GS 2009, November 2015), www.churchofengland.org/sites/default/files/2017-12/gs_2009_-_the_migrant_crisis.pdf.
[40] Paul Butler, "Debate on the Migration Crisis" (Church of England General Synod, Westminster Abbey, November 25, 2015).
[41] Butler, "Debate on the Migration Crisis."

while calling on the UK government to expand the numbers of refugees it would receive and establish "safe and legal routes to places of safety, including this country." Surprisingly for a topic that captured the public imagination from September 2015 to December 2019, this was the only time the church's governing body carried out a debate on broad questions of migration.[42]

In the second episode, Butler led a debate in the House of Lords in response to a report for which he was partly responsible as member of the All-Party Parliamentary Group on Refugees.[43] From 2015 to 2019, as Bishop of Durham, Butler not only served his diocese and the General Synod of the Church of England, he also sat as a governing member in the upper house of Parliament. There among twenty-six bishops and hundreds of other peers, the Bishop of Durham could debate legislation originating in the House of Commons, propose amendments, and pose spoken and written questions that a Minister from the governing party had to answer. In the House of Lords, Butler continued beyond 2019 to be active in pursuing an agenda of advocating for refugees and asylum seekers, especially children.[44]

In the 2017 Lords' debate, he began by arguing for a national refugee integration strategy and the creation of a role of Minister for Refugees. The terms in which he framed his argument reveal insight into the opportunity and paradox of being pastor and legislator at the same time. For much of the speech, he spoke as a member of a "we" among Britain's lawmaking body. He states that when "our systems left [refugees] bereft and destitute, … we can and should fix these structural and process issues." Because an integration strategy for refugees will not only benefit refugees but also the "wider society," an integration strategy is "in our own best self-interest." As he turns to the report's

---

[42] In addition to this broad discussion, the General Synod considered two focused legal questions about migration. The first was a debate on a motion seeking a lowered fee for naturalization, *Report of Proceedings* 48, no. 1 (July 10, 2017), www.churchofengland.org/sites/default/files/2017-10/General%20Synod%20-%20February%202017%20w.%20index.pdf. The second was a motion arguing that refugee professionals should be able to work, *Report of Proceedings* 50, no. 2 (July 7, 2019), www.churchofengland.org/sites/default/files/2020-02/General%20Synod%20-%205%20-%209%20July%202019%20%28003%29.pdf.
[43] H.L. Deb. (July 19, 2017), vol. 783, cols. 1688–91, hansard.parliament.uk/lords/2017-07-19/debates/02FCEA8A-3782-431D-9C2C-DEA8D4783847/Refugees; "Refugees Welcome? The Experience of New Refugees in the UK" (All Party Parliamentary Group on Refugees, April 2017), www.refugeecouncil.org.uk/wp-content/uploads/2019/03/APPG_on_Refugees_-_Refugees_Welcome_report.pdf.
[44] For example, see H.L. Deb. (January 25, 2017), vol. 778, cols. 722–24, hansard.parliament.uk/Lords/2017-01-25/debates/B510EEDD-43EC-4FA9-8222-865249D8A3D2/HigherEducationAndResearchBill#contribution-C0B2C4B4-6D09-41ED-907E-FDAA9CEF737F.

recognition of the work of churches "welcoming refugees to our country," he began to shift to another "we," a different point of belonging: "We do so to join in the work of the one whom the psalmist describes as 'a father to the fatherless, a defender of widows,' who 'sets the lonely in families.' We are a welcomed people who desire to welcome others."[45]

As these comments exhibit a British voice and a Christian one, they may not say what Butler believes. Instead, they play out and perform this role assumed by bishops in the House of Lords, where a Christian clergyperson sits in a governing body because he is a leader within one church communion. The comments from Butler in this 2017 debate display the tension inherent in being a bishop in the House of Lords who cares deeply about an issue of justice. In the same speech, Butler speaks as a member of a "we" who have the power to change systems of government, or with the privilege of calling publicly for reform, and at the same time as a member of a "people" welcomed and joining in the work of the God spoken of in the Psalms.

That the Bishop of Durham stands in between church and state is something Butler articulated eloquently in the third episode of this survey. He was among the UK's representatives as a leader in refugee resettlement at the Annual Tripartite Consultations on Resettlement in Geneva, a global multilateral forum (sponsored by the UNHCR) with representatives of governments, non-governmental organizations, and refugees. There he spoke as "someone whose initial training is in fecundity" to those who are trained in "productivity."[46] Recognizing the question his audience may have had about why they should listen to a Christian clergyperson, he questioned the assumption that "scarcity and competition is the fundamental reality." He noted, "I keep finding evidence of another story, rumors of a possible abundance rather than scarcity." He suggested that where productive systems "are put in the service of fecundity, of possibility, of fruitfulness, of life—it makes good policy." Again, Butler spoke of unexpected partnerships between faith groups, schools, charities, and local authorities. While drawing on the writing of Jean Vanier, John 10, and testimonies of refugees in the Diocese of Durham, he named generosity and the willingness he saw in refugees to contribute to their new communities.[47] He spoke of refugees as individuals, not justifying that turn because

---

[45] H.L. Deb. (July 19, 2017), vol. 783, cols. 1688–91.

[46] Paul Butler, "Fecundity, Productivity, and Resettlement" (Annual Tripartite Consultations on Resettlement, Geneva, July 2, 2019), durhamdiocese.org/bishop-paul-speaks-at-annual-tripartite-consultation-on-resettlement-conference-in-geneva/. He attributes the pairing of "productivity" and "fecundity" to Jean Vanier, *Drawn into the Mystery of Jesus Through the Gospel of John* (London: Darton, Longman & Todd, 2004), 189. This speech was given before revelations were made about Jean Vanier's deplorable pattern of sexual abuse.

[47] See the comment about Vanier in the preceding footnote.

they have dignity, but because "each individual, each family group is a gift." He hoped that each person might be enabled to flourish. He noted that both those who find new homes and those who welcome them report increased thankfulness for what they have and the new possibilities they discover. Resettlement must be seen, he urged, not first in terms of burdens, but through the image of "refugees as gifts." He invited a shift of mindset in refugee resettlement from the scarce allocation of resources to a world of abundant gifts, alluding to the working of a gift-giving God.[48]

As the three previous episodes suggest, the Syrian exodus amidst the Brexit debate prompted action, and teaching followed. That teaching took a wide range of forms, from speeches in the Church's General Synod and the House of Lords to editorials, press releases, one statement, and one book relating to migrants. In the most prominent case of a church leader speaking on migrants, Butler's comments arose out of extensive practical commitment to refugees. Church interventions on migrants tended to focus on vulnerable migrants like refugees, asylum seekers, children, and detainees rather than on those who come to the UK to join family, work, or study, with an occasional mention of EU migrants of all types. The Church of England's House of Bishops did not issue any pastoral letters or collective statements during the September 2015 to December 2019 period, and the range of sources that did appear came from bishops speaking individually. The existing teaching tended to be brief, and only a portion of those statements contained theological or biblical content. This teaching did not provide trails or references that led to longer explanations of what Christians believe about migrants. The teaching that did come from Church of England bishops on migrants, then, was short, widely dispersed, and in the best case, flowed out of churches standing with refugees.

US Roman Catholic Bishops: The Case of the Tex-Mex Border Bishops

In the US, the Trump Administration's decision to separate families at the US-Mexico border and force refugees and asylum-seekers to remain in Mexico moved Roman Catholic border bishops to respond. They did so through statements, lobbying efforts, and by echoing Pope Francis's calls to welcome, protect, promote, and integrate immigrants and refugees. Catholic social teaching is evident in the bishops' responses to populist immigration policies, which aimed to acknowledge migrants' dignity through solidarity. In light of Cardinal Joseph Cardijn's see, judge, act method (taken up by John XXIII in

---

[48] After the period considered in this article, in autumn 2020 Butler gave speeches in the House of Lords and wrote an editorial that drew more explicitly on migrants' perspective on biblical stories. This came after his then-assistant Josh Harris read a draft of this article.

Mater et Magistra),[49] border bishops turned their gazes and ours to places along the border that US Christians may not wish to see: airports where the Muslim ban led to the detention of permanent residents and refugees; detention centers filled at first with mothers and children and then with children that officers took from their parents; ports of entry with armed troops surrounded by concertina wire as they awaited the arrival of migrant caravans; the scene of the *matanza*, the mass shooting in El Paso, Texas, where, in the words of Mark Seitz, bishop of the Roman Catholic diocese, a young man spilled Latinx blood, immigrant and not, "in sacrifice to the false god of white supremacy."[50]

Since 1986, the bishops of Roman Catholic dioceses along the Texas-Mexico border—at present five on the US side and five on the Mexican side—have met every other year. At the end of each meeting these border bishops publish a statement identifying their shared pastoral concerns. While the US Conference of Catholic Bishops (USCCB) would be a closer analogue to the Church of England's General Synod in the UK, we focus instead on this core group of US and Mexican Catholic bishops. Because of their consistency, it influences the Roman Catholic episcopate's ministry—including its teaching—across the binational border region (where 31 million people live) and their respective national conferences of bishops.[51] In that time, they have been constant witnesses of the suffering migrants experience at the border. As a case in point, their 2017 meeting took place a month after the Trump Administration announced its policy of family separation, a policy reflective of populist sentiments. Front and center was the suffering the recently announced policy was already causing. "We have seen the pain," the bishops write, that immigrants in their dioceses are suffering because of potential family separations (a threat that ultimately became real). "We can sense the pain," they continue, "of the separation of families, loss of employment, persecutions, dis-

---

[49] John XXIII, *Mater et Magistra: Encyclical on Christianity and Social Progress*, 1961, no. 236, www.vatican.va/content/john-xxiii/en/encyclicals/documents/hf_j-xxiii_enc_15051961_mater.html.

[50] Mark Seitz, *Night Will Be No More: Pastoral Letter to People of God in El Paso* (El Paso, TX: Diocese of El Paso, 2019), no. 1, www.hopeborder.org/nightwillbenomore-eng.

[51] 31 million people lived within one hundred miles of each side of the border, and 90 million live on border states on each side of the border. See Erik Lee, Christopher E. Wilson, Francisco Lara-Valencia, Carlos A. de la Parra, Rick Van Schoik, Kristofer Patron-Soberano, Eric L. Olson, and Andrew Selee, *The State of the Border Report: A Comprehensive Analysis of the U.S.-Mexico Border*, ed. Christopher E. Wilson and Erik Lee (Washington, DC: Woodrow Wilson Center, El Colegio de la Frontera Norte, and the North American Center for Transborder Studies, 2013), www.wilsoncenter.org/sites/default/files/media/documents/misc/mexico_state_of_border.pdf.

crimination, [and] expressions of racism," all of which are leaving immigrants "empty and without hope."[52] Two years later, their 2019 meeting focused on the Trump Administration's "Remain in Mexico" policy. The policy, also reflective of populist sentiments in relation to migrant caravans finding their way from Central America, forced asylum seekers to wait in Mexico for their immigration court hearings. Inspired by the parable on the judgments of nations (Matthew 25), when their meeting ended, the bishops affirmed their commitment to stay the course in providing humanitarian assistance to migrants across their dioceses (shelter, food, medicine). "We urge everyone to discover, in these brothers and sisters who are suffering, Christ in need," they wrote, "and to give them the support they require, without assuming they are criminals, as they are sometimes perceived."[53] Before concluding that the policy must be opposed because it undermines the right to seek asylum, among other legal reasons, they appeal "to governments, in the name of our Lord Jesus Christ, not [to] adopt policies that have the effect of increasing the suffering of the most vulnerable."[54]

As to their lobbying efforts in Congress and the public square more broadly, border bishops were remarkably consistent with their turn to the principles of human dignity and solidarity to critically reflect on the suffering they are witnessing at the border. Like most Americans, the bishops reached the conclusion that the country's immigration system is broken.[55] What is distinctive about the border bishops' communications was their attempt to offer accounts that are *both* legally and theologically grounded as to why the system is broken and at what cost. To that end, for the most part their press releases tended to emphasize legal or policy analyses, while Seitz's pastoral letters (more on them in the following section) tended to offer more robust theologically informed critical reflections. Statements by the Tex-Mex bishops fell somewhere in between. Thus, for example, the bishops mostly

---

[52] Tex-Mex Border Bishops and Obispos de la Frontera, *Statement of the Bishops of the Border between Texas and Northern Mexico: The Cry of Christ in the Voice of the Migrant Moves Us* (San Juan, TX: Bishop of Brownsville, 2017), nos. 6–7, www.dioceseoflaredo.org/sites/default/files/files/Immigration%20Statement%20Bishops.pdf.
[53] Tex-Mex Border Bishops, "Statement of the Bishops of the Border between Texas and Northern Mexico: I Was a Stranger and You Welcomed Me (Mt 25:35)," *Ignatian Solidarity Network*, ignatiansolidarity.net/blog/2019/03/10/remain-in-mexico-catholic-bishops/.
[54] Tex-Mex Border Bishops, "Statement of the Bishops of the Border between Texas and Northern Mexico."
[55] For an argument that the US immigration system is *not* broken but indeed functioning as intended, please see Victor Carmona, "Mixed Status Families and Brokenness: Will our Fractured Relationships Heal?" in *Human Families: Identity, Relationships, and Responsibilities*, ed. Jacob Kohlhaas and Mary M. Doyle Roche (Maryknoll, NY: Orbis Books, 2021), 151–72.

expressed opposition to the Muslim ban through press releases that identify it as un-American, for example, because it denies due process to individuals or curtails the freedom of religion. While they also identify the ban's failure to respect the human dignity of Muslim refugees, that reasoning was usually not as central a point. That may well be because their intended purpose was to engage the country's immigration debate to shape immigration policy in targeted ways. Statements by the Tex-Mex bishops and Seitz's pastoral letters addressing family separations offer more robust accounts of human dignity, a principle which claims that all persons are made in the image and likeness of God (Genesis 1) and should be treated accordingly, as the basis for a person's right to "find in their own countries the economic, political, and social opportunities to live in dignity" and, failing that, of their right to migrate "to support themselves and their families."[56] That may well be because their intended purpose has been to shape the conversation within Catholic communities on both sides of the border, if not to form them so they may be able to acknowledge the human dignity of all alike: Muslim and Christian, citizen and immigrant, Latinx and European-American. The texts reflect a similar treatment with regard to the principle of solidarity, which John Paul II defined "not [as] a feeling of vague compassion or shallow distress at the misfortunes of so many people, both near or far [but as] a firm and persevering determination to commit oneself to the common good; that is to say to the good of all and of each individual, because we are all really responsible for all."[57] That principle, however, presents an added difficulty in that most readers may have an elusive understanding of what it means or how it may lead one to the *praxis* of Christian discipleship in the context of a violent immigration system that Seitz discerns to be an expression of institutionalized racism, and thus ultimately of personal and structural sin.[58]

---

[56] Conferencia del Episcopado Mexicano and United States Conference of Catholic Bishops, *Strangers No Longer: Together on the Journey of Hope: A Pastoral Letter Concerning Migration from the Catholic Bishops of Mexico and the United States* (Washington, DC: USCCB, 2003), nos. 34–35, www.usccb.org/issues-and-action/human-life-and-dignity/immigration/strangers-no-longer-together-on-the-journey-of-hope.cfm.

[57] John Paul II, *Sollicitudo Rei Socialis: On Social Concern*, 1987, no. 38, www.vatican.va/content/john-paul-ii/en/encyclicals/documents/hf_jp-ii_enc_30121987_sollicitudo-rei-socialis.html.

[58] Both letters point to the wounds, physical and psychological, past and present that immigrants and others in the border communities of the diocese of El Paso are experiencing as a result of the country's broken immigration system; see Mark Seitz, *Sorrow and Mourning Flee Away: Pastoral Letter on Migration to the People of God in the Diocese of El Paso* (El Paso, TX: Diocese of El Paso, 2017), no. 15, www.elpasodiocese.org/uploads/5/4/9/5/54952711/sorrow_and_mourning_pastoral.pdf; Seitz, *Night Will Be No More*, nos. 18, 19, 43, closing prayer.

Border bishops also lent indirect opposition to populist immigration policies by echoing Pope Francis's calls to welcome, protect, promote, and integrate immigrants and refugees. While our analysis purposefully does not include papal texts during the timeframe in question because they tend to receive the bulk of the attention, papal texts clearly support and shape the US bishops' press releases, statements, and pastoral letters. During that time, border bishops referenced seven documents and statements by the pope, but one stands out: his 2018 World Day of Peace message, which addressed migration as a global reality. In it, Francis argues that offering "asylum seekers, refugees, migrants, and victims of human trafficking an opportunity to find the peace they seek requires a strategy combining four actions: welcoming, protecting, promoting, and integrating."[59] The message further lays out those actions and offers brief grounds from Scripture to support each (Hebrews 13:2; Psalm 146:9; Deuteronomy 10:18–19, and Ephesians 2:19, respectively). Those same actions frame the Vatican's support of the Global Compact for Migration at the United Nations, which advanced a comprehensive and integral approach to managing international population movements worldwide. They also framed the pope's call to Catholic bishops to use those same actions to frame their pastoral response to immigrants and refugees in their dioceses.[60] Echoing Francis, the Tex-Mex bishops encouraged Catholics in their 2019 statement opposing the Administration's "Remain in Mexico" policy "to join ourselves to the God of hope and life, so that he may help us to welcome, protect, promote, and integrate immigrants, as requested by Pope Francis."[61]

REMAINING GROUNDED IN SCRIPTURE
Church of England Bishops: The Case of Justin Welby, Archbishop of Canterbury

The Church of England's teaching on migration in the context of Brexit reflects the importance of grounding ecclesial responses in Scripture and the challenges involved in doing so in the public square. The ministry of Justin Welby, Archbishop of Canterbury, is a case in point, as his teaching demonstrates a commitment to valuing migrants while also tending to read Scripture from the perspective of someone who is settled and established.

Much of what Welby has said and written on the matter concurs with Butler's teaching: they share an emphasis on the dignity of all

---

[59] Francis, "Migrants and Refugees: Men and Women in Search of Peace," January 1, 2018, www.vatican.va/content/francesco/en/messages/peace/documents/papa-francesco_20171113_messaggio-51giornatamondiale-pace2018.html.
[60] Migrants and Refugees Section, *Towards the Global Compacts on Migrants and on Refugees 2018* (Vatican City: Holy See, 2018).
[61] Tex-Mex Border Bishops, "Statement of the Bishops of the Border between Texas and Northern Mexico."

human beings, including migrants, and a message of "welcoming the stranger." Welby differs in other respects. As for genre, he too has written press releases, spoken to the General Synod and in the House of Lords. His speaking and writing have special prominence because he is the Church of England's leading member of clergy as Primate of England and Metropolitan.[62] Welby gave a speech in the House of Lords just after the EU referendum vote responding to its implications, and many other Lords responded to this speech, indicating his special role in speaking to Britain in moments of crisis.[63] In response to Brexit, he published a book entitled *Reimagining Britain*, expressing views he said were his own rather than the official position of the Church of England.[64] While Butler tended to focus on refugees, Welby said more in the wake of Brexit about the connection of immigration to integration. His comments that fears of migrants were not necessarily racist drew note in the tabloid press,[65] and he has said that the response should be to recognize those fears, transferring more resources to communities experiencing a high level of immigration.[66] Alongside this advice to government, he has called on churches to be involved with integration, mentioning Near Neighbours as a Church of England effort linking local communities.[67] Connected to a commitment he made during his archiepiscopate to reconciliation, Welby sometimes addressed Brexit as a division internal to Britain and mentioned the migrant residents of Britain "who feel fearful and rejected

---

[62] Martin Davie, *A Guide to the Church of England* (London: Mowbray, 2008), 9.

[63] H.L. Deb. (5 July 2016), vol. 773, cols. 1859–61, hansard.parliament.uk/Lords/2016-07-05/debates/D80BBB95-5A60-4084-B3DF-F83312E031C2/OutcomeOfTheEuropeanUnionReferendum#contribution-44BD09F4-F5BD-4D11-BB04-B817DADBD89A. For other Lords' comments, see Justin Welby, "Archbishop of Canterbury on the Future for the United Kingdom after the EU Referendum," *The Church of England in Parliament*, July 5, 2016, churchinparliament.org/2016/07/05/archbishop-of-canterbury-on-the-future-for-the-united-kingdom-after-the-eu-referendum/.

[64] Welby, *Reimagining Britain*, x.

[65] James Slack, "It's NOT Racist to Fear Migration, Says the Archbishop of Canterbury: Justin Welby Believes It Is 'Outrageous' to Dismiss Public's Genuine Concerns about Housing, Jobs, and the NHS," *Daily Mail*, March 10, 2016, www.dailymail.co.uk/news/article-3486397/It-s-fine-fear-migrant-influx-says-Archbishop-Canterbury-Justin-Welby-believes-absolutely-outrageous-people-voice-concerns-condemned-racist.html.

[66] Justin Welby to the Home Affairs Committee, Oral Evidence, the Work of the Immigration Directorates (Q1 2016), H.C. 151 (June 7, 2016), data.parliament.uk/writtenevidence/committeeevidence.svc/evidencedocument/home-affairs-committee/the-work-of-the-immigration-directorates-q1-2016/oral/34208.html; Welby, *Reimagining Britain*, 189, 206.

[67] Justin Welby, "Debate on a Motion on the EU Referendum," Church of England General Synod, *Report of Proceedings* 47, no. 2 (July 8, 2016), www.churchofengland.org/sites/default/files/2017-10/July%202016%20Report%20of%20Proceedings%20w.index_.pdf.

... with ... good reason" as well as the uncertainties of British "expatriates" in the European Union.[68] Besides integration, Welby spoke more often than Butler in terms of concepts or middle axioms that those of many persuasions might share, some of these drawn from Catholic social teaching, terms like justice, peace,[69] relationship,[70] common good, generosity, hospitality, gratuity, and solidarity,[71] though he applied "solidarity" to inequalities internal to Britain rather than to standing with migrants.[72]

In the speeches and writing considered here, Welby's handling of Scripture in relation to migrants draws on many of Butler's themes as well as a few others. After the Syrian exodus, Welby wrote that we should love strangers as ourselves, from the legal texts of Leviticus 19:34,[73] and said that "Jesus was a refugee," with reference to the Holy Family's flight to Egypt in Matthew 2:13–15.[74] His book includes two lengthier considerations of Scripture in relation to migration, interpreting the Parable of the Good Samaritan (Luke 10:25–37) in relation to British foreign policy and the Book of Ruth in relation to immigration and integration. From the parable, the book makes the suggestive claim that the neighbor is not only someone nearby or within the in-group but includes the enemy and reaches across boundaries, even in today's interconnected world.[75] It argues for increasing Britain's intake of refugees, sending development aid to prevent migration push factors, and using hard power and soft power together.[76] And it tells the moving story of Ruth as a love story between members of two enemy groups.

Yet in Welby's book, the interpretation of Luke and Ruth does not bring to the fore the strong role that foreigners play as bearers of divine mercy, love, and joy. The section on the Parable of the Good Samari-

---

[68] Welby, "Debate on a Motion on the E.U. Referendum." See also H.L. Deb. (5 July 2016), vol. 773, col. 1860.
[69] Justin Welby, "Archbishop of Canterbury on the Refugee Crisis," Church of England, September 3, 2015, www.archbishopofcanterbury.org/speaking-and-writing/latest-news/news-archive-2015/archbishop-canterbury-refugee-crisis.
[70] Welby to the Home Affairs Committee, H.C. 151 (June 7, 2016).
[71] H.L. Deb. (5 July 2016), vol. 773, cols. 1859–61.
[72] For the influence of Catholic Social Teaching on Welby, see his *Reimagining Britain*, 286. For an Anglican account of using social principles (following William Temple) and middle axioms (following Ronald Preston) that stand between church and society, see Alan M. Suggate, "The Temple Tradition," in *Anglican Social Theology: Renewing the Vision Today*, ed. Malcolm Brown (London: Church House, 2014).
[73] Welby, "On the Refugee Crisis."
[74] Tom Pugh, "Jesus Was a Refugee, Says Archbishop of Canterbury in New Year Message," *The Independent*, January 1, 2016, www.independent.co.uk/news/uk/home-news/jesus-was-a-refugee-says-archbishop-of-canterbury-in-new-year-message-a6792706.html.
[75] Welby, *Reimagining Britain*, 187.
[76] Welby, *Reimagining Britain*, 176, 183, 190.

tan fails to point out that the person who follows one of the great commandments and loves his neighbor as himself is the Samaritan, the stranger that the parable's hearers would have viewed with suspicion as a half-breed heretic and outsider.[77] The treatment of the Book of Ruth praises Boaz, the settled person in the story, for risking a marriage to Ruth, obeying God, and showing courage. The book does not appear to praise Ruth who courageously moves to an enemy country, risks her reputation in approaching Boaz at night, and is the only one in the story said to display *ḥesed*, the faithful love that characterizes God in the Hebrew Scriptures.[78] This exploration of immigration and integration from *Reimagining Britain* does not read the stories from a migrant's perspective, missing the spotlight each story places on a migrant. It misses the Samaritan as bringer of God's mercy and Ruth the Moabite as bringer of God's love and joy.

As for whether Welby's writing and speaking on migrants counters the worst of populism with a Christian vision of what a people is, his teaching continues Butler's pattern of speaking of the dignity of migrants and the value of welcoming them. Still, his statements from September 2015 to December 2019 do not seem to say much to support fellow feeling for migrants or oppose racism. As for a vision of the people that might counter populism, Welby's teaching exhibits more of a singular picture of being both British and part of the church—and not only British, but a member of a ruling class in Britain. There are moments when his book hints at a disunity between Britain and the church, like when he says that the role of the church is to bear witness to Jesus Christ, which is not something he expects of the UK. He sees the church's witness as happening "in the political system" so that it "live[s] as the people of God in such a way that society is both preserved and illuminated."[79]

Most of the time, however, Welby's statements hold Britain and the church close together. When he speaks in the first-person plural, "we" tend to be the British people and British rulers, like when he moves from interpreting the Parable of the Good Samaritan directly to the claim, "Applying our values to foreign policy has to take account of our interests."[80] He gives reasons for holding Britain and the church closely together, for example, when he writes: "Because of the Christian foundations of our society in Britain, it draws frequently on more or less well-known traditions and stories in the Bible."[81] The reasons

---

[77] Welby, *Reimagining Britain*, 178–81, 186–87; see Robert W. Heimburger, *God and the Illegal Alien: United States Immigration Law and a Theology of Politics* (Cambridge: Cambridge University Press, 2018), 192–93.
[78] Welby, *Reimagining Britain*, 200–05; Susanna Snyder, *Asylum-Seeking, Migration, and Church* (Farnham: Ashgate, 2012), 180–83, 191.
[79] Welby, *Reimagining Britain*, 21.
[80] Welby, *Reimagining Britain*, 187–88.
[81] Welby, *Reimagining Britain*, 4.

he gave to a House of Commons committee that Britain should take in more refugees are similar: "Are there really good reasons why the overwhelming claims of our historic culture of Christian compassion, which is deeply embedded for believers and non-believers and goes back centuries, and has received refugees for centuries, should be overruled?"[82] Speaking to a church gathering, the General Synod, he also speaks with what sounds like one "we" who both takes refuge in God and has a foreign policy.[83] Welby does not speak as a strange voice with strange stories, or as a migrant voice with migrant stories, but as a historic voice speaking from Britain's foundations. He speaks as someone embodying Britain and church, British and church leadership. With that voice he speaks for a different vision of a welcoming British people, but it is not clear that he speaks for a Christian people that includes migrants.

In terms of the interaction of Anglican bishops' teaching on migrants with Scripture, then, the most frequent themes are that migrants are human beings with dignity, a claim sometimes connected with their being made in the image of God, and that churches or the British nation should welcome the stranger. In two cases, biblical themes are expounded at more length, in a speech on John 10 and refugees as gifts, and in a book drawing on Ruth and the Parable of the Good Samaritan to praise love for neighbors that crosses ethnic and national boundaries. What that book misses in these passages, as noted earlier, is the way they feature foreigners as agents of divine grace, focusing instead on praising charity among settled persons. Other biblical themes rarely appear in Church of England teaching if at all; only the lay, non-British voice of Meg Warner in a General Synod debate talks about migration as central to the church's foundation stories in Abraham's call and the Exodus.[84] Butler touches on church identity as a "welcomed people" in one House of Lords speech, but other ways of framing the church as a community of outsiders, whether Gentiles welcomed into Israel or the diaspora sent out in mission, do not appear in the dozens of documents. Beyond biblical themes, the bishops follow the tradition of William Temple in appealing to concepts shared by church and wider society, concepts like hospitality and integration. Unlike their Catholic counterparts, the Anglican bishops do not seem to appeal to solidarity. Instead of implying a posture of standing with

---

[82] Welby to the Home Affairs Committee, H.C. 151 (June 7, 2016).
[83] Welby, "Debate on a Motion on the E.U. Referendum."
[84] "Debate on the Migration Crisis," Church of England General Synod, *Report of Proceedings* 46, no. 3 (25 November 2016), www.churchofengland.org/sites/default/files/2017-10/RoP%20November%202015%20%28final%20version%20with%20index%29.pdf.

immigrants and their struggles, a conflictive stance, the Anglican emphasis on welcome and integrating implies a posture of seeking harmony within society.

US Roman Catholic Bishops: The Case of Mark Seitz, Bishop of El Paso

In the US, Roman Catholic bishops' responses to Trump Administration actions also reflected the importance of grounding ecclesial responses in Scripture along with the challenges of doing so beyond the walls of the church. In Roman Catholicism, a bishop has the right to write pastoral letters to his diocese. As William Clark explains, "The bishop's authority to teach in this way is secured by his position as the chief pastor of his diocese."[85] Mark Seitz, Roman Catholic bishop of the diocese of El Paso, wrote two pastoral letters during the Trump Administration that address migration. The first, *Sorrow and Mourning Flee Away*, from July 2017, sets out to name, confront, and transform the reality of migration in his diocese—particularly in terms of the suffering that immigrant detentions and family separation are causing his people.[86] The available evidence suggests that no other bishop had dedicated a pastoral letter to the topic of migration since 2003. Seitz wrote the second one, *Night Will Be No More*, in the aftermath of the shooting—the *matanza*—of August 3, 2019, that left 22 people dead in El Paso.[87] It addresses the shooting as a consequence of the white privilege and racism his people suffer under, especially the Latinx community and immigrants.

Generally, the statements of Catholic border bishops reflect two methodological characteristics of Catholic social teaching on migration: (1) a reliance on general principles to discern what doing the good entails, particularly in terms of their stance on specific immigration policies; (2) a necessary eschatological reservation as they do so. The last point is key because it allows them to address a temptation that may be influencing US Christians, including Catholic officials and policy makers. Echoing the insights of Butler, Seitz observes that fear and the desire for complete security may be shaping people's thinking in unrealistic and spiritually distorted ways. Seitz writes: "We will never build a utopia in this broken world of ours. Guarding mere passing possessions is not our goal. We serve a God of abundance who provides for the needs of those who serve Him with charity and generosity. We trust that God did not create a world without room

---

[85] William A. Clark, "Pastoral Letter," in *An Introductory Dictionary of Theology and Religious Studies*, ed. Orlando O. Espín and James B. Nickoloff (Collegeville, MN: Liturgical Press, 2007), 1009.
[86] Seitz, *Sorrow and Mourning Flee Away*.
[87] Seitz, *Night Will Be No More*.

for all at the banquet of life."[88] Immigration reform, the texts seem to suggest, will only be possible when that kind of utopic thinking—grounded in fear and scarcity rather than abundance and hope—gives way.

While the previous characteristics shed light on how Catholic teaching addresses populist immigration policies at the border, they also point to its superficial engagement with Scripture to substantiate theological-ethical claims regarding such policies. Others have critically analyzed the contours of Catholic social teaching's engagement with the Bible.[89] In the case of the texts in question, their limited use of Scripture might reflect their purpose. For instance, what *would* proper use of the Bible look like in a press release addressing a specific immigration policy? As for the statements by the Tex-Mex bishops, for the most part they simply referenced Jesus's parable of the judgment of nations (Matthew 25:31–46). Their 2019 statement, reflecting the fact that the struggle for immigration reform is now over a quarter of a century old, also closes prayerfully with Galatians 6:9 ("Let us not grow tired of doing good"). While the prayerful use of the text might be sufficient, is its use without any further attention to the passage or its context (historical, literary, etc.) appropriate?

Pastoral letters tend to offer bishops more room to maneuver; to read Scripture and, as Gustavo Gutiérrez writes, allow ourselves (and our ecclesial and political communities) to be read by Scripture.[90] Seitz's pastoral letters, for example, engage Scripture with care and consistency. For instance, he frames *Sorrow and Mourning Flee Away* as a reflection on his border community's experience with immigration in light of Isaiah 35:7, 10 ("The burning sands will become pools, and the thirsty ground, springs of water. ... And the ransomed of the Lord shall enter Zion singing, crowned with everlasting joy. They meet with joy and gladness ... sorrow and mourning flee away"). As Michael Sean Winters observed, the passage "reflects the view from that of the migrant ... entering Zion, a once distant and harsh land made fertile and welcoming. It is the view of the migrant arriving at her destiny, under the shadow of God's protection."[91] The passage al-

---

[88] Seitz, *Sorrow and Mourning Flee Away*, 14.
[89] See, for instance, "The Bible and Catholic Social Teaching: Will This Engagement Lead to Marriage?" *Modern Catholic Social Teaching: Commentaries and Interpretations*, 2nd ed., ed. Kenneth Himes, Lisa Sowle Cahill, Charles E. Curran, David Hollenbach, and Thomas Shannon (Washington, DC: Georgetown University Press, 2005), 9–40.
[90] Gustavo Gutiérrez, *Beber en su Propio Pozo: en el Itinerario Espiritual de un Pueblo*, 9th ed. (Lima: CEP, 2011), 58.
[91] Michael Sean Winters, "Bishop Seitz's Remarkable Pastoral Letter," *National Catholic Reporter*, July 19, 2017, www.ncronline.org/blogs/distinctly-catholic/bp-seitzs-remarkable-pastoral-letter.

lows the bishop to acknowledge "the pain and the hardships," as Winters observes, "but doesn't give them the last word." Even so, the letter does not make explicit that original context or explain why it speaks so powerfully to our own. One may argue that it is a matter of writing style, an author's prerogative to let a pastoral letter unfold itself slowly, in time; or that a practice is developing in the community to interpret the pastoral letter accordingly. Seitz's pastoral letter on racism engages Revelation 22:5 ("Night will be no more, nor will they need light from lamp or sun, for the Lord God shall give them light, and they shall reign forever and ever") to similar effect. Perhaps the texts' limited use of Hebrew and Christian Scriptures are an implicit acknowledgment of the ambivalent ways and complex perspectives in which they engage the experiences of people on the move—more so in light of the cultural and historical distances that span the worlds of the Bible and ours.[92] And yet, such grappling should be at the heart of texts such as these, if not at least somehow evident in them.

THE TEACHING OF TWO CHURCHES' BISHOPS ON MIGRATION: AN ASSESSMENT

In this paper, we have outlined how populism in the US and UK depends on and furthers the perception of immigrants as a threat, particularly in the case of right-wing populism. Then-candidate Trump and the "Leave" campaign leveraged that perception successfully by invoking racism and xenophobia, encouraging the notion among voters that elites favor immigrants and refugees to their detriment. We analyzed how Roman Catholic bishops in the US and bishops in the Church of England marshaled their churches' teaching on migration to inform their communion's response and their government's actions after the election and referendum. We turn now to assess how the teaching on migration by bishops from both churches reckons with the influence of populism during the Brexit-Trump era.

First, how have the two churches responded to the claim that migrants represent a threat? Here, the US Roman Catholic bishops are a step ahead of their Church of England counterparts, working in groups with bishops across the border in Mexico and writing letters, especially in the case of Bishop Mark Seitz. The Church of England bishops' interventions on migration tend to be short, occasional, and written individually. Given the way that xenophobic discourse harms those on the margins of society and twists the imaginations of our countries, we propose that Church of England bishops can learn from

---

[92] For penetrating scholarship that illustrates the point, see Gilberto A. Ruiz, "'Out of Egypt I Called My Son': Migration as a Male Activity in the New Testament Gospels," *Latinxs, the Bible, and Migration*, ed. Efraín Agosto and Jacqueline M. Hidalgo (Basingstoke: Palgrave MacMillan, 2018), 89–108.

US Catholic bishops by devoting more attention to writing and speaking about migration. Alongside commitment to practical work alongside migrants, the Church of England bishops can gather to study, discuss, and write on the issue, as the Mission and Public Affairs division of the Church plans to do. Given the limits of their time and expertise, the bishops can draw on or foreground the works of laypeople and priests on theology and migration. Following the example of the Tex-Mex and Alta-Baja bishops who meet across the US-Mexico border to examine issues together, the bishops of the Church of England can take up the theme of migration in gatherings with other churches, whether Anglican communions beyond England or ecumenical discussions. Finally, following the example of Mark Seitz, Church of England bishops can write pastoral letters on issues of migration, as they have done on political life and creation.[93]

Second, how are the churches' bishops reckoning with Scripture in responding to the fear of migrants? In the sources analyzed, we find that some US Catholic and English Anglican bishops tend to advance their teaching about migration by appealing to national values or interests, whether American or British. Many of their interventions focus on making changes in law and policy. Those interventions may be motivated by worship and faith nourished by the Scriptures, but sometimes that motivation is not clear in the writings and speeches. Exceptions come in two cases where bishops draw upon the deep wells of Scripture. Roman Catholic Bishop Mark Seitz's pastoral letter, *Sorrow and Mourning Flee Away*, interprets a border community's experience within the world of Isaiah 35 so that the migrant's experience is set within the experience of crossing burning sands to reach Zion, singing and full of joy. By resting in the world of Scripture, Seitz enables the framing of church and government actions toward migrants in a manner that acknowledges God as a God of abundance. This insight aligns remarkably well with a second case where Church of England Bishop Paul Butler speaks from John 10 that abundance is a deeper reality than scarcity. Both bishops zero in on how the belief that this is a world of scarcity motivates fear of migrants and shapes government policies. The insight that this is a world of abundance offers the clearest evidence of the distinct way in which our churches' teaching may reckon with the influence of populism on immigration policy.

---

[93] The House of Bishops issued a letter before the period considered in this article: "Who Is My Neighbour? A Letter from the House of Bishops to the People and Parishes of the Church of England for the General Election 2015," February 2015, www.churchofengland.org/sites/default/files/2017-11/whoismyneighbour-pages.pdf. See also "Anglican Primates Respond to Archbishop of Canterbury's Request on Letters for Creation," *Anglican Communion News Service*, September 18, 2018, www.anglicannews.org/news/2018/09/anglican-primates-respond-to-archbishop-of-canterburys-request-on-letters-for-creation.aspx.

Bishops Seitz and Butler are able to perceive that abundance runs deeper than scarcity because their vision firmly rests in the universe of Scripture or, as Hans Ulrich describes it, finds its resting place in God's story.[94] They are able to speak about a God who gives and refugees *as* gifts when they allow themselves to be read by Scripture, in Gustavo Gutiérrez's words.[95] They speak in different contexts; Seitz writes to his diocese and quotes Scripture more, while Butler speaks to refugee resettlement workers and recognizes their doubts as to whether they can learn something from a bishop. Butler gently expresses what he, like Seitz, has gained by listening—listening to Scripture where they hear God's Word, and listening to stories from refugees, asylum seekers, and their neighbors. Butler passes on what he has heard, much like Seitz: a reality of gift-giving and fecundity runs alongside the apparent realities of scarcity and productivity.

A more complex case comes from Welby's book *Reimagining Britain*. The work interacts with Scripture at some length, examining Luke and Ruth and expecting to receive new insights about immigration and integration, and for that it ought to be commended. But the book's insights draw attention to the settled persons in the story rather than persons on the move: it praises settled Boaz more than the brave migrant Ruth, and does not seem to point out that the one who reaches across boundaries to become a neighbor is not the settled person but the Samaritan, the hated foreigner. While the book goes part of the way, we hope that texts about migration would dwell more in the biblical stories. As the bishops teach and preach from the Bible, can they read the Bible more like foreigners and outsiders and not mostly as settled citizens? If bishops can read Scripture alongside migrants as Seitz and Butler sometimes do, their teaching might do better at inviting hearers into life as an exodus people, an exiled people, and a dispersed church—a redeemed people of God.

Third, our analysis suggests that bishops' statements necessarily have a dual function: shaping more just immigration policies and forming faith communities that acknowledge migrants' human dignity and act accordingly. However, concern for the former appears to outweigh attention to the latter when both must go hand in hand. It may seem that the most efficient approach to protecting vulnerable migrants is to appeal to national interests and values, whether American or British, in the public square, but that move overidentifies the hierarchy (if not the churches themselves) with Pharaoh rather than Israelite migrant slaves, with Nebuchadnezzar rather than the exiles in Kings, with the chief priests and scribes rather than the persecuted diaspora in Acts. If bishops' statements in both churches could more

---

[94] Hans G. Ulrich, *Transfigured Not Conformed: Christian Ethics in a Hermeneutic Key*, ed. Brian Brock (London: T&T Clark, 2022), 29–50.
[95] Gutiérrez, *Beber en su Propio Pozo*, 58.

fully dwell in the narratives of Scripture, they would be better equipped to address the fear feeding into extremely restrictive immigration policies and laws. They will also be better able to form faith communities that fully acknowledge migrants and refugees as people with whom God journeys. If, as with Seitz and Butler's statements, they can inhabit the story of God's loving embrace of a damaged world first, then the surplus from that story will spill over into questions of civil politics. They might approach speaking in Parliament or writing to governors and Congresspeople more like Esther who speaks to protect God's exiled people in Persia. They might call on their faith communities to learn from the best examples among them to say, "Refugees and the undocumented are our people; we as church are a migrant people who stand alongside these multiply marginalized migrants." From there a truer solidarity will arise. Such an approach might seem weak; it might seem less politically expedient or productive. Yet, it will be more consistent with the bishops' prophetic calling and, in Butler's words, more fecund.

In conclusion, the influence of right-wing populism in the US and UK migration debates will continue (if not deepen). Catholic and Anglican churches in the US and UK, respectively, have spoken in the public square to confront populist immigration policies in light of Scripture directly and indirectly. In the future, bishops' texts and statements can respond better to populism, xenophobia, and racism by attending to migrants as they meet, speak, and write. Anglican Bishop Butler and Catholic Bishop Seitz embody that approach in distinct ways. Our bishops' teaching can respond better, then, not by foregrounding or starting with legal and policy goals but by inhabiting the world of Scripture alongside migrants who "read Scripture" with their lives and challenge non-migrants to be read by it. In this way, the vision of the reign of God can bring new life to tired discourses and festering wounds, being truer still to Christ's subversive hope.

Victor Carmona is an Associate Professor of Theology and Religious Studies at the University of San Diego. Recent pieces include "Amar en medio del conflicto: la teología de la liberación ante la migración" in *Memoria, presencia y futuro: A los 50 años del libro Teología de la liberación* (CEP, 2021) and "Mixed Status Families and Brokenness: Will our Fractured Relationships Heal?" in *Human Families: Identity, Relationships, and Responsibilities* (Orbis Books, 2021). His current writing brings insights from the discipline of spirituality to migration ethics.

Robert W. Heimburger is a Research Fellow in Theological Ethics at the University of Aberdeen in Scotland. He is author of *God and the "Illegal Alien": United States Immigration Law and a Theology of Politics* (Cambridge University Press, 2018). With Fe y Desplazamiento, the Faith and Displacement Project at the Seminario Bíblico de Colombia (FUSBC), he co-authored curricula for internally displaced persons and published on forgiveness, conflict, and the parable of the unforgiving debtor. His current writing asks what the Book of Acts has to say about ethics and politics today.

A Synodal Alternative for Ecclesial Conflict: Marshall Rosenberg's Nonviolent Communication

Mary Lilian Akhere Ehidiamhen

THROUGHOUT ITS HISTORY, CONFLICTS HAVE shaped various doctrines in the Roman Catholic Church. The contemporary Church struggles with controversies about racism, gender, reproductive rights, sexual abuse, power abuse, same-sex relationships, and intra/interreligious conflicts. In these situations, Church leaders can apply different strategies to address conflict, including negotiation, dialogue, or repression. Often, such strategies presume interpretative patterns of unity and stability or narrowly perceive conflict simply as "public opposition to the magisterium."[1] What often happens may be likened to what Thania Paffenholz, of the Center on Conflict, Development, and Peacebuilding at the Graduate Institute, Geneva, refers to as conflict management: this approach by leaders is largely diplomatic and top-down, excludes the people at the grassroots, and does not go deep into the roots of the conflict.[2]

The Church sometimes resorts to this top-down approach when it comes to discernment and communication around issues concerning reproductive rights, gender, and interreligious conflict.[3] At other times, the Church uses conflict resolution strategies which attempt to build relationships. Unfortunately, this latter approach may sometimes

---

[1] Anthony J. Figueiredo, *The Magisterium–Theology Relationship: Contemporary Theological Conceptions in the Light of Universal Church Teaching since 1835 and the Pronouncements of the Bishops of the United States*, Tesi Gregoriana, Serie Teologia 75 (Rome: Pontificia Università Gregoriana, 2001). Cited in Judith Gruber, "Consensus or Dissensus? Exploring the Theological Role of Conflict in a Synodal Church," *Louvain Studies* 43, no. 3 (2020): 246.
[2] Thania Paffenholz, "Understanding Peacebuilding Theory: Management, Resolution, and Transformation," *New Routes* 14, no. 2 (2009): 3.
[3] I shall further reflect on this in the application section. See Alan C. Robles, "Bishops versus Majority," www.dandc.eu/en/article/catholic-church-opposes-reproductive-health-bill-philippines; Barbra Mann Wall, "Conflict and Compromise: Catholic and Public Hospital Partnerships," *Nursing History Review* 18, no. 1 (2010): 100–17; Paul VI, "Encyclical Letter on the Regulation of Birth *Humanae Vitae*, July 25, 1968," www.vatican.va/content/paul-vi/en/encyclicals/documents/hf_p-vi_enc_25071968_humanae-vitae.html.

exclude leaders, given its great emphasis on grassroots.[4] Gerald Powers, of the Kroc Institute for International Peace Studies, therefore advocates an approach that "promotes greater integration and involves the different sectors of the Catholic community."[5] One may refer to such approach as "conflict transformation." However, any inclusive method that does not support groups and individuals with skills to deal with conflicts becomes an illusion. My hypothesis is that Marshall Rosenberg's notion of *nonviolent communication* offers sustainable tools for mediating and transforming conflicts.

Marshall Rosenberg was an American Jew who experienced anti-Semitism and violence while growing up in Detroit, Michigan. This experience led him to examine violence, compassion, and the role language plays in human relationships and peacebuilding through the lens of clinical psychology.[6] He would later study comparative religions and was convinced that religion offered a deeper understanding of human relationships. Rosenberg also observed that the central teaching of comparative religions about the human person is love, and he became more interested in how to put this into action.[7] From his knowledge of psychology and religion, he developed the idea of *nonviolent communication* which involves both speaking and listening as tools to practice love and foster human relationships. Rosenberg's conflict mediation offers tools that have the potential to satisfy the needs of everyone involved in a conflict.[8] His approach resists all forms of power asymmetry and pays attention to people's needs in justice and love. Rosenberg highlights four elements that cause conflict: making moralistic judgments, making comparisons, denying responsibility, and making demands.[9] To mediate conflicts, he suggests four actions: observing the situation without evaluation, acknowledging one's feelings, identifying the needs behind the feelings, and making an actionable request.[10] Fulfilling human needs is at the heart of Rosenberg's approach, whereas conflict arises when a person's need is unmet and every action a person performs is an attempt to meet a

---

[4] Paffenholz, "Understanding Peacebuilding Theory," 4.
[5] Gerard Powers, "Towards an Integral Catholic Peacebuilding," *Journal of Social Encounters* 2, no. 1 (2017): 1.
[6] Rosenberg, *Nonviolent Communication: A Language of Life,* 3rd ed. (Encinitas, CA: PuddleDancer, 2015), 1–2.
[7] Marshall B. Rosenberg, *Practical Spirituality: Reflections on the Spiritual Basis of Nonviolent Communication* (Encinitas, CA: PuddleDancer, 2004), 5.
[8] Rosenberg, *Nonviolent Communication,* 162.
[9] Rosenberg, *Nonviolent Communication,* 15–22.
[10] Rosenberg, *Nonviolent Communication,* 25–89.

need.[11] Nevertheless, some strategies used to meet needs result in conflict. Knowing various strategies used for meeting needs and choosing less conflict-inducing ones reduces tension.[12]

Therefore, the key objective in this investigation is to take Rosenberg's theory of nonviolent communication developed in the context of civil-political conflicts and explore its applicability to conflictual moral issues within an ecclesial context. Hence, it will briefly discuss conflict and sketch three common approaches to it: conflict management, resolution, and transformation. It will situate Rosenberg's approach within a conflict transformation approach. Against this background, it will further present Rosenberg's view of conflict, his conflict mediation principles, and their application to intrapersonal, interpersonal, and intergroup conflict. Finally, this essay will evaluate Rosenberg's approach and examine how his strategy offers practical tools for mediating diverse forms of conflict, using examples from an ecclesial context, specifically, the Reproductive Health Bill in the Philippines which affected the relationships both within the Catholic community as well as between the Church and the state.[13]

COMMON APPROACHES TO CONFLICT IN THE CHURCH: A CONCEPTUAL ANALYSIS

Conflict is basically a disagreement between opposing views or interests, which can be either intrapersonal, interpersonal, or between groups striving for discordant ends.[14] In addition, disparities in values

---

[11] Rosenberg, *Nonviolent Communication*, 52–54.
[12] Rosenberg, *Nonviolent Communication*, 49–88.
[13] "The Philippine bishops objected to 'micro-measures' of the government aimed at encouraging contraceptives and sterilization as means for family planning. The bishops emphasized responsible parenthood education as the proper way to assist married couples to plan their families." They condemned the state approach through organized protests and pastoral letters, of which one was titled 'Choose Life, Reject the RH Bill.' In the letter, the bishops argued that "the very name contraceptive already reveals the anti-life nature of the means that the RH Bill promotes." On the contrary, the state accused the bishops of "promoting a theocratic view of society that privileges Catholic teaching as the basis for legislation. Bishops have used political threats to pressure legislators to vote against the RH Bill." Consequently, the RH Bill divided the Catholic community even though the bishops claimed that the Church unanimously rejected the RH Bill. However, "A survey taken in 2008 showed that 71 percent of Filipino Catholics supported the bill. Additionally, the debate on the RH Bill provided opportunity for Filipinos to disagree with and openly criticize the Hierarchy not only about its position on the RH Bill but also on a variety of issues such as the Church's treatment of women, the sex scandal, and clergy involvement in partisan politics" (Eric Marcelo O. Genilo, "The Catholic Church and the Reproductive Health Bill Debate: The Philippine Experience," *Heythrop Journal* 55, no. 6 [2014]: 1044–51).
[14] Berghof Foundation, ed., *Berghof Glossary on Conflict Transformation: 20 Notions for Theory and Practice* (Berlin: Berghof Foundation Operations, 2012), 10. See Paul Wehr, *Conflict Regulation* (Boulder, CO: Westview, 1979), 7.

and needs stimulate social conflict[15] such that it becomes "an expressed struggle between at least two interdependent parties who perceive incompatible goals, scarce resources, and interference from others in achieving their goals."[16] To become interpersonal, a conflict must have happened at the intrapersonal level and been expressed.[17] For Paul Wehr, conflict occurs because of "poor communication, misperception, miscalculation, socialization, and other unconscious processes."[18] Conflict implies misunderstanding of perceptions, needs, interests, and values. It can occur within an individual or between individuals and groups, which involves communication and conflictual behaviors. Yet conflict also promotes social change by demonstrating that something is not right and there is need for improvement. Absence of conflict leads to stagnation.[19]

Conflict is part of human experience, and it cuts across various institutions, including the Catholic Church. Although it can have a positive dimension because it leads to transformation when properly understood and handled, some institutions do not fully understand this. For example, some centuries ago, the Catholic Church "aggressively struggled against dissenters within and without; Christians who disagreed with the Church's teachings were considered heretics and could be physically punished or killed."[20] However, in recent times, Pope Francis's retrieval of synodality can make a valuable contribution to the Catholic engagement with conflict and dissent.[21] Along this line, Judith Gruber observes that diverse evaluations of Church conflict show that "a conceptualization of synodality calls for a theology of conflict and contestation." She further argues for the need to search for a strategy to understand disagreements within the Church so that they are not immediately dismissed as heresies, and resolved in a synodal manner.[22] Yet while "a theological understanding of conflict is an integral component of synodality," the Catholic Church has not advanced a sustainable theology of conflict that can effectively deal in a nuanced way with the constructive effect contestation has on the

---

[15] Ho-Won Jeong, *Understanding Conflict and Conflict Analysis* (Singapore: Sage, 2008), 9.
[16] Joyce L. Hocker and William W. Wilmot, *Interpersonal Conflict* (New York: McGraw–Hill Education, 2018), 3.
[17] Hocker and Wilmot, *Interpersonal Conflict*, 3–4.
[18] Paul Wehr, *Conflict Regulation*, 7.
[19] Peter Harris and Ben Reilly, eds., *Democracy and Deep-Rooted Conflict: Options for Negotiations* (Stockholm: International IDEA, 1998), 32.
[20] Alixe Bovey, "The Medieval Church: From Dedication to Dissent," April 2015, www.bl.uk/the-middle-ages/articles/church-in-the-middle-ages-from-dedication-to-dissent.
[21] Judith Gruber, "Consensus or Dissensus? Exploring the Theological Role of Conflict in a Synodal Church," *Louvain Studies* 43, no. 3 (2020): 241.
[22] Gruber, "Consensus or Dissensus?," 242.

Church's way of life.²³ It is important to consider how best to accept "conflict and disagreement as a formative dimension of ecclesial traditions without falling back on interpretative patterns of unity and stability."²⁴ Hence, synodality is crucial in dealing with conflicts in the Catholic Church over against the traditional hierarchical management of conflict.

Furthermore, when there is conflict, it is either managed by leaders, resolved by those at the grassroots without the leaders, or transformed in a synodal way. Conflict management is an approach that intends to limit conflict or war through diverse diplomatic strategies by diplomats from two or more countries or organizations.²⁵ For theorists of this approach, the way to deal with conflict is to control it and eventually reach an agreement to minimize violence so that everyday politics can begin again. Additionally, conflict management engages leaders of the parties in negotiation and manages conflict for the short-term.²⁶ Despite its advantages, one weakness of conflict management is that it is a top-down approach that does not bring all actors of the conflict into negotiation. In other words, it pays little or no attention to the root of conflicts²⁷ and mainly involves leaders. Consequently, underneath what seems to be peace, there may still be boiling issues to resolve. For instance, in the ecclesial context, the efforts of leaders to address questions regarding gender, same-sex attraction, racism, sexual abuse, power abuse, issues regarding reproductive rights (a typical instance is the conflict between the Catholic Bishops and the Philippines' state on the Reproductive Health Bill),²⁸ and other conflicts managed by Church leaders without involving those at the grassroots.

Conflict resolution, which is the next focus, emerged to respond to the limitations of conflict management. Unlike the management approach, conflict resolution considers the root causes of conflict and aims at restoring damaged relationships between parties in conflict.²⁹ This method tends to enhance connections between conflicting parties by examining the origin of the conflict. It investigates the conflict's structural dimension, conflict behaviours, and the attitudes of the conflicting parties, by supporting them to examine the origin of the conflict and reframe their perspectives and goals.³⁰ This approach does not always lead to a solution because it essentially builds a network at

---

[23] Gruber, "Consensus or Dissensus?," 243.
[24] Leuven Encounters in Systematic Theology XIII, "Dissenting Church: Exploring the Theological Power of Conflict and Disagreement," theo.kuleuven.be/en/lest/lest-xiii/cfpprintable.
[25] Berghof Foundation, *Berghof Glossary on Conflict Transformation*, 18.
[26] Paffenholz, "Understanding Peacebuilding Theory," 3.
[27] Paffenholz, "Understanding Peacebuilding Theory," 3.
[28] Genilo, "The Catholic Church and the Reproductive Health Bill Debate," 1051.
[29] Paffenholz, "Understanding Peacebuilding Theory," 4.
[30] Berghof Foundation, *Berghof Glossary on Conflict Transformation*, 18.

the grassroots without necessarily involving those at the leadership level.³¹ Additionally, it may not address conflicts at the root because of structural factors, such as socioeconomic and political issues in society.³² In the ecclesial context, at local levels people at the grassroots tend to use this approach to address conflicts. Because it excludes leaders, it does not necessarily lead to agreement in resolving conflicts and does not necessarily end conflict since it does not establish structures preventing reoccurrence.

For these reasons, conflict transformation promises a better way forward. Conflict transformation aims at changing "deep-rooted armed conflicts into peaceful ones."³³ John Paul Lederach—of the Kroc Institute for International Peace Studies—advanced this approach when he focused on the root of the conflict as a way of resolving the limitations of conflict management, whose result is short-term, and conflict resolution, which has a long-term effect.³⁴ Lederach notes that "conflict transformation ... envision[s] and respond[s] to the ebb and flow of social conflict as life-giving opportunities for creating constructive change processes that reduce violence, increase justice in direct interaction and social structures, and respond to real-life problems in human relationships."³⁵ This approach pays attention to context, "mid-level individuals or groups," and strengthens them to promote peacebuilding³⁶ and reconciliation. The focus of this approach in addressing conflict from the root cause involves all conflicting parties in negotiation and creates structures to prevent reoccurrence.

Despite the high prospect for conflict transformation, Paffenholz observes, based on her experience in Mozambique and Somalia, the following weaknesses: first, "The linkage between the tracks is not sufficiently elaborate, as conflict management is still necessary but is under-conceptualised in Lederach's approach." Second, external actors need to broaden their scope beyond insiders to look at peacebuild-

---

[31] Paffenholz, "Understanding Peacebuilding Theory," 4.
[32] Brad Spangler, "Settlement, Resolution, Management, and Transformation: An Explanation of Terms," www.beyondintractability.org/essay/meaning-resolution.
[33] Paffenholz, "Understanding Peacebuilding Theory," 4.
[34] Paffenholz, "Understanding Peacebuilding Theory," 4.
[35] John Paul Lederach, "Defining Conflict Transformation," www.restorativejustice.org/10fulltext/lederach.html.
[36] "Peacebuilding engages all sectors of society and all the relevant partners—people living in the local communities who perpetrate the violence or who are directly victimized by it, national elites in the government, business, education, religion, and other sectors; and diplomats, policymakers, scholars, international lawyers, religious leaders, and other professionals who often operate at a geographical remove from the conflict." See R. Scott Appleby, "Peacebuilding and Catholicism: Affinities, Convergences, Possibilities," in *Peacebuilding: Catholic Theology, Ethics, and Praxis*, ed. Robert John Schreiter (Maryknoll: Orbis Books, 2010), 3.

ing from the wider perspective up to the regional or transnational levels.[37] Thus, conflict transformation transcends the other two approaches by extending towards post-conflict peacebuilding and social change. However, the weaknesses pointed out by Paffenholz suggest the need to further enhance the approach. Hence, for conflict transformation to support the ecclesial context in promoting integral peacebuilding, Rosenberg's nonviolent communication and conflict mediation holds promise as a complementary approach.

MARSHALL ROSENBERG ON VIOLENT COMMUNICATION

Rosenberg's approach begins with his idea of violent communication. He conceptualizes violent communications as those that make moralistic judgments and comparisons, deny responsibility for thoughts, feelings, actions, and make demands. His critique of moralistic judgment is similar to the biblical injunction in Matt 7:1: judge not, to avoid being judged. For Rosenberg, a moralistic judgment is life-alienating communication which seeks to explain the rightness and wrongness of people's actions. It involves the use of expressions judging the morality of a person's action such as, "he is a liar," and "John is right or wrong." These judgements manifest themselves in "blame, insults, put-downs, labels, criticism, comparisons, and diagnosis."[38] Such forms of moralistic judgments are apparent in the ecclesial context. For instance, in the Philippines' ecclesial context, one observes the labelling of those who opposed the Reproductive Health Bill as "team life," and those who supported the bill as "team death" and supporters of abortion.[39] Additionally, a person can also make moralistic judgment of self by seeing the self as inadequate; for instance, "I am a failure."[40] Moralistic judgment also involves using "must" or "mustn't," "should" or "shouldn't," which tends to deny a person's choice.[41] Hence, moralistic judgment involves evaluating people in terms of good, bad, right, and wrong, should and shouldn't, must and mustn't. It also includes labelling and criticizing people.

For Rosenberg a second form of violent communication is making comparisons. This involves examining the similarities and differences of two or more objects or persons in terms of quality, quantity, size, achievements, etc. Rosenberg sees making comparisons as another way of judging others. For example, when a person compares their

---

[37] Paffenholz, "Understanding Peacebuilding Theory," 5.
[38] Rosenberg, *Nonviolent Communication,* 15.
[39] Genilo, "The Catholic Church and the Reproductive Health Bill Debate," 1050–51.
[40] Mary Mackenzie, *Peaceful Living: Daily Meditations for Living with Love, Healing, and Compassion* (Encinitas, CA: PuddleDancer, 2005), 16.
[41] Thom Bond, *The Compassion Book: Lessons from the Compassion Course* (Orange Lake, NY: One Human, 2018), 217–18.

achievements with those of others, it reduces the compassion the person has for self and others.[42] Additionally, comparison exposes people to pain and envy.[43] Envy is one of the emotions and a moral vice people hardly discuss because of the pain and destructive effects that go with it.[44] According to Timothy Perrine and Kevin Timpe, envy refers to "sorrow over another's good because of a perception of inferiority regarding the other's good."[45] They note that envy results from comparing one's self-worth to another.[46] Gabriel Taylor affirms that interpersonal comparison leads to envy because a person feels that the other person is better than he/she.[47] Envy can also lead to violence against the other perceived as superior, more fortunate or successful than oneself.[48] Thus, making comparisons contributes to envy, violence, and mutual disconnections. The envy observed within some of the diverse organizations in the ecclesial context might be induced by making comparisons.

Rosenberg notes that a third form of violent communication, denying responsibility for actions, involves using "language which denies choice and implies that people are not responsible for their thoughts, feelings, and actions."[49] The inability to claim responsibility for personal actions, emotions, and thoughts contributes to alienating communication. Denial of responsibility functions in the form of "have to"; for instance, "I have to obey my superior." Such an expression might indicate that the person is under obligation or being compelled to perform certain actions the person would not ordinarily execute. In addition, expressions such as "makes me feel," "she makes me feel angry" shift the responsibility for a person's feelings and actions to something external or someone else. Finally, denial of responsibility for actions also functions in expressions such as: "'superiors' orders,' 'company policy,' and 'it was the law.'"[50] In the ecclesial context, denying responsibility for actions is sometimes supported with expressions such as: "it is natural law," "bishop's order," "the supreme pontiff has declared," and "I have to obey." Such expressions exonerate

---

[42] Rosenberg, *Nonviolent Communication*, 19.
[43] Mackenzie, *Peaceful Living*, 31.
[44] Ann and Barry Ulanov, *Cinderella and Her Sisters: The Envied and the Envying*, 4th ed. (Philadelphia: Westminster, 2012), 9.
[45] Timothy Perrine and Kevin Timpe, "Envy and Its Discontents," in *Virtue and their Vices*, ed. Kevin Timpe and Craig A. Boyd (Oxford: Oxford University Press, 2006), 232. See Aaron Ben-Ze'ev, "Envy and Inequality," *Journal of Philosophy* 89 (1992): 554.
[46] Perrine and Timpe, "Envy and Its Discontents," 231.
[47] Gabriel Taylor, *Deadly Vices* (Oxford: Oxford University Press, 2006), 41.
[48] Perrine and Timpe, "Envy and Its Discontents," 233.
[49] Rosenberg, *A Model for Nonviolent Communication* (Philadelphia: New Society Publishers, 1983), 5.
[50] Rosenberg, *Nonviolent Communication*, 19.

the actor from the action and shift the responsibility to the superior, company, and policy and might lead to disconnection and conflict.

A fourth form of violent communication is making demands. Demand implies blaming a person who fails to comply with a request.[51] When a person makes a demand of another person, they carry the disposition to disagree with the receiver if they refuse to comply. The only option available to the receiver is to either submit or rebel. In addition, a demand does not give people the space to respond joyfully to needs.[52] Moreover, some demands sound like a request.[53] For instance, "please help me to get the key." The person making the demand might need to check the feelings that emanate if the receiver does not acquiesce to the demand. If the action triggers judgment, it is a demand.[54] When making a demand of others to contribute to a person's needs, the person making the demand does not consider if the receiver also has their own needs to handle.[55]

The custom of making demands fixes a person to a particular strategy, and the receiver is seen as the only person who could satisfy the needs.[56] When people express their needs in the form of demands, they speak a language that tends to resist compassion because a demand implies willingness to blame the receiver if they do not comply.[57] Hence, placing demands on others indicates compelling them to comply without paying attention to their own needs. Making demands (could lead to disagreements if there is no willingness to accept the recipients' refusal. In the ecclesial context, the hierarchy sometimes places demand on people with their declarations without considering the needs of the people, for instance, the demand of *Humanae Vitae*, no. 11, which "condemned every use of artificial means to regulate fertility (i.e., contraception) and demanded that 'each and every marital act [sexual intercourse] must remain open to the transmission of life.'"[58] Several persons in developed countries refused to accept the teaching. Joseph Selling refers to the action as "a failure in communication." Hence, placing demands on people is one of the sources of conflict in the Church.

In sum, Rosenberg's articulation of violent communication demonstrates sources of conflict in human relationships both in the Church

---

[51] Rosenberg, *A Model for Nonviolent Communication*, 7.
[52] Mackenzie, *Peaceful Living*, 96.
[53] Demand may be understood as a synonym of request. The distinction will be clarified below.
[54] Mackenzie, *Peaceful Living*, 21.
[55] Liv Larsson and Katarina Hoffmann, *Cracking the Communication Code: Nonviolent Communication by 42 Key Differentiations* (Svensbyn: Friare Liv, 2011), 163.
[56] Larsson and Hoffmann, *Cracking the Communication*, 33.
[57] Rosenberg, *Nonviolent Communication*, 22.
[58] Joseph Selling, *Reframing Catholic Theological Ethics* (Oxford: Oxford University Press, 2016), 17.

and the state. His idea exposes the alienation that occurs when people make moralistic judgments and comparisons, deny responsibility for actions, and place demands on others, without giving them the space to accept or refuse demands. However, Rosenberg also provides some basic principles that can transform violent communication and support conflict mediation. These will be explored in the next section.

ROSENBERG ON NONVIOLENT COMMUNICATION AND MEDIATION OF CONFLICT

Rosenberg highlights four steps of nonviolent communication (NVC), which include (a) making an observation, (b) connecting with feelings, (c) identifying needs, and (d) making feasible requests. The first step in NVC is observation without evaluation, which denotes explaining what one sees, hears, or touches, while evaluation refers to drawing conclusions on what one observes. Making an evaluation (moralistic judgment) from what one observes disconnects an interlocutor from listening to what is being said, and the person might resort to defence when he or she feels judged.[59] Contrarily, observation involves expressing clearly what one hears or sees in the manner one hears or perceives it without adding the reasons why it occurred that way. When situations are described the way they are, the observer may enjoy more connection with the other. For instance, instead of saying "you always come home late" it is crucial to use observation language by saying "you arrived home beyond the agreed time three times this week." This statement might lead the hearer to offer an explanation instead of feeling guilty or critiqued.[60] In addition, instead of labelling a person deviant or sadist, it is crucial to describe the person's action captured by such labels. Observation involves describing one's experience without drawing inference from it or labelling the other.

Furthermore, observation is a substitute for changing conversation from judgment to quality connection. It frees one's thoughts and communication from judgment when talking about one's action or another person's action. For instance, if I say to my friend, "Can you remember you were screaming and complaining about your mother two days ago?" My friend will respond, "I was not screaming or complaining, I was only relaying what happened." However, if instead I say, "Remember when you were telling me about what transpired between you and your mother two days ago," my friend might be willing to talk more connectedly about what happened.[61] In addition, making observation without judgement is important because, first, of the lack of adequate facts (such as circumstances) and knowledge about the other. Second, nobody is entirely impartial in judgment because a person can

---

[59] Rosenberg, *A Model for Nonviolent Communication*, 11.
[60] Mackenzie, *Peaceful Living*, 24.
[61] Thom Bond, *The Compassion Book*, 110–11.

be emotional at the subconscious level, which could affect his/her judgment. Third, no one is faultless and as such entitled to judge others.[62] Thus, making an observation by describing the specific behaviour can prevent judgment and bring clarity and understanding.

Additionally, by expressing an observation, one describes the stimuli that results in dialogue.[63] Consequently, NVC dissuades fixed generalizations and promotes using observation language considering the "time and context" because reality is not static but continues to change.[64] Making observation resolves the problem posed by moralistic judgment and making comparison. In the ecclesial context, learning and using observation language in communication could reduce conflicts arising from moralistic judgment, labelling, and comparison which promote envy. Observation promotes connection and compassion when a person can connect with the feelings emanating from what he/she observes.

Rosenberg posits a second step in NVC: connecting with feelings. Feelings, he argues, arise when a situation is observed. They are the gateway to connect with what is happening within a person and create a vocabulary to express it to others. Feelings show evidence of how a person is, whether they are comfortable or not. For instance, the way persons feel shows whether they are hot, cold, warm, interested, or confused.[65] Feelings help humans understand how situations impact them positively or negatively.[66] They are messengers who support people to connect with what is alive in them.[67] Additionally, a feeling could be understood as "an emotion, body sensation, mood, or state of mind."[68] Rosenberg promotes connecting with how a person feels, identifying and naming the feelings, and separating feelings from thinking. It is crucial to connect with feelings and take responsibility for the feelings without blaming others for them. For instance, "I feel worried and forlorn," instead of blaming others by saying, "I feel

---

[62] William Barclay, *The Gospel of Matthew*, vol. 1 (Edinburgh: Saint Andrew, 1965), 266–68. See Lloyd J. Ogilvie and Myron S. Augsburger, eds., *The Communicator's Commentary: Matthew* (Waco, TX: Word, 1982), 96.

[63] Raj Gill, Lucy Leu, and Judi Morin, *Nonviolent Communication (NVC) Toolkit for Facilitators: Interactive Activities and Awareness Exercises Based on 18 Key Concepts for the Development of NVC Skills and Consciousness* (Charleston, SC: Createspace Independent, 2009), 103.

[64] Rosenberg, *Nonviolent Communication*, 26.

[65] Rosenberg, *A Model for Nonviolent Communication*, 18.

[66] Rosenberg, *A Model for Nonviolent Communication*, 19.

[67] Thom Bond, *The Compassion Book*, 37.

[68] Gill, Leu, and Morin, *Nonviolent Communication (NVC) Toolkit for Facilitators*, 119.

abandoned."[69] Therefore, feelings tend to imply connecting with inward and outward bodily sensations, which could be expressed in the form of emotions: joyful, sad, surprised, and upset.

Rosenberg further notes that people do not cause how another person feels, but their actions could stimulate personal feelings. He argues that feelings depend on a person's choice on how to receive and react to stimuli.[70] In other words, a person feels a certain way because of his/her needs.[71] To overcome this, Rosenberg suggests transcending feelings to identify the needs behind actions.[72] Hence, a person's action could trigger another person's feelings. However, no one can cause a person to feel the way he/she feels except the person's needs. It is crucial to express feelings in a manner that does not place blame on another person. Connecting with feelings supports one in taking responsibility for one's actions and feelings. This principle resolves the problems of moralistic judgment, comparison, and denying responsibility, examined in the previous section. In the ecclesial context, paying attention to people's feelings could support understanding one another and avoiding actions that could lead to conflict and disconnection.

Since feelings arise due to human needs, it is crucial to further examine Rosenberg's third step in the NVC process, the ability to connect with need. This enables people to identify the needs their feelings reveal.[73] Needs involve the daily assets human beings require for sustenance. These could be *physical needs* such as air, water, food, and rest or *emotional needs* such as mutual understanding, care, authenticity, and meaning.[74] In addition, need is an inborn compelling force, universal irrespective of culture and context, which helps people grow and survive as humans.[75] Consequently, all human actions are efforts to meet needs.[76] NVC involves learning how to translate words and actions into needs, which can promote connection and transformation of conflict.[77] Hence, need is what motivates human actions.

Moreover, feelings direct humans to their needs. When people can identify the needs behind their actions and feelings, they are more inclined to support others compassionately.[78] NVC encourages a person

---

[69] Gill, Leu, and Morin, *Nonviolent Communication (NVC) Toolkit for Facilitators*, 119.
[70] Rosenberg, *Teaching Children Compassionately*, 17–18.
[71] Marshall B. Rosenberg, *Life-Enriching Education: Nonviolent Communication Helps Schools Improve Performance, Reduce Conflict, and Enhance Relationships* (Encinitas, CA: PuddleDancer, 2003), 30.
[72] Rosenberg, *Teaching Children Compassionately*, 18.
[73] Rosenberg, *Nonviolent Communication*, 60.
[74] Rosenberg, *Nonviolent Communication*, 165.
[75] Larsson and Hoffmann, *Cracking the Communication Code*, 21.
[76] Thom Bond, *The Compassion Book*, 1.
[77] Rosenberg, *Nonviolent Communication*, 168.
[78] Rosenberg, *Nonviolent Communication*, 53.

to connect a feeling to a need by expressing, for example, "I feel angry because I need connection." This statement explains what is happening within that is stimulating a subjective feeling.[79] Deborah Hunsinger and Theresa Latini relate needs to Christian virtues and argue that

> What we called virtues [justice, compassion, mercy, forgiveness, prudence, temperance][80] in the Christian life are here identified simply as universal human needs. All persons need love, integrity, hope, and purpose. Christians may define each of these words in a specifically Christian way, and they can use the words as pointers toward universal qualities of being that enable them to connect meaningfully with the humanity of others.[81]

Hence, virtues are human needs which motivate human actions; they could be identified through connecting with feelings.

Identifying needs helps individuals and groups search for strategies to meet the needs. Rosenberg refers to strategies as means of meeting needs by making a request of oneself or another person about an action to perform to satisfy needs.[82] However, efforts to meet human needs could result in conflict when there is lack of adequate strategies.[83] One reason that some strategies result in conflict could be because they are not in agreement with societal norms.[84] Consequently, unmet needs due to scarcity could retard an individual's or group's development. If this experience is widespread, society will experience large-scale conflict at personal, interpersonal, intrastate, and interstate levels.[85] In the ecclesial context, it can be argued that diverse conflicts (gender, same-sex relationships, reproductive rights, racism, power, and sexual abuse) result from unmet needs (equity, collaboration, recognition, inclusion, choice, well-being, support, acceptance, sharing, consideration, justice, and respect). Specifically, some clergy who perpetrate sexual abuse might be having need for companionship, connection,

---

[79] Rosenberg, *A Model for Nonviolent Communication*, 26.
[80] The bracketed words are mine, for emphasis.
[81] Deborah van Deusen Hunsinger and Theresa F. Latini, *Transforming Church Conflict: Compassionate Leadership in Action* (Lousville, KY: Westminster John Knox, 2013), 24.
[82] Rosenberg, *Nonviolent Communication*, 67.
[83] Christopher Mitchell, "Necessituous Man and Conflict Resolution: More Basic Questions about Basic Human Needs Theory," in *Conflict Resolution and Human Needs: Linking Theory and Practice,* ed. Kevin Avruch and Christopher Mitchell (London: Routledge, 2013), 155.
[84] Larsson and Hoffmann, *Cracking the Communication Code*, 21–22.
[85] Ramashray Roy, "Social Conflicts and Needs Theories: Some Observations," in *Conflict Resolution and Human Needs*, 125. See Ronald J. Fisher, "Needs Theory, Social Identity, and an Eclectic Model of Conflict," in *Conflict: Human Needs Theory*, ed. John Burton (London: Macmillan, 1990), 109.

and support. However, some tragic strategies are being used in communicating and satisfying needs. Therefore, conflict ensues when persons attach themselves to a particular strategy without the disposition to explore diverse options. Rosenberg's idea of connecting with human needs addresses the four types of violent communication investigated in the previous section. Instead of engaging in moralistic judgment, comparison which leads to envy, denying responsibility for actions, and making demands of people, it is more supportive to connect with the needs they are attempting to meet with their actions and support them with less conflicting strategies to meet those needs.

This leads to the fourth step in the NVC process and one of the strategies for satisfying needs: to the examination of request. Making requests is a way of asking someone to do something willingly.[86] It implies a language that suggests dialogue and contrasts with a language of demand, which implies order or ultimatums. A request includes mentioning a specific action a person wants the other to perform. It involves using polite language such as "would you be willing to," which gives a person the space to either accept or refuse the request without being blamed.[87] Furthermore, the process of making a request begins with observing a situation without mingling it with judgment. Then the feelings concerning the situation are expressed and the needs emanating from the feelings are identified. Finally, a request is made to meet the identified need.[88] Thus, a request is a respectful way of asking someone or a group to perform an action instead of placing a demand as discovered in the previous section.

People might sometimes find it difficult to differentiate between demand and request. A request creates space for others to accept what people ask for as "an opportunity to exercise their generosity and not as demands, threats, or orders."[89] The receiver's response to what is asked is an act of compassion, which gives them the joy of contributing to needs and receiving support. In contrast, a demand threatens people's freedom of choice, and they react with guilt and shame.[90] The willingness to accept the refusal of a request by connecting with the feelings and needs of the receiver shows that it is a request and not a demand. Contrarily, when persons make a demand, they might not be willing to accept any refusal or connect with the feelings and needs of the receiver.[91] Thus, a request is a strategy for asking others to contribute to needs, which is different from a demand that imposes an

---

[86] Larsson and Hoffmann, *Cracking the Communication Code*, 33. See Hunsinger and Latini, *Transforming Church Conflict*, 69.
[87] Martha Lasley, *Facilitating with Heart: Awakening Personal Transformation and Social Change* (Charleston, SC: Discover, 2010), 104.
[88] Rosenberg, *Nonviolent Communication*, 67.
[89] Rosenberg, *A Model for Nonviolent Communication*, 36.
[90] Rosenberg, *A Model for Nonviolent Communication*, 36.
[91] Rosenberg, *A Model for Nonviolent Communication*, 36.

order on another person with the goal of satisfying needs. In the ecclesial context, some hierarchical declarations appear in the form of demands, and some people at the grassroots struggle with such demands because they sometimes affect their freedom of choice. Placing a demand on people might lead to disconnection and conflict. However, using request language will increase people's willingness to collaborate in achieving certain tasks.

In sum, Rosenberg's nonviolent communication is ground-breaking work that offers people tools of observation, feelings, needs, and request to connect with their compassionate nature and others for peaceful coexistence. The principles promote empathy for self and others. They are very useful and learnable even though training is required to enable people to use them efficiently. So, how might these principles be applied in mediating and transforming conflicts? Rosenberg's mediation approach follows five steps. First, the conflicting parties communicate their needs. Second, the mediator helps the conflicting parties clarify their needs. Sometimes, the parties express their observations/experiences by mixing them with judgments, while the mediator listens to them and translates the expressions and judgments into needs. Third, the mediator checks with each of the conflicting parties whether they have been able to discern the needs of the speaker correctly by reflecting to the speaker what they said.[92] The mediator continues to reflect to the speaker until the speaker confirms that their needs have been articulated properly. Fourth, the mediator engages empathically with the speaker (especially when emotions—arguments, pains, tears—are high) to coherently understand their needs. Fifth, after the mediator has gained clarity on both parties' needs, and the parties are clear about their needs as well, the mediator can support them with suggestions about the strategies needed to resolve the conflict by guiding them on making doable requests.[93] Rosenberg's mediation style involves establishing quality connection between conflicting parties by supporting them to identify their feelings and needs, and collaborate in searching for feasible strategies to satisfy needs.

Furthermore, Rosenberg's analysis of the mediation of conflicts is very clear and practical; however, it requires training, emotional intelligence, literacy, and constant practice. Since Rosenberg's approach is more structured, it could complement and provide structure to the gen-

---

[92] Carefulness is important when rephrasing what was said by any of the conflicting parties. The restating by a mediator of what he heard from the parties increases trust and reassures them that the mediator understands what they are saying. See Liv Larsson, *A Helping Hand: Mediations with Nonviolent Communication* (Svensbyn: Friare Liv, 2010), 85.
[93] Rosenberg, *Nonviolent Communication,* 164. Marshall Rosenberg, *Living Nonviolent Communication: Practical Tools to Connect and Communicate Skilfully in Every Situation* (Boulder, CO: Sounds True, 2012), 2.

eral conflict transformation approach. In addition, discussions of Rosenberg's conflict mediation paradigm have contributed to an understanding of the mediation process that is life-enriching, promotes power sharing, and empowers people to resist compromise, bias, corruption, favouritism, and the use of persuasion in mediation. Rosenberg's mediation process tends to be more efficient because it focuses on satisfying disputed needs.

ROSENBERG'S MODEL, THE REPRODUCTIVE HEALTH BILL, AND GENDER JUSTICE

In the introduction, I highlighted some of the issues the Roman Catholic Church struggles with, such as racism, gender inequality, reproductive rights, sexual and power abuses, same-sex relationships, as well as intra/interreligious conflicts. Church leaders use different methods to deal with conflicts. One of these is conflict management, which however excludes people at the grassroots. Such an approach creates doctrines on how to manage problems without connecting with the experiences of people who differ in opinion and, as a result, have little impact at the grassroots level.

Pope Francis's rediscovery of synodality (journeying together),[94] which involves "all members of the people of God in the life of the Church,"[95] offers the Church a new hope and a different way of dealing with conflicts. For Pope Francis, "Conflict should not be ignored or concealed; it has to be faced. The best way to deal with conflict is the willingness to resolve it and to make a link in the chain of new process."[96] As a result, Rosenberg's nonviolent communication and conflict mediation offers the Church some practical tools to transform conflict in a synodal manner. This suggests applying the principles of observation, feelings, needs and request to the Church's approach to conflict. Rosenberg's approach could shift the Church's attention from conflict management to conflict transformation using NVC skills.

Instances for applying Rosenberg's principles within the Catholic Church include issues of reproductive rights, abortion right/prohibition, gender issues, sexual and power abuse, other conflicts, and communication around these. Generally, the case of *Humanae Vitae*, no. 11 (on birth regulation), that stirred a massive controversy could be transformed with the NVC approach. Such a strategy would begin by observing and listening to the reproductive experiences of people at

---

[94] Gruber, "Consensus or Dissensus?," 241.
[95] Gruber, "Consensus or Dissensus?," 241. See Pope Francis, "*Evangelii Gaudium*: Apostolic Exhortation of the Holy Father Francis to the Bishops, Clergy, Consecrated Persons and the Lay Faithful on the Proclamation of the Gospel in Today's World," November 24, 2013, nos. 27–33, www.vatican.va/content/francesco/en/apost_exhortations/documents/papa-francesco_esortazione-ap_20131124_evangelii-gaudium.html#II.%E2%80%82Pastoral_activity_and_conversion.
[96] Francis, "*Evangelii Gaudium*," no. 227.

the grassroots (both married and young people) without judgment, criticisms or labelling them as dissenters or heretics, in order to understand what they are not comfortable with in the document that is affecting their well-being. Such listening could be organized in the form of seminars at the local and global levels. The next step would be to connect with people's feelings about what the Church proposed in the document and identify their needs (what is important to them that will support their well-being). Such needs might include the desire to be heard and respected, as well as collaboration, given the yearning to be involved in making decisions on issues affecting them. This collaboration implies a co-participatory dimension in Church life instead of limiting the decision-making process to only a small number of male clergy who have no experience of conjugal or parental life. Having identified their needs, the next step would be to collaborate by involving them in searching for less conflicting strategies that will satisfy everybody by making feasible requests using positive and action-oriented language.

Consider as a possible case study the Reproductive Health Bill (RHB) conflict between the Catholic Church and the Philippine state, which escalated due to communication issues. Here we saw the Church engage in actions of judging in terms of right and wrong, labelling opponents of the bill "team life" and supporters "team death" and supporters of abortion.[97] Such sloganeering revealed a judgmental and belligerent mindset. Such a mindset at times affects the Catholic Church's communication and willingness to dialogue with those who differ in opinion. The Church needs to consider the experiences (poverty, inadequate access to good health care, family violence, and the cost of raising a large family) and needs of people at the grassroots when making ethical decisions. Consequently, nonviolent communication processes could support the Church with practical communication skills that focus on connecting with people's experiences and feelings, identifying, and satisfying their needs with diverse and less conflicting strategies in a collaborative manner.

The process implies training NVC mediators (both clergy and laity) to facilitate dialogues within the Church and between the Church and the state. Such dialogues could take the form of conferences and seminars to create space to listen to the experiences of dissenters, for example, people at the grassroots and leaders directly and indirectly involved in the RHB conflict—without judgment, criticism, and labelling. This would enable the Church to understand the circumstances surrounding the people and why they are supporting the bill. The second step would require connecting with the feelings of all parties to understand how they feel about supporting and opposing the bill. In

---

[97] Genilo, "The Catholic Church and the Reproductive Health Bill Debate," 1051.

this situation, the feelings could be anger, frustration, worry, exclusion, fear, etc. The next step would be identifying the needs behind the feelings, which motivate their actions. Such needs could be respect, mutual understanding, participation, collaboration, recognition, and support. The Church's ability to focus on identifying and satisfying people's needs would support effective pastoral care for the people. The role of the mediators in this regard would be to ensure that all parties are heard and their needs adequately articulated. Once they are sure that the needs of the parties have been mutually identified, the last step would involve the collaborative efforts of all parties to search for less conflicting strategies to satisfy these needs, which would involve making feasible requests, using clear, positive, and action language.

Gender justice in the church is a structural problem related to reproductive health and another arena in which NVC could make an interesting contribution. Regarding gender issues, women have articulated their needs for respect, participation, collaboration, and inclusion in the clerical life of the Church, and have made some requests to the Church. However, the Church's hierarchy is slow in granting these requests. This is not to say that the Church is not responding to the issue. Collaborative effort between women and men is needed to achieve the flourishing of people in the Church. Excluding women from participating in priesthood, studying in Catholic seminaries, and holding certain functions in the Church could be seen as forms of gender injustice. Justifying such an exclusion with some biblical passages is being insensitive to the needs of people and the signs of the times. The Bible was written from the lived experiences of people at the time it was written. Consequently, though the Bible stands as a template, it is important to pay attention to the experiences and needs of people in the present time to avoid being fixated on lived experiences of the past while ignoring the needs of the present times. It is crucial to use NVC principles to respond to instances of gender conflict through a collaborative process of dialogue between the hierarchy and people at the grassroots in the attempt to discover less-conflicting strategies that will satisfy the needs of all parties in the conflict. To achieve this, the Catholic Church needs to make a shift from its moralistic judgement stance that perceives women as unfit for certain tasks in the Church.

Consequently, the current reflection on the synodal process is a golden opportunity for the Church to re-examine gender justice by first empathically listening to the experiences (observation) of women to understand the areas where they experience exclusion. Such a listening forum could be organised at local, diocesan, and global levels facilitated by priests and laity trained in the NVC mediation process. Second, connect with the feelings of women to understand how exclusion impacts them. Connecting with their feelings will enable facilitators to identify their needs because feelings reveal people's needs.

Third, the facilitators identify their needs such as inclusion, collaboration, acceptance, support, and so on. After identifying the needs—when the facilitators are convinced and have checked with women that their needs have been adequately articulated—they collaborate in exploring strategies to satisfy these needs by making actionable requests. The process also involves using the same steps to listen to the needs of the Church (through representatives), such as order, collaboration, ease, courage, and so on. After identifying the needs of both women and the Church, both the laity and clergy could collaborate in searching for peaceful strategies to satisfy these needs without anyone compromising their needs for the other. The process might take a long time, but it will reduce gender tension in the Church and promote the flourishing of all Christians, if the Church is willing to make a shift to respond to the needs of people by paying attention to the signs of the times.

Exploring the NVC process could support the Church at all levels to regain its moral voice in creating sustainable norms through dialogue for effective pastoral care that will respond to people's needs rather than insisting on rigid interpretation of doctrines lacking compassion, alienating and negatively impacting people. NVC will shift the Church from conflict management to conflict transformation that involves all parties in transforming conflicts and creating structures to prevent future reoccurrence. It will support the Church to become an empathic and listening Church caring for the needs of people, sharing power *with* not exercising power *over* people. Therefore, this paper recommends general education on peacebuilding and specifically trainings on Rosenberg's nonviolent communication and conflict mediation skills by including them in Catholic schools' curriculum. More concretely, seminaries, religious congregations, and the entire laity need to pay attention to trainings in peace education and NVC. At local levels, parishes need to train groups and families in NVC skills for daily intrapersonal, interpersonal, and intergroup interactions, to promote dialogue and satisfactory relationships responding to human needs and rights.

CONCLUSION

An investigation into ways of dealing with conflicts benefits greatly from a perspective grounded in Rosenberg's nonviolent communication and conflict mediation. This approach which I applied in this article began by highlighting the Catholic Church's struggle in dealing with conflicts. The study further examined the general meaning of conflict which indicates disagreement between needs, interests and values, linking it with the Catholic understanding of conflict and attitude towards dissenters. Furthermore, the paper examined the three common approaches to conflict: management, resolution, and transformation, arguing that the Catholic Church tends towards conflict management which focuses mainly on leaders and excludes those at the grassroots. The paper appeals to Rosenberg's nonviolent communication, given its capacity to enhance previous approaches as a way of providing robust support to the Church in conflict. In order to attain some of the goals addressed in this investigation, I advocate for training on nonviolent communication to equip individuals and groups with practical skills to dialogue and engage empathetic listening as a way of supporting the Church in its synodal mission.

Mary Lilian Akhere Ehidiamhen, from Nigeria, is presently a doctoral researcher and assistant at the Faculty of Theology and Religious Studies, Catholic University of Leuven, Belgium. She majors in Theological Ethics with specific interest in Social and Peace Ethics. Her academic orientation involves paying attention to the experiences of people from their frame of reference (context) and its relationship to their belief system. This is realized through focusing on people's needs and bringing them into dialogue with academics in an interdisciplinary manner. She is interested in contributing to the realization of United Nations' Sustainable Development Goals 4 and 16. Thus, her research focuses on how Marshall Rosenberg's nonviolent communication can contribute to Catholic social teaching on peace and address the violent conflicts in Nigeria and contribute to peacebuilding in Nigeria and beyond.

Review Essay

Theological Ethics of Life: A New Volume by the Pontifical Academy for Life

Roberto Dell'Oro and M. Therese Lysaught

*E*TICA TEOLOGICA DELLA VITA: SCRITTURA, TRADIZIONE, SFIDE PRATICHE (Theological Ethics of Life: Scripture, Tradition, Practical Challenges) is a hefty tome, 520 pages of primary text, discussion, and response.[1] It brings together the papers presented at an interdisciplinary study seminar organized by the Pontifical Academy for Life in October 2021, in which leading theologians and philosophers provided a series of substantive, targeted responses to a primary text (or *testo base*) that aimed to recast a "theological ethics of life" in light of Pope Francis's more recent doctrinal impulse, especially his encyclicals and apostolic exhortations.[2]

This *testo base*—which opens with the words "the joy of life" or *gaudium vitae*—was the fruit of the collaborative work of eight authors who engaged in a long process of progressive formulation and redaction, discerning how the insights of the Catholic bioethical tradition (e.g., *Humanae Vitae, Evangelium Vitae*) receive further articulation in light of Pope Francis's developing theological corpus from *Evangelii Gaudium, Amoris Laetitia*, and *Laudato Si'* to *Veritatis Gaudium*, and more.[3] Catholic scholars were invited to offer their support or, conversely, critical assessment, of the *testo base*, keeping alive a dialogue within the church on the delicate field of bioethics beyond any artificial division between conservatives and liberals, traditionalists and revisionists. In *Etica teologica della vita*, the *testo base* is

---

[1] Vincenzo Paglia, ed., *Etica teologica della vita: Scrittura, tradizione, sfide pratiche* (*Theological Ethics of Life: Scripture, Tradition, Practical Challenges*) (Libreria Editrice Vaticana, 2022).
[2] "Archbishop Paglia on Pope's Teaching on 'Theological Ethics of Life," *Vatican News*, June 30, 2022, www.vaticannews.va/en/vatican-city/news/2022-06/archbishop-vincenzo-paglia-pope-francis-interview-theological-et.html.
[3] As the introductory note to *Etica teologica della vita* clarifies, the eight scholars who drafted the *testo base* were: Carlo Casalone, Maurizio Chiodi, Roberto Dell'Oro, Pier Davide Guenzi, Anne-Marie Pelletier, Pierangelo Sequeri, Marie-Jo Thiel, and Alain Thomasset.

offered in Italian, followed by responses in Italian, Spanish, French, and English from figures hailing from Europe, the US, Africa, Latin America, and the Philippines. As such, the volume stands out for its strong international character and scope, highlighting the *global* nature of the church as reflected in the works of the seminar.

There is much to recommend about the volume—for what it represents, i.e., a meditative and respectful conversation among scholars of diverse theological inspiration in the tradition of *questiones disputatae*—but also for what it signals with respect to the premises that sustain such an extraordinary exchange. The latter—embodied in the concrete practices of study, reflection, argument, and face-to-face interactions that unfolded between real persons in real time over the years necessary for in-depth theological discourse—may not always come across as clearly in the finished product, which might be perceived as a static artifact. Unpacking the critical premises that undergird the volume, therefore, may provide a helpful framework for readers, who are invited to enter into the dynamism of the text and continue the deliberations it offers.

In this article, we highlight three such premises, provide an overview of the volume itself, and offer some final considerations about its potential impact upon the current theological discussion on an ethics of life inspired by Christian anthropology.

HERMENEUTICAL PREMISES OF *ETICA TEOLOGICA DELLA VITA*

The first premise concerns the relation between *theology and magisterium*. Overcoming the stereotypical rendition of the two as alternative, the volume pleads for a shared *diakonia* to the "intelligence of faith," which both magisterium and theology, in their respective space and function, serve in obedience to the objectivity of the Christian revelation. Thus, the unrelenting work of theological reflection, as an attempt to unpack the meaning of the "joy of life," aims, ultimately, at conveying the beauty and significance of the Gospel's ethical message for both believers and non-believers.

In turn, the magisterium articulates the multifaceted richness of the Christian revelation by pointing, with its doctrinal articulation, to the heart of the kerygma, the "ever fresh and attractive good news of the Gospel of Jesus Christ."[4] Such a premise results in an understanding of the inseparable nexus of theology and pastoral care, beyond an intellectualist ethics detached from faith, on the one hand, and a magisterial message disincarnated from history, on the other.

To retrieve a different appreciation for the dialogue between theology and magisterium entails recognizing the dynamic character of the ecclesial tradition and the importance of *doctrinal developments* in matters of morals. This is the second premise.

---

[4] Pope Francis, *Veritatis Gaudium* (2018), Foreword, no. 4a.

The issue here is one of fidelity to the origins and continuity of doctrinal statements consistent with a *lived* attunement to the challenges of the times, rather than abstract repetition of formulas. The Christian message is born of an "event of life" that neither immediately depends on a particular system of thought nor can be fixed within the measure of a timeless normative articulation. The Gospel of life is not a "statement" about life, nor a rigid normative system defined once and for all, but an experience of the overwhelming mystery of its origin in God.

As the *testo base* suggests, "*The life* of faith *explains itself, thinks itself*, it makes itself intelligent" (no. 5, emphasis in original).[5] This means that the attempt to articulate doctrinally the significance of such an original experience cannot simply "reassemble life by means of an abstract conceptualization, but restores to it its *own* understanding in words of wisdom that come from the roots of its mystery" (no. 5).

In this light, it becomes clear that the dynamic character of church doctrine on matters of life ethics does not answer to spurious requests for accommodation, nor is it a kind of linguistic adjustment aimed at making the Gospel of life more suitable to contemporary ears. The Christian tradition moves between the two poles that nourish its self-understanding: the Christ event, finding its mediation in Scriptures and tradition, and the reality of contemporary society, to whose complexity and cultural expectations it tries to respond. Benedict XVI described this tradition in the beautiful image of "the living river that links us to the origins, the living river in which the origins are ever present."[6]

Because it is *living*, such tradition is also constantly in motion, beyond any pretense to realized completeness. Thus, as Pope Francis suggests,

> The theologian who is satisfied with his complete and conclusive thought is mediocre. The good theologian has an open, that is, an incomplete thought, always open to the *maius* of God and of the truth, always in development, according to the law that Saint Vincent of Lérins described in these words: *annis consolidetur, dilatetur tempore, sublimetur aetate*.[7]

Dialogue, and this third premise is, therefore, an exigence internal to theological thinking, an intellectual necessity rather than a concession to "good will" or an optional disposition by amiable thinkers in search

---

[5] The English quotations from the *testo base* offered here were made directly from the Italian text. All parenthetical in-text citations in this article are to the *testo base* as included in *Etica teologica della vita*.
[6] Pope Francis, *Veritatis Gaudium*, Foreword, 4d.
[7] Pope Francis, *Veritatis Gaudium*, Foreword, 3.

of self-congratulatory recognition. *Etica teologica della vita* gives testament to the fruitfulness and need for intra-ecclesial dialogue, especially around issues that, though hotly debated, do not always pay heed to foundational dimensions necessary to ground their more mindful articulation. Among the issues addressed in the *testo base*, subsequently becoming an object of discussion during the seminar, are artificial contraception, *in vitro* fertilization, and end of life care, among others.

ETICA TEOLOGICA DELLA VITA: A PRÉCIS

Etica teologica della vita, seeking to capture the dynamics of a theological conversation unfolding under the aegis of the Pontifical Academy for Life, is organized following the timeline of the seminar, presenting sections of the *testo base* and the targeted commentaries under the headings of Prima Giornata, Seconda Giornata, and so forth. The *testo base* proceeds in roughly three parts. After the introductory chapter, Chapters II-V take up traditional loci in Catholic bioethics; Chapters VI-X take up a series of "Great Anthropological, Ethical, and Theological Questions"; and the final two chapters consider emerging questions and eschatology. For the sake of simplicity, we outline in this section the content of the *testo base*. Given the multiplicity of discussants and respondents, it would be too cumbersome to detail here the individual analyses of the *testo base* and the ensuing dialogue amongst seminar participants.[8] Beyond the "materiality" of the dialogue between the authors of the *testo base* and their interlocutors, we provide a snapshot of the nature of the dialogue in which they engaged, whose hermeneutical premises and potential impact we articulate in this piece.

Chapter I, entitled "The Joy of Life—Inheritance and Project," sets both the tone of the *testo base*, and signals key methodological moves that shape its vision. This vision is grounded in the preceding tradition of magisterial reflection on bioethical questions but locates that tradition in a more robust theological framework. In language that echoes *Laudato Si'*, the document opens boldly—affirming not only that life is a gift, but that this gift is rooted in and discerned through joy, relationship, contemplation, and attentiveness, and manifest in the ordinary, concrete lives of real people. Its opening paragraphs are worth quoting in full:

> The joy of life (*Gaudium vitae*) is manifested in human history in many ways and has its origin in the gift of life itself. It is a sentiment that is born of the gratuitousness of personal relationships, but also of

---

[8] In the seminar, invited *discussants* responded critically to the *testo base;* authors of the *testo base* served as *respondents* to those critical presentations.

> a "contemplative distance" and of a deep attentiveness vis-à-vis created things and the universe. It is the grateful joy of the one who receives an act of welcome, a cup of water, a smile, or a hand in moments of difficulty. It is the joy of the child who is happy to see again the face of its father who is playing hide-and-seek with it. It is the pleasure of the grandmother when she sees her little grandchild running towards her and taking its first steps. It is the joy of the poet who is struck with wonder at the manifestation of things, even the simplest things that are apparently insignificant. It is the tremor of one in love when he recognizes the approaching steps of his beloved. It is the profound joy of one who in prayer feels within oneself the words of Jesus: "I have called you friends ..." (Jn 15:15). It is the marvelous joy of the one who has recovered from Covid-19 and lies on the grass under the tepid March sun and lets himself be welcomed by the maternal embrace of the earth. The joy of life implies freedom from the claim to control and manipulate everything. It is generated by an attitude of "let it be" that reveals openness to welcome the revelation of good in the promise that is inscribed upon existence itself. This joy, accordingly, is not far from the life of human persons, nor is it an impossible mirage for them. (no. 1)

Yet the joy of life is not simply captured in these myriad minute incarnations; it is primordial and cosmic as well—an ontology of gift, joy, and life rather than of scarcity, death, darkness, pointing recursively toward Christology:

> In its concrete history, humanity recognizes with surprise that the joy of living is a quivering that is spread throughout the entire universe. Joy goes ahead of us, because it belongs to life itself, in its essence: it is manifested in the sensitive and sensuous character of its glorious presence, which is the opposite of a cold seriousness or an inert neutrality. The joy of life is the very glory of the being that asserts itself over against pure nothing and detaches itself from the inertness of pure Being [*Sein*], with the incessant vibration and dance of the living being. Joy belongs to life in its essence, because life enjoys from the very first moment its victory over the blinkered identity of the being that remains standing where it is, as it is, in itself. This means that the cultures and the religions, the philosophies and the theologies, art and poetry, and many other works of the human being are, in their various ways, a testimony to the joy that is born of the promise of life, the promise that has found its full realization in Jesus. The Church bears witness to this with amazement and gratitude. The present document wishes to put words to the "symphonic truth" that makes its way through the world and through history in an authentic hymn to joy. (no. 2)

Other key affirmations resound throughout the chapter—that the joy of life: springs from God's own joy in complementing the goodness and abundance of creation (no. 3); is for every single person, persisting through the pain of the world as "an authentic act of spiritual resistance to the blackmail of evil" (no. 4); challenges the false divorce between theology (theory) and pastoral work (practice) (no. 5); and affirms that "the truth is not an abstract idea, but is Jesus himself, the Word of God in whom is the Life that is the Light of the human race" (no. 6).

Drawing on Pope Francis's corpus broadly—including, for example, *Veritatis Gaudium*—the opening chapter also reflects on the task of theology. It affirms that "the church is ever open to new situations and ideas" and that "the good theologian has an open, that is, an incomplete thought, always open to the *maius* of God and of the truth, always in development" (no. 6). It reprises Pope Francis's four criteria for revivifying ecclesiastical studies—and hence, the whole of theology—going forward. The first criterion is that theology is first and foremost a contemplative practice, a discipline that proceeding "in a manner that is spiritual, intellectual, and existential, is able to go 'to the heart of the kerygma'" (no. 7). Second, it is dialogical. Citing Benedict XVI, we are reminded that from the encounter that is at the origin of theology "truth is *logos* that creates *dia-logos*" (no. 8). Third, theology must be both inter- and trans-disciplinary; revelation "does not annul other knowledge; on the contrary, it requires it" (no. 9). And finally, it requires a rich collaboration (no. 10) among theological institutions, cultural fields, scientific disciplines, those who are poor, the laity and clergy who participate in parish life, and more. The *testo base* articulates a broadly synodal vision for the practice of theology.

Setting the rhythm for the entire document, Chapter I is followed by analyses of two discussants: Piero Coda, Ordinary Professor of Trinitarian Ontology at the University of Sophia in Loppiano; and Emilce Cuda, Faculty member at the Pontifical Catholic University of Argentina and the Secretary of the Pontifical Commission for Latin America.

Taking to heart the counsel of the Second Vatican Council, the systematic work of the document, which begins in Chapter II, begins with a substantive reflection on "Sacred Scripture and Life." After a series of caveats on the loss of engagement with scripture for baptized persons (no. 14) and potential misuses of scripture (nos. 15–17), the document traces the scriptural witness not only to "life" (as in *Evangelium Vitae*) but to the *joy* of life and its goodness from Genesis through the witness of the Hebrew Scriptures to the incarnation, beatitudes, Christ's ministry, and his glorified body (transfigured and raised). The overriding message here—captured in many of the subheadings—is *blessing*. Andrzej S. Wodka, president of the Holy See Agency for the evaluation and promotion of the quality of university and ecclesiastical faculty (Avepro) and former dean of the Alphonsian Academy, Rome, serves as the discussant for Chapter II.

Following the pattern established with *Rerum Novarum,* Chapter III—"Interpreting the Present Time"—outlines the particular "signs of the times" that challenge those faithfully seeking to navigate the church's witness to the blessing and joy of life in our contemporary context. These include, in keeping with the tradition, distorted anthropologies and sociologies, the "individualism and the privatization of the subject, whose narcissism and self-centeredness increase all the time.... the deep fraying of family and societal relationships in a logic of self-sufficiency that sees only one's own interests" (nos. 46–47). We hear as well of the two-edged sword of new technologies, offering extraordinary new knowledge and benefits (nos. 56–59) as well as equally profound challenges. In keeping with Pope Francis's insight that "everything is interconnected," this chapter highlights the close connection between the "'emerging and converging' processes" of twenty-first century technologies, that promise to transform not only the natural world but also ourselves (nos. 63–66). This survey of the contemporary landscape also foregrounds another hallmark of Pope Francis's papacy, one largely absent in Catholic bioethics—the role played in all these issues by economics. As the *testo base* notes, we are faced with

> a dramatic paradox: precisely at the moment when humankind possesses the technical-scientific capabilities to achieve a widespread prosperity that could promote an effective universal distribution of goods in according with God's desires, what we observe is an exacerbation of conflicts, fomented by increasing inequalities.... The technological structure of the industrial revolution and of the digital expansion has resulted in a unilateral and dominant technological-scientific paradigm that has deleted the questions about the meaning of life and about the bonds that create solidarity among human beings. This trajectory intersects with the predominance of the laws of the market, interpreted in the sense of greed and rapacity, and leading to indifference vis-à-vis those who are weakest; here, the wisdom of the peoples and of the poor is forgotten, and there is an erosion of the time devoted to what is more fundamental, such as the search for the good. (no. 46)

The discussant for Chapter III is William Desmond, the David Cook Chair in Philosophy, Villanova University; the Thomas A. F. Kelly Visiting Chair in Philosophy, Maynooth University; and Professor of Philosophy Emeritus, Institute of Philosophy, KU Leuven, Belgium.

Chapter IV demonstrates the debt of this document to *Evangelium Vitae* in turning next to an extended reflection on the fifth commandment: "'Thou Shalt Not Kill': Historical-Theological Hermeneutic and Hermeneutic of the Magisterium." As the *testo base* notes, it "concentrate[s] in particular on the interpretation of the fifth commandment concerning the prohibition of the direct killing of an innocent person" (no. 74). It traces the interpretation of this commandment beginning in thirteenth century Scholasticism and the *Summa Theologiae* II-II, Q. 64 (nos. 75–76), continuing through the development of moral theology (nos. 77–85) and the history of interventions from the ecclesiastical magisterium through the post-conciliar period (nos. 86–108). The discussant for Chapter IV is Angel Rodríguez Luño, Professor Emeritus of Fundamental Moral Theology, Pontifical University of Santa Croce, Rome. Pierdavide Guenzi, Ordinary Professor of the Moral Theology of Marriage and Family, John Paul II Pontifical Theological Institute for Marriage and Family, responds to Professor Luño's remarks.

Where Chapter IV traced the primacy of the fifth commandment for Catholic bioethics from the thirteenth century forward, Chapter V—"Theological Ethics: Conscience, Norm, and Discernment"—does the same for other key components of the pre-conciliar moral tradition. Here, reflections on moral responsibility, conscience, the moral law, and norms are framed by a theoretical reflection on theological anthropology (nos. 110–18). Discussions of this chapter are provided by Sigrid Müller, Professor of Moral Theology, University of Vienna, and William Murphy, Jr., Professor of Moral Theology, Pontifical College Josephinum, Columbus, Ohio. Alain Thomasset, Professor of Fundamental Moral Theology, Centre Sèvres - Facultés Jésuites de Paris, offers a response to Müller and Murphy.

After considering fundamental topics in moral theology—scripture, the signs of the times, the fifth commandment, conscience, norms—the document then shifts to a longer section on "The Great Anthropological, Ethical, and Theological Questions." These questions are taken up in Chapters VI–X. As the opening to Chapter VI, "Our Common Home and Global Perspectives," asks:

> Are there fundamental experiences in human life that we could recognize as common and shared by everyone, within and beyond cultural and religious differences? And what are they? This is the great question posed by *nature*. The affirmative answer to this question is at the origin of the following reflection, in which our theme will be the anthropological, ethical, and theological structure of the experience of life, in order that it can be lived in the joy of the Beatitudes (Matt 5). (no.134)

This chapter—focused largely on questions of ecology—reads almost like an excerpt from *Laudato Si'*, distilling its concerns in similar language. Discussants for Chapter VI are Gaël Giraud, Professor, the McCourt School of Public Policy and the Directeur of the Environmental Justice Program, Georgetown University; Director of Research, CNRS (Centre National de la Recherche Scientifique), Paris, and Marie-Jo Thiel, Professor of Ethics and Moral Theology and the

Director of the European Center for the Study and Teaching of Ethics, Université de Strasbourg, France.

Chapter VII pivots from the ecosystem on a global scale to a specific focus on the beginning of life, "Being Born, Loving, Generating." While this chapter takes up traditional questions—reproductive technologies, contraception, marriage, sexuality—it seeks to shift from a juridical framework to "the anthropological question about the body, the incarnation, and the 'filial' character of the 'incarnate self'" (no. 151). This reframing pushes into, through, and beyond phenomenology to the touchstone of joy:

> How can one make sense of such a love, and what explains a joyful vision of life and makes possible gratitude for its gratuitous gift? Certainly, joy must be understood and *described*, because pain and misery are aspects of reality that are just as *true* as joy. How can one regain a sense of the ontological primacy of the latter, without ingenuously passing over the obvious character of the former? (no. 147, emphasis in original)

Carlos Castillo Mattasoglio, Archbishop of Lima, Peru, offers the discussion; Maurizio Chiodi, Ordinary Professor of Bioethics, John Paul II Pontifical Theological Institute for the Science of Marriage and the Family, Rome, responds to the Archbishop.

Chapter VIII shifts from the beginning of life to the end of life in taking up the great anthropological, ethical, and theological questions surrounding "Suffering and Life 'Put to the Test.'" From scripture to phenomenology to *Salvifici Doloris,* this chapter offers a beautiful reflection for reimagining the joy and blessing of life amidst the suffering, pain, and illness negotiated within the realities of modern end-of-life health care. Here the discussion is led by Richard-Nazzareno Farrugia from the Università di Malta in conversation with Roberto Dell'Oro, the Austin and Ann O'Malley Chair in Bioethics and the Director, Bioethics Institute; Professor, Department of Theological Studies, Loyola Marymount University.

Chapter IX extends these reflections to the anthropological, ethical, and theological questions surrounding aging in "The Various Ages of Life and the Joy of the Life that is Offered." Importantly, this chapter locates questions of aging within a reflection on the entirety of the lifespan, covering topics such as time and the ways it is constrained and transformed in the modern era; personal identity as it shifts from childhood, through adolescence and youth, to adulthood; finally turning to consideration of old age. This section is notably marked by a constant and creative engagement with scripture. Théophile Akoha, lecturer at Cames University and Vice-President of the African Section of the Theological Pontifical Institute John Paul II of Cotonou (Benin), serves as discussant. Noël Simard, Bishop of Valleyfield, then provides a response to the entirety of reflections on Chapters VI–IX.

The reflection on "The Great Anthropological, Ethical, and Theological Questions" closes in Chapter X, as the *testo base* takes up the themes of "Death, the Fulfillment of Existence, and the Care of the Dying." Building on the previous reflections on suffering and aging, here the document takes up questions at the end of life, highlighting hospice and palliative care, the traditional considerations surrounding prudent decision-making at the end of life, as well as medically-assisted nutrition and hydration, euthanasia, and assisted-suicide. Carlo Casalone, of the Pontifical Academy for Life, responds to two discussants: Chris Gastmans, Professor of Medical Ethics and Head of the Centre for Biomedical Ethics and Law at the Faculty of Medicine, KU Leuven (Belgium), and Pablo Requena Meana, Professor of Bioethics in the Faculty of Theology of the Pontifical University of Santa Croce, Rome.

Having pondered these great questions, the document turns to its final two chapters. In Chapter XI, it takes up "Ethical Challenges and Themes that are Emerging in the Present Epoch." These cover New Digital Technologies; Cooperation between Human Being, Machine, and Robot; The Relationship between Human Beings and Animals; Screening and Perinatal Diagnoses; Vaccines: Personal Health and Protection of the Community; Individual Medicine, Public Health, Allocation of Health Resources; and The Theologian and the Public Debate. The discussant for Chapter XI is Laura Palazzani, Professor of Philosophy of Law in the Free University Maria Santissima Assunta, Rome, and Vice President of the National Italian Committee for Bioethics.

The final chapter of the document moves to a theologically-fitting end, considering in Chapter XII, "Eschatology and the Drama of Life." Here it returns to contemplation, relationship, and attentiveness to both the particular and the cosmic, the now and the historical, the finite and the infinite, and more, as outlined in the opening paragraphs. Two discussants reflect on this eschatological horizon: Luis Antonio G. Cardinal Tagle, the Prefect for the Congregation on the Evangelization of Peoples; and Andrea Bozzolo, Rector of the Pontifical Salesian University, Rome.

Philippe Bordeyne, President of the John Paul II Pontifical Theological Institute for the Sciences of Marriage and the Family and moderator of the three-day symposium at which the document was discussed, offers a set of closing observations. In addition, the volume closes with homilies offered during the event by Cardinal Mario Grech and Cardinal Marcello Semeraro, for the Thirty-First Sunday in Ordinary Time and the Solemnity of All Saints, respectively.

THE POTENTIAL IMPACT OF *ETICA TEOLOGICA DELLA VITA*

It is not easy to predict the impact of a volume like *Etica teologica della vita* on the current theological discussion. One of the hopes of our presentation is to signal its importance and to call for an open disposition by attentive readers who seek to further its vision that moves beyond polarizations and fractures toward a robust and renewed practice of theological dialogue. In closing, let us name four future directions for engagement that we find most pressing.

To begin, there is in *Etica teologica della vita* a preoccupation with *foundational* questions—in fact, it explicitly calls Catholic scholars to attend more closely to the anthropological premises that ground a theological ethics of life. This call may be difficult to heed both for theologically-minded and secular thinkers alike, currently working in the field of bioethics. For the latter, bioethics tends to be driven by public policy preoccupations. It is alert to the new ethical quandaries of the day, though aiming less at defining their specific conceptual contours, resting mindfully on the challenges they raise for our understanding of the human condition. For the most part, secular bioethics foregrounds a strategy for the *ethical* solution of moral problems, that is, for a workable approach consistent with basic commitments to respect for person, beneficence, and justice. Furthermore, it assumes the latter in their validity, as principles of common morality, but fails to offer a coherent ontological framework capable of justifying them in light of a meaningful anthropological vision.

The call for deeper thinking is no less challenging for Catholic bioethicists, when the preoccupation for the normative dimension of the Catholic tradition takes precedence over a more considered articulation of its grounding theological and philosophical premises. *Etica teologica della vita* points in a different direction: without eschewing the need for discussion about moral norms, it invites scholars to focus on the vision for human beings.

Secondly, *Etica teologica della vita* shows, with a multiplicity of approaches yet in an uncanny unanimity of method, that theological reflection brings to completion the movement toward transcendence, rooted in an anthropology hospitable to the religious dimension. The openness to theology pushes bioethics toward intermediation with the final, most radical, dimension of ultimacy, but without breaking from previous engagements. The *religious* gesture thus recapitulates the deeper intentionality at work in the philosophical searching of *secular* bioethics. It does not appear on the methodological scene like a bolt out of the blue sky.

Such a realization sustains both the openness of theology to philosophical reflection, on the one hand, as well as the recognition by philosophy that a theological ethics of life may offer a journey into new dimensions of meaning. If so, the hospitality of bioethics to a theological anthropology responds to an exigence of philosophical depth rather than ambiguous tolerance toward "irrational" raptures, incommensurable with its own "rational" premises.

In this light, it becomes possible to give a full account of a *theological* ethics of life, whose *novity* unfolds in the ethical implications of a hyperbolic historical beginning that demands constant reinterpretation and deepening. The ethical truth of the original event is not given once and for all. This is why dialogue among theological perspectives is necessary within the church, for it sustains the effort of an ever-growing process of understanding and experiential articulation. Implicit in the difficult, yet always rewarding, exchange of theological differences is the conviction that normative *determinations* are kept in motion by a more original process of *determining*. Without relation to the latter, all Christian ethical principles and rules atrophy, they become "letters" devoid of "spirit."

Theology offers reasons to support a *eudaimonistic* and communitarian turn in ethics: it recognizes the primacy of the good, the relevance of virtuous moral agency, its rootedness in community, the need to articulate criteria for rightness of actions and practices in light of full narratives of human fulfilment and flourishing. At the same time, theology underlines the *teleological* orientation of ethics with a more original confidence in the *archeology* of the good. The good given in the gift of life grounds the search for a final good.

An ethics of life (*bio-ethics*), theologically grounded, reflects such ontological confidence (*cum-fides*) in all its articulations. The matrix of ethical insights flowing from the Christ event redefines the meaning of all ethical principles and norms. A new *action theory* follows from the metaphysical and anthropological premises of theology. This is so because the primacy of love, in this case, a *love for life*, informs the status of moral normativity, the relevance of ethical rules, and ultimately, the very shaping of *praxis*. Moreover, it defines our fundamental attitude toward the challenges involved in practices of life shaping, from medicine to scientific research, to the application of technology.

Finally, *Etica teologica della vita* demonstrates in rich detail how these directions—the exploration of foundational questions, of the religious dimension of bioethics, and the theological grounding of the tradition—all find new impetus and insight in the deeply post-conciliar theology of Pope Francis. It surfaces the inexorable and recursively generative connections inherent in Pope Francis's as-yet-unfinished-oeuvre between the theological and pastoral, the theoretical and practical, the clarity of abstraction and the epistemologically imperative realities of the poor, all grounded in the heart of the church—the life of prayer, sacrament, contemplation, and discernment. As Archbishop Vincenzo Paglia notes in his introductory note to the volume, Pope Francis has recognized the importance of this initiative, as it critically integrates his discourse into a theological ethics of life. *Etica teologica della vita* now invites the broader theological community to join that conversation, articulating together an ethic, theology, and witness infused with the joy of life and the gospel. M

Roberto Dell'Oro, PhD, is the Austin and Ann O'Malley Chair in Bioethics, the Director of the Bioethics Institute, and professor in the Department of Theological Studies at Loyola Marymount University. He earned a doctorate in moral theology at the Pontifical Gregorian University in Rome and specialized in bioethics at Georgetown University. Roberto is the author/co-author of four books: *Pope Francis on the Joy of Love: Pastoral Reflections on Amoris Laetitia* (Mahwah, NJ: Paulist, 2018); *Health and Human Flourishing: Religion, Moral Anthropology, and Medicine* (Washington, DC: Georgetown University Press, 2006); *Esperienza morale e persona* (Rome: Gregorian University Press, 1996); and *History of Bioethics: International Perspectives* (San Francisco: International Scholars, 1996). He has translated Klaus Demmer, *Shaping the Moral Life* (Washington, DC: Georgetown University Press, 2000). He is a corresponding member of the Vatican's Pontifical Academy for Life.

M. Therese Lysaught, PhD, is Professor of Moral Theology and Healthcare at the Neiswanger Institute for Bioethics and Health Care Leadership at the Stritch School of Medicine, Loyola University Chicago. Her scholarly work brings into conversation the fields of theology, medicine, bioethics, and global health. Her books include *Biopolitics after Neuroscience: Morality and the Economy of Virtue* (Bloomsbury Academic, 2022, co-authored with Jeffrey P. Bishop and Andrew Michel); *Catholic Bioethics and Social Justice: The Praxis of US Healthcare in a Globalized World* (Liturgical Press, 2019, co-edited with Michael McCarthy); *Caritas in Communion: The Theological Foundations of Catholic Healthcare* (Catholic Health Association, 2014); *On Moral Medicine: Theological Perspectives on Medical Ethics*, 3rd edition (Eerdmans, 2012, co-edited with Joseph Kotva); *and Gathered for the Journey: Moral Theology in Catholic Perspective* (Eerdmans, 2007, co-edited with David Matzko McCarthy). She is a founding member and editor of the *Journal of Moral Theology* and a corresponding member of the Vatican's Pontifical Academy for Life.

Teaching Catholic Social Thought: A Symposium Introduction

Jon Kara Shields

THE FOLLOWING ESSAYS WERE SELECTED FROM submissions to an open call on pedagogy and Catholic social thought. Several articles in revision, including my own, were not completed for this collection, and some persons who planned to write as part of this symposium found themselves unable to do so. In addition to the increasing demands upon instructors across ranks and levels of contingency in higher education, the effects of the global COVID-19 pandemic on our ability to support one another materially, spiritually, and mentally in health and wellbeing continue to ripple through our learning communities even two years later. Perhaps it calls for some explanation, then, as to why this symposium remains important to me. Why do I recommend that you read these essays now when student engagement is at an unprecedented low and many teaching faculty and staff are demoralized and burnt out?[1]

Since the USCCB's *Sharing Catholic Social Teaching: Challenges and Directions* published in 1998, several good collections of essays on teaching Catholic social thought have touched on a number of the issues discussed here: Where should one start? How and why should we integrate community-engaged learning or service learning with CST? What can we learn about how to teach CST from scholar-practitioners? What are the results of adopting an issue-driven focus or case study approach? How do students reflect on learning CST in their

---

[1] On low student engagement, see Jonathan Malesic, "My College Students Are Not Okay," *The New York Times*, May 13, 2022, www.nytimes.com/2022/05/13/opinion/college-university-remote-pandemic.html; Beth McMurtirie, "A Stunning Level of Disconnection," *The Chronicle of Higher Education*, April 5, 2022, www.chronicle.com/article/a-stunning-level-of-student-disconnection; and Beth McMurtirie, "'It Feels Like I'm Pouring Energy Into a Void,'" *The Chronicle of Higher Education*, April 11, 2022, www.chronicle.com/article/it-feels-like-im-pouring-energy-into-a-void. On burnout and exiting the profession among instructors, see Joshua Dolezal, "The Big Quit," *The Chronicle of Higher Education*, May 27, 2022, www.chronicle.com/article/the-big-quit.

own words?[2] Numerous works have been written that facilitate instructors' own appreciation for the development of the tradition and argue for the vital importance of various documents and themes for introducing the Catholic social tradition to new audiences.[3] This reflection is critical for teaching.

Despite the range of teaching and the diversity of Catholic social movements and important figures in Catholic social thought, many faculty members only get one semester to expose, engage, enlighten, and/or transform students on its themes while modeling means of navigating its depth, scope, and arc—even when teaching at Catholic institutions. Instructors must make difficult choices. Do they give a wide-angle exposure to the tradition or focus on the depth of the tradition for a single issue, place, or theme? Such choices and interaction with students' fresh perspectives can be developmental keys to our ongoing reflection on teaching.

Practices of issue-focused immersion or encounters across lines of difference that help instructors to open educational opportunities beyond the transmission of intellectual content are "costly" in terms of course time, instructor attention, and student commitment.[4] Commu-

---

[2] See, for example, Kathleen Maas Weigert and Alexia K. Kelly, eds., *Living the Catholic Social Tradition: Cases and Commentary* (Lanham: Sheed and Ward, 2005); Michael Galligan-Stierle, *A Vision of Justice: Engaging Catholic Social Teaching on the College Campus* (Collegeville, MN: Liturgical Press, 2014); Jeff Gingerich and Nicholas Rademacher, eds., Special Issue on "Reframing Catholic Social Teaching," *Praxis* 1, no. 1 (2018): www.pdcnet.org/collection-anonymous/browse?fp=praxis&fq=praxis%2fVolume%2f8999|1%2f8999|Issue%3a+1%2f; Michelle Nickerson and Harry Dammer, "Catholic Social Teaching in Their Own Words: Oral Histories of College Students Learning CST," *Journal of Catholic Higher Education* 37, no. 1 (2018): 111–25.

[3] See, for example, Francis P. McHugh, *Catholic Social Thought Renovating the Tradition: A Key Guide to Resources* (Leuven: Peeters, 2008); Marvin L. Krier Mich, *Catholic Social Teaching and Movements* (Mystic, CT: Twenty-Third Publications, 2008); David Matzko McCarthy, *The Heart of Catholic Social Teaching: Its Origins and Contemporary Significance* (Grand Rapids, MI.: Brazos Press, 2009); Thomas Massaro, *Living Justice: Catholic Social Teaching in Action* (Lanham, MD: Rowman and Littlefield, 2012); Susan Crawford Sullivan and Ron Pagnucco, eds., *A Vision of Justice: Engaging Catholic Social Teaching on the College Campus* (Collegeville, MN: Liturgical Press, 2014); Meghan J. Clark, *The Vision of Catholic Social Thought: The Virtue of Solidarity and the Praxis of Human Rights* (Minneapolis, MN: Fortress, 2014); Bernard V. Brady, *Essential Catholic Social Thought*, 2nd edition (Maryknoll, NY: Orbis Books, 2017).

[4] Roger Berman's *Catholic Social Learning: Educating the Faith That Does Justice* (New York: Fordham University Press, 2011) has become a key text on encouraging students to study CST out in the world beyond the classroom in order that relationships with individual persons, places, and actions can enrich or deepen sincere dialog on Catholic social themes. The student engrossed in the needs of the world is no longer driven by transactional expectations and competitive personal achievement alone. This requires personal risk and intimacy with the problems Catholic social teaching

nity engagement or service-learning opportunities for students engaging primarily or entirely online due to forced isolation (COVID) or because of material conditions (studying while a full-time parent or laborer) are more difficult for instructors to arrange and manage.[5] Intellectual engagement often needs further embodiment and experience to unfold into deeper understanding—learning that continues long after the semester is over. Nevertheless, semester-limited decisions may hold new insights for our scholarly understanding and personal lived-reception of the tradition.

This symposium includes short articles from highly experienced and new teachers about what they have learned within the Catholic social thought "classroom" and beyond. Each short essay focuses on a transformative experience, contextual adaptation, or pedagogical intervention reflecting how the experience of teaching has inspired productive reflection over time. Such reflection is a vital part of the work of those called to teach: we are always engaged in the process of learning with our students not only about the performative aspects of teaching effectiveness, but by affirming the vitality of this tradition for our lives, discerning anew how we are called to "witness with our very lives."[6] We are witnesses to ourselves, our communities, our congregations, our countries, our world as sites of ongoing struggle for a good larger than ourselves.

As Monika Hellwig wrote in 2005, "There is no lack of good will about passing on the social teaching of the church at Catholic colleges and universities."[7] Not only in Catholic colleges but in other Christian and pluralist contexts, the Catholic social tradition has become a resource for deliberative discourse on why and how to pursue the common good.[8] However, in addition to the obstacles Hellwig names to teaching CST (e.g., its interdisciplinary demands, the difficult style of

---

addresses. Two other recent works on education beyond transmission of content which insist on the need to adopt relational pedagogical methods which encourage the student to go outside the self, tarry in the pain and suffering of others, and see "themselves as a site of struggle" are Mara Brecht, "See–Judge ... Act? The Role of Action in the Anti-Racist Catholic Theological Classroom," *Religious Education* 114, no. 3 (2019): 202–13, text cited at 212; and Timothy Hanchin,"Encounter and/as Pedagogy for Catholic Higher Education in Our Time," *Religious Education* 114, no. 5 (2019): 565–80.

[5] See Teofil Giovanni Pugeda's essay in this symposium, "Teaching Catholic Social Thought Online in the Philippines; From a Challenge to an Opportunity" (105–16), for one strategy.

[6] See Daniel Cosacchi's essay, "Formative Figures for Catholic Social Witness" (117–26), in this symposium.

[7] "Preface: Curricular Contexts and Challenges for Catholic Social Thinking," in *Living the Catholic Social Tradition: Cases and Commentary*, ed. Kathleen Maas Weigert and Alexia K. Kelly (Lanham: Sheed and Ward, 2005), xi.

[8] See, for example, Simon Cuff, *Love in Action: Catholic Social Teaching for Every Church* (London: SCM, 2019).

encyclical documents, a general lack of prior theological and scriptural formation), in 2022 those teaching in higher education must own that an instructor's goodwill will not suffice where our education institutions measure profit and status as the markers of success among themselves and in their meritocratic assumptions about student outcomes.[9] Instructors often face challenges from the formative impacts of the environments in which they teach to the challenges of creating opportunities for transformative learning and the capaciousness of the subject. This means that our "living testimony" to Catholic social teaching often demands greater participation in student affairs, faculty governance, or campaigns for organized labor than is easily accommodated by the teaching and research load of instructors, whether contingent or tenure-track.

Pope Francis has said, "No teacher is ever alone: they always share their work with other colleagues and the entire educational community to which they belong."[10] We may be especially renewed, therefore, by the extension of this remark to the larger formative community. The university and the pulpit are not the only places where one might be formed in the Catholic social tradition. This symposium contains several essays that remind us that formation into Catholic social thought and traditions extends and *should* extend beyond the classroom and the pulpit into other formative social environments such as young adult groups, base communities, communal living spaces, or protests. When we educate others as formators (formally or informally), we prepare them to engage others in the ongoing process of interpreting, extending, and living the Catholic social tradition. Every student of Catholic social thought is a potential future teacher of Catholic social thought beyond the classroom.

The first few essays in this collection focus explicitly on what instructors have learned from the challenges of the classroom, sharing their strategies for perpetual obstacles instructors face alongside unprecedented challenges. Bernard Brady's essay maps a series of course development decisions that model an ongoing responsiveness to development in the tradition and changes in student engagement. Brady's emphasis on primary texts gives students guided practice reading, interpreting, and assessing the documents themselves. His narrative construal of the tradition as an invitation to live in a certain way—marked by principles to be experienced rather than merely declared—flows naturally into comparison with other "invitations" from

---

[9] Gerald J. Beyer, *Just Universities: Catholic Social Teaching Confronts Corporatized Higher Education* (New York: Fordham University Press, 2021).
[10] Pope Francis, "Address of His Holiness Pope Francis to Members of the Italian Union of Catholic School Teachers, Managers, Educators, and Trainers," March 14, 2015, www.vatican.va/content/francesco/en/speeches/2015 /march/documents/papa-francesco_20150314_uciim.html.

traditions or ideological commitments which are in partial agreement or fundamental opposition to the tradition. This critical encounter can be engaged intellectually and reflectively in the pluralist classroom as preparation for a world with others who think and live differently—so that students may not only evoke the tradition but be *formed* by their commitments in their means of engagement.

Brady raises an important issue—every instructor of Catholic social teaching (Catholic or not) must be ready to respond to student questions about the legitimacy of the Catholic Church's moral wisdom given the sex abuse crisis and an ongoing failure of clergy and high profile Catholics to "walk the talk" on racism, climate change, and poverty.[11] While all are significant, I think the challenge of addressing the sex abuse crisis with appropriate sensitivity to students' personal concerns and legitimate universal skepticism is especially important.[12] Brady suggests that instructors be prepared with personal and thoughtful responses; I would go further to advise that instructors be wary of a temptation to rely on the historic separation of Catholic social and sexual ethics.[13] We should also be reminded that ordinary people have responsibilities in the aftermath of the abuse crisis, because while all are *not* equally culpable, the failure to protect children and young adults (including seminarians) from abuse was *a collective failure*, not limited to Church leaders or institutions. We can participate in transforming the institutions, processes, and expectations of both sacred institutions and their secular and civil counterparts towards reparations for past harms and the prevention of future injustices, as well as

---

[11] "Walking the talk" on racism and public justice is an issue also raised in Daniel Cosacchi and Casey Mullaney's essays in this symposium which both emphasize the necessity of the instructor or peer-mentor's own authentic walk in the emotional and practical dispositions of anti-racism and pacifism. See Cosacchi, "Formative Figures for Catholic Social Witness" (117-26) and Mullaney, "Solidarity, Praxis, and Discernment at the Catholic Worker" (127–35).

[12] Instructors may want to consult works such as Darryl W. Stephens and Kate Ott, eds., *Teaching Sexuality and Religion in Higher Education: Embodied Learning, Trauma-Sensitive Pedagogy, and Perspective Transformation* (New York: Routledge, 2020).

[13] While different histories of these two parts of Catholic moral theology may be a way to reflect on why these discourses have become separated, that must not undermine drawing from a common understanding of how God's revelation makes use of the *sensus fidelium*, conscience mediated by faith, and secular and scientific forms of knowledge-creation. For further discussion of their historic separation and recent rapprochement see Todd Salzman and Michael G. Lawler, "*Amoris Laetitia*: Towards a Methodological and Anthropological Integration of Catholic Social and Sexual Ethics," *Theological Studies* 79, no. 3 (2018): 634–52, doi.org/10.1177/0040563918784772; and Alexandre Andrade Martins, "From Vatican II to *Amoris Laetitia*: The Catholic Social and Sexual Ethics Division and a Way of Ecclesial Interconnection," *Fronteiras-Revista de Teologia da Unicap* 2, no. 2 (2019): 69–89, doi.org/10.25247/2595-3788.2019.v2n2.p69-89.

in maintaining such transformations. As Sally Scholz writes, "Catholic social teaching helps to provide a framework for thinking through some of the obligations of ordinary folks in the aftermath of the collective failure to protect children from abuse and the structural injustices that encouraged it to continue."[14]

Joyce A. Bautch's essay on the dangers of gnostic spiritualism for students studying Catholic social teaching reflects on the differences between the conceptual and evaluative and suggests that teaching Catholic social thought, while inevitably an introduction to an *intellectual* tradition, should not be thought of as exhausted or encapsulated by its intellectual content. The danger of taking mere intellectual mastery as a sufficient learning objective for course development and instruction is that it robs students of an opportunity for a direct personal encounter with the transformational nature of Catholic social teaching. While not dismissive of the investments of time and energy that meaningful service-learning demands, Bautch makes a compelling case for its pedagogical returns.[15] In this way, she picks up on the theme of invitation in Brady's essay. She suggests that the theoretical and historical underpinnings of the tradition need to be matched with practical experiential learning and dialogical reflection so that the invitation to the tradition as an embodied tradition of reflective *living* be fully "received."

In his essay, Teofilo Giovan Pugeda discusses how COVID-19 pushed him to new deliberations on how to offer to God the best out of an undesirable and difficult situation.[16] Guided by emphasizing the Ignatian-Jesuit commitment to care for the entire person, even in the context of online teaching, Pugeda emphasizes how an instructor as designer, facilitator, and coach can practice ongoing reflection throughout a course to best serve students in a unique situation. During the COVID-19 pandemic there has been no shortage of contact with the reality of injustice in the world, but Pugeda's course facilitated and encouraged students' assessment of local issues in the Philippines, collaboration in mutual formation, and sharing the burden of learning through difficult circumstances (intrinsic and extrinsic to the learning

---

[14] Sally J. Scholz, "The Sexual Abuse Scandal in the Church: Social Morality after Social Sin," *Praxis* (2022): 126–133, www.pdcnet.org/praxis/content/praxis_2022_0999_5_31_20.

[15] For additional resources on service-learning and CST, see Erin Brigham, *See, Judge, Act: Catholic Social Teaching and Service Learning* (Winona, MN: Anselm Academic, 2019); and Andrés Peregalli and M. Beatriz Isola, eds., *Service-Learning Pedagogy and the Teachings of the Catholic Church* (Buenos Aires: Uniservitate, 2021), www.uniservitate.org/es/2021 /10/26/la-pedagogia-del-aprendizaje-servicio-y-las-ensenanzas-de-la-iglesia-catolica/.

[16] For further discussion of Catholic educational institutions' preliminary response to the COVID-19 pandemic, see the 2020 special issue of *Catholic Education* 23, no. 1 (2020): digitalcommons.lmu.edu/ce/vol23/iss1/.

goals). The organization of his course furthered the depth of students' understanding through lived commitments to subsidiarity and solidarity within the learning community formed by the course.

The next two essays in the collection draw explicitly on the witness of particular persons or communities. Daniel Cosacchi's essay emphasizes the value of concrete examples of life that model abstract concepts for "novice learners"—calling them to see anew and know more deeply. His emphasis on the necessity for conversion minimizes the distance between instructor and student—emphasizing the Catholic social vocations for all of us which are evoked when we see our social reality through the commitments of the saints and martyrs who have gone before us. Casey Mullaney's essay describes the power of Catholic Worker communities as schools of solidarity where students have long been an active part of multigenerational and cross-class community-building.

Mullaney frames the formation into Catholic social thought at the Worker as a part of the practice of clarification of thought in the life of the community, which is pervasive beyond the periods set aside for intentional deliberation in "conversations held across a weedy garden bed or a dishpan full of coffee cups." Mullaney's essay is particularly poignant in its appeal for us to be attentive to the seriousness and sincerity that students display in seeking moral evaluation of local and world circumstances in the context of a community of mutual aid. She shows us the holiness they embody in their readiness to respond to a world full of injustice and the corresponding gift of stability and continuous access to a living spiritual tradition offered to them by the network of Worker communities. Mullaney's essay is eloquent in how it makes visible the bodily and emotional disciplines that must accompany intellectual development and which can begin to be acquired even by "novice" learners in the learning laboratory of the Worker where everyone is welcome to labor and learn for justice.

The symposium is crowned with a small collection of essays by Sarah DeMarais, a coordinator at the Loyola Institute for Ministry (New Orleans, LA), and three East African women religious LIM alumnae. DeMarais's essay describes the model of program development at work at LIM and how its shows respect for the particularity of geographically and culturally diverse contexts through inculturated, adaptable programs which enable the development of living theologians. Her description of how the sisters embody subsidiarity by interviewing wise practitioners as formative witnesses to local knowledge exemplifies how students do not have to abandon the fragments of knowledge they or their communities already hold in order to take hold of the Catholic social tradition. Similarly, comparisons with secular approaches to development questions are not merely instructive intellectual comparisons but preparation for mobilizing collective action with diverse stakeholders in their communities. They come prepared to rely on what different approaches have in common and to examine and work toward accommodation or protection for Catholic distinctives. We are always engaged in ongoing discernment of how the Church's social tradition intersects with our present context. For these sisters, this discernment is both one of cultural translation and personal vocation. How does CST integrate with their local situation, congregational charism, and mission? And how does God use it to call them to respond to the needs of their local communities with their abilities and knowledge?

The essay that follows integrates reflections by LIM alumnae Srs. Charity Bbalo, Lucy Kimaro, and Jane Frances Mulongo. Together they demonstrate that community-level benefits are made possible by students' own growth—something that LIM can anticipate as an ongoing result as congregations they have worked with are integrating CST into their earlier stages of formation.

Sr. Bbalo describes how sharing her learning with a group of widows, some with limited educational background, resulted not only in further exploration of relevant local proverbs, but in a project to supply alternative fuel made from recyclables to slow deforestation due to irresponsible tree harvesting practices.

Sr. Kimaro reflects on her work as an example of solidarity, exhorting and accompanying others in both material and spiritual ways around the Catholic University of East Africa. She models how works of mercy reflect our love of God by honoring what God has made in creation and our neighbor. Our desire to help that life flourish would not shirk from speaking in economic terms—even when we face material hardships ourselves. As with Pugeda's and Cosacchi's essays, Kimaro emphasizes that support for students requires community building that enables material, spiritual, and intellectual solidarity.

Lastly, Sr. Mulongo's essay reflects on building knowledge of CST among lay people in Kenyan small Christian communities, where she notes there is much goodwill but insufficient formation. These SCCs are one way the Church is in constant contact with the daily life situations and concerns of the people; they are a living system in which people know each other's home and families and can speak and show deep solidarity in one another's lives. She emphasizes that different age groups require different roles: youth need a more deliberately structured, planned engagement as a teacher, whereas older adult groups may benefit from "facilitation," which enables individuals within the group to share their experiences and reflect on what they have already accomplished in light of the themes and principles of Catholic social thought.

Our symposium leaves many themes untouched and opens many lines of inquiry that deserve further reflection. We can be confident that this issue contributes to a conversation on pedagogy and Catholic social thought which we hope will continue for many years to come. Ⓜ

Jon Kara Shields is an instructor in the Religion department at Simpson College in Indianola, IA. She holds degrees in liberal studies and religion from St. John College (Annapolis) and Cambridge University, an MDiv from Yale Divinity School, and a PhD in Theology from the University of Notre Dame.

Catholic Social Living: Teaching Students To "Live Wisely, Think Deeply, and Love Generously"[1]

Bernard Brady

IN WORDS THAT ACKNOWLEDGE THE COMPLEXITY of modern social structures, suggest a certain humility in addressing them, and advocate the moral agency and responsibility of persons to respond to them, Paul VI writes in *Octogesima Adveniens*: "In the face of such widely varying situations it is difficult for us to utter a unified message and to put forward a solution which has universal validity" (no. 4). As I think about teaching Catholic social teaching (CST) in the context of our "widely varying situations," I am struck by Paul VI's words and, at the same time, guided by John XXIII's in *Mater et Magistra*: "There are three stages which should normally be followed in the reduction of social principles into practice ... look, judge, act" (no. 236).

The development of a CST course syllabus can follow John XXIII's advice. We begin by looking, and then design our courses for audiences in particular contexts, reflecting the needs of our students and the world in which they live. As instructors, we also bring our interests, concerns, and loves to bear. I want my students to leave the course with a good sense of Catholic social teaching and a more developed sense of themselves as persons serving the common good. My deep objective is to encourage students to "live wisely, think deeply, and love generously." After "looking," we must judge and make choices on course specific objectives and content. Then, of course, we "act" on our pedagogical decisions. The aim of this essay is to share my thoughts "judging" content for the course. My approach rests on a preference for primary texts, a particular understanding of the core ideas of the tradition, and ways to enrich the course by going beyond the basics. Specifically, I advocate for reflecting on the method of CST, bringing in conversation partners outside the tradition and inviting students to engage the local community.

---

[1] Francis, *Encyclical Letter on Care for our Common Home* (*Laudato Si'*), May 24, 2015, no. 47. All papal documents, documents from the Second Vatican Council, and documents from pontifical councils and commissions can be found on the Vatican website: www.vatican.va.

ON USING PRIMARY TEXTS

I use more primary than secondary texts and invite students to work through and interpret the texts. I want my students not simply to be told what is in the tradition but to read the tradition. CST is an intellectual tradition, in dialogue with alternative visions of the good society, as well as a moral tradition directing personal and social behavior. It is an intellectual practice[2] that embraces community and dialogue,[3] promotes human agency and invites discernment and decision making,[4] recognizes a common humanity and takes seriously the claims of other traditions,[5] offers prophetic critiques in the face of harmful social practices,[6] has developed and will continue to develop,[7] and is profoundly linked to the transcendent—holding that one's love for

---

[2] It is an "intellectual" practice as it appeals to "persons of good will" and offers reasoning based not only on Scripture and Christian tradition, but also on the grounds of common human experience. These six categories in the paragraph are derived from Pontifical Biblical Commission, *The Bible and Morality: Biblical Roots of Christian Conduct*.

[3] The idea that humanity is a family is a dominant theme in the literature. See, for example, Second Vatican Council (*Gaudium et Spes*, nos. 2, 3, 26, 29, 33, 37, 38, 39, 42, 45, 53, 567, 57, 63, 74, 75, 77, 91), John XXIII (*Pacem in Terris*, nos. 25, 97, 98, 117, 132), Paul VI (*Dignitatis Humanae*, no. 15; *Populorum Progressio*, no. 17; *Octogesima Adveniens*, nos. 21, 37), John Paul II (*Laborem Exercens*, nos. 10, 16, 18, 27; *Centesimus Annus*, nos. 26, 51, 58, 62), Benedict XVI (*Caritas in Veritate*, nos. 7, 33, 42, 50), and Francis (*Evangelii Gaudium*, nos. 183, 245; *Laudato Si'*, nos. 13, 52, 102, 192; *Fratelli Tutti*, nos. 8, 16, 17, 18).

[4] On human agency and social responsibility, see for example John XXIII, *Mater et Magistra*, no. 236; Paul VI, *Populorum Progressio*, no. 81: *Octogesima Adveniens (A Call to Action)*, no. 48; and Benedict XVI, *Deus Caritas Est*, no. 29.

[5] This is most clearly illustrated in *Fratelli Tutti* where Pope Francis writes of his relationship with the Grand Imam Ahmad Al-Tayyeb, see nos. 5, 136, 192, 285. He notes, "In these pages of reflection on universal fraternity, I felt inspired particularly by Saint Francis of Assisi, but also by others of our brothers and sisters who are not Catholics: Martin Luther King, Desmond Tutu, Mahatma Gandhi and many more" (no. 286).

[6] This is a consistent theme in the tradition. In the first paragraphs of *Rerum Novarum*, Leo XIII describes an impetus for the encyclical, "A small number of very rich men have been able to lay upon the teeming masses of the laboring poor a yoke little better than that of slavery itself" (no. 2). Francis titled the first chapter of *Fratelli Tutti*, "Dark Clouds over a Closed World." Social critique appears in all the documents between these two bookends.

[7] Compare, for example, Pope Leo's description of work and working in *Rerum Novarum* with John Paul II's in *Laborem Exercens*. Note also their differing moral evaluations of labor strikes. See *Rerum Novarum*, nos. 36 and 39 in relation to *Laborem Exercens*, no. 20. Also compare *Octogesima Adveniens* (esp. no. 21) to *Laudato Si'* on the environment. An interesting class project is to trace the movement in the tradition from supporting (or assuming) set class structures in society to promoting a certain egalitarianism in society.

God is expressed in one's love for the neighbor.[8] Students read selected sections from the encyclicals to highlight the contributions of a particular text or pope in relation to a broader narrative.

The narrative they discover can tell the story of development in three stages, each highlighting a certain claim within a broader sense of morality.[9] The first stage, from Leo XIII to John XXIII, stresses rational responses to injustice within an ordered society. The second, from Pius XII to John Paul II, builds on the first while moving toward a global vision highlighting human dignity and the consequent human rights. The third, which runs from John Paul II to Francis, includes justice and dignity, but also addresses the affective responses of persons in love and solidarity. A key to the narrative is the tradition's growing understanding of human dignity, its expressions of the moral demands of dignity, as well as its call for persons to experience the dignity of others.[10]

This semester, I will start my course with chapters two and three of *Fratelli Tutti*. Here, Pope Francis reflects on the Parable of the Good Samaritan and its implications for universal love. These chapters provide an opening for my objectives. The text grounds social ethics in the biblical tradition. It appeals to the head, offering a critical interpretation of the Good Samaritan, as well as to the heart, inviting the reader into the parable. *Fratelli Tutti* provokes moral agency and offers a perspective on the development of Church teaching. To cite the *Compendium of the Social Doctrine of the Church*, it provides motivations, directions, and deliberative elements (no. 73) to build a society worthy of human persons (no. 580).

After a discussion of *Fratelli Tutti* and an introduction to basic themes of the course, we move to engaging foundational ideas in the tradition with excerpts from encyclicals. Reading *Rerum Novarum*, nos. 1–12, 15–17, 20, 34–38, highlights Pope Leo's understanding of rights, duties, private property, wages, workers' groups, and the role of government. Students often balk at the objective tone and the top-down moral view of the text. I try to move them toward subjective reflection. Most of my students have had jobs. Some have had "good" employers and others have not. They can describe a "good" employer or "good" work experience. I turn to the language of rights and responsibilities, or perhaps the idea of culture and workplace expectations, as ways to articulate their experiences. What about wages? What

---

[8] See Second Vatican Council, *Gaudium et Spes*, no. 24, Benedict XVI, *Deus Caritas Est*, no. 18, and Francis, *Evangelii Gaudium*, no. 187.

[9] See Bernard Brady, "From Catholic Social Thought to Catholic Social Living: A Narrative of the Tradition," *Journal of Catholic Social Thought*, 15, no. 2 (2018): 317–52.

[10] See Bernard Brady, "The Evolution of Human Dignity in Catholic Moral Theology," *Journal of Moral Theology*, 10, no.1 (2021): 1–25.

is the difference between a minimum wage and a living wage? I ask students to think about the justification for the private ownership of things, examining both their sense of owning things and the broader "theories" of private property. Leo offers a complex set of reasons in this text. While his answers to these issues may not be immediately applicable today, his questions about responsibilities of owners, workers, and the governments remain highly pertinent. These excerpts are examples of the first stage of CST, that is, a rational response to injustice within an ordered society.

Quadragesimo Anno, nos. 57–58, 71, and 79–80, set up two important themes in the tradition: social justice and subsidiarity.[11] The first prioritizes relationality and responsibility. The second stresses moral agency and relative autonomy. Under this lies the anthropological claim of the tradition. We are individuals, autonomous beings responsible for our own lives, and we are interconnected and intertwined with various spheres of others and are to be responsive to them within the frameworks of those relationships. Students can easily articulate their sense of themselves as decision-makers and can recognize the many ways they are and have been dependent and interrelated with others. *Mater et Magistra*, no. 65, gives us what has become the official description of the common good in the tradition. To understand the latter, we must unpack this description. In no. 236, John XXIII encourages moral agency with the Look, Judge, Act methodology.

At times, reading *Pacem in Terris*, nos. 1–37, on human rights and responsibilities stuns my students. The Church really believes that all people have these rights? This section puts moral muscle on the idea of human dignity. Even more surprising are nos. 98–119 on peace and disarmament. Ban nuclear weapons? These excerpts exemplify the second stage of CST, a global vision highlighting human dignity and the consequent human rights.[12]

Catholic anthropology is addressed more systematically in *Gaudium et Spes*, nos. 1–32. We see that it is part of a larger methodology. At its core is an understanding of God and God's intentions for creation. Flowing from this understanding is an anthropology, its claims about personhood. Moral claims, for example about justice and rights, flow from this anthropology. See *Populorum Progressio*, nos.

---

[11] Subsidiarity is an expression of the dignity of the person as it empowers the moral agency of individuals and groups in relation to overarching powers and authority. Yet, in certain cases, particularly in situations of injustice or incompetence, the responsibility of larger bodies overrides the autonomy of lower groups. See Benedict XVI, *Caritas in Veritate*, no. 57. Thus, subsidiarity does not appear as a separate "central idea of the tradition" in the list here. It is part of "promoting, protecting, and encountering the dignity of persons."

[12] John XXIII, *Pacem in Terris*, no. 171 contains a moving statement, a longing for peace which with a few simple edits becomes a welcoming prayer.

12–32, 43–49, 76–77 for a reflection on integral development and persons. This idea of development can be linked to students' understandings of their own holistic development. It can also be related to the mission statements or charisms of their institutions, many of which assert they are concerned with developing the whole person.

Laborem Exercens returns us to and advances some themes from *Rerum Novarum* and offers deeper reflections on work, working, and workers' rights (nos. 4–6, 11–12). This provides an opening to have students think about how they feel when they work and question why they work or why they would prefer certain jobs or careers over others. Indeed, they all have or will have majors. They should be able to experience the levels of work addressed here.

In *Sollicitudo Rei Socialis*, nos. 35–45, Pope John Paul develops the key ideas of social sin (applicable to discussions on racism and climate change) and solidarity, ideas that may well be his enduring intellectual contribution to Catholic moral theology. *Centesimus Annus* nos. 30–43 invite students to reflect on the morality of capitalism, which for many of them may seem as strange as reflecting on the morality of the weather. In their minds, capitalism just "is" and not liable to moral judgment.

If John Paul reminds us of the affective and emotive nature of the moral life with his reflections on solidarity, then Pope Benedict digs deeper with his writing on the social requirements of love. See *Deus Caritas Est*, nos. 2–18, 25, 28b, 31c, and 33–35, as well as *Caritas in Veritate*, nos. 1–9. Read nos. 53–67 in the latter text for his reference to basic elements of Catholic social teaching. Christian morality always comes back to love. Love, according to Augustine, is a movement of the soul to that which we perceive to be good.[13] For Benedict and Augustine, we were created to love and be loved, and this love has the potential to grow and develop throughout our lives. The love addressed in these texts is expansive, yet one that students may have experienced and need to name. These excerpts, as well as the ones from *Sollicitudo Rei Socialis* above and *Laudato Si'* below, are examples of the third stage of CST, calling forth the affective responses of persons in love and solidarity.

It is hard to abridge or cut-and-paste sections from *Laudato Si'*, which is such a significant document. In the Introduction, I assign nos. 1–2, and 10–16. This invites reflection about how to think about an issue as much as it serves as an introduction to integral ecology. From chapter two read nos. 66–68, 76–77, 79, 81, 84, 89, and 91–93, a

---

[13] See, for example, Augustine, *City of God*, trans. Robert W. Dyson (Cambridge: Cambridge University Press, 1998), book 14, sec. 7, and Augustine, *Eighty-Three Different Questions*, trans. David Mosher (Washington, DC: Catholic University of America Press, 1982), question 35.

deeply rich set of readings with theological and anthropological insights. I would suggest nos. 106–21 in chapter three for the technocratic paradigm. *Laudato Si'* is structured around the "See, Judge, Act" model with two chapters devoted to each. The "Act" chapters address discernment from the global level to the deeply personal.

ON USING THE PRINCIPLES/THEMES

I use the principles/themes of Catholic social teaching as organizing elements for the class, trying to put all parts into a whole. Since these ideas have been popular teaching tools for the tradition, students should know them. In practice, this suggestion is not as clear as it may seem. There is no "official" list of the principles and, indeed, there is no universally agreed on terms to describe these core points. Are they principles, themes, or lessons?[14] Compare, for example, the USCCB's list of themes with the *Compendium*'s list of principles.[15] Some sources list seven, another has nine, and many have ten.[16] Students should know that these come out of a history. They have grown from the tradition even as they come to direct the tradition. The Pontifical Council for Justice and Peace, for example, describes the tradition as in "continuous renewal" and open to "new things."[17] They would not have been written in the same way in 1891 or 1962.

To my mind, there are seven central ideas in the tradition, which ought to be understood in ordered fashion. The ordering reflects the role each plays in the tradition and thus tells the narrative of the whole. There are two foundational convictions in Catholic social teaching: *Promote, protect, and encounter the dignity of persons* and *Work for the common good*. There are four themes in Catholic social teaching: *Give priority to the poor, the powerless, and the marginalized; Work for peace and the development of peoples; Recognize the dignity of*

---

[14] For "principles," see Pontifical Council for Justice and Peace, *Compendium of the Social Doctrine of the Church*; J. Milburn Thompson, *Introducing Catholic Social Thought* (Maryknoll, NY: Orbis Books, 2010); and Therese Lysaught, ed., *Catholic Bioethics and Social Justice* (Collegeville: Liturgical Press Academic, 2018). For "themes," see Thomas Massaro, *Living Justice: Catholic Social Teaching in Action* (Lanham: Sheed & Ward, 2000) and the United States Conference of Catholic Bishops, www.usccb.org. For "lessons," see Edward DeBerri and James Hug, *Catholic Social Teaching: Our Best Kept Secret* (Maryknoll, NY: Orbis Books, 2003).

[15] See www.usccb.org and chapters three and four of the Pontifical Council for Justice and Peace, *Compendium of the Social Doctrine of the Church*.

[16] For seven, see United States Conference of Catholic Bishops and Thompson, *Introducing Catholic Social Thought*. For nine, see Massaro, *Living Justice*. For ten, see William Byron, "The 10 Building Blocks of Catholic Social Teaching," *America*, October 31, 1998, www.americamagazine.org/faith/1998/10/31/10-building-blocks-catholic-social-teaching. For eleven, see Lysaught, *Catholic Bioethics and Social Justice*. The Byron article describes the origins of these ideas as teaching categories.

[17] Pontifical Council for Justice and Peace, *Compendium of the Social Doctrine of the Church*, no. 85.

work and the rights of workers; and *Care for creation*. Finally, there is an integrative principle: *Live mercy, solidarity, and love.*[18]

Starting the statement of each principle/theme with a verb makes the point that these are not simply "objective" principles but rather invitations to live one's life a certain way. A class can explore the ways that the university community or a local parish or diocese lives these. They are, of course, an invitation for students to live their lives in certain ways. Perhaps we should rename our courses Catholic Social Living instead of Catholic Social Teaching.

GOING BEYOND THE BASICS

If this was all the material a class covered, it might be judged successful. But there can be more to this story. In this section, I urge instructors to go beyond familiarizing students with the content of CST. I believe we must also consider the method and authority of CST, engage the tradition with complementary or critical sources, and consider community engagement experiences within the course.

Reflecting on Methodology: What is the Moral Authority of this Tradition?

Why study CST? What is the moral authority of the documents? Indeed, we may ask, what gives any reflection on social life moral authority for persons?

The basic form of CST is the papal encyclical, one of the highest levels of authoritative teaching of the Church. Thus, for Catholics, CST ought to play a directive role in their thinking about, feelings toward, and actions in society. The tradition, however, is not authoritarian; it is intellectual. The authors want to influence people, Catholics or otherwise, not simply by stating their authority. They want to influence people through accessible and intelligible—that is to say, rational—descriptions of and responses to social issues. Studying CST then is an invitation to students to respond to and develop the tradition.

Yet there is a another "source" of moral authority along with the position/office of the contributor and the reasonableness of the claims, that is, simply stated, the sense of how the contributor "walks the talk." This is relevant as much for institutions as for individuals. Instructors may be challenged by students here on, for example, the role of women in the Church—why are there no women priests, what does that say about the dignity of women?; the sexual abuse crisis—how can the Church now speak with moral authority?; the rejection of same-sex relationships by the Church—students in the room are in

---

[18] For descriptions of these seven points see Bernard Brady, "The Practices of Catholic Intellectual Tradition," *Journal of Catholic Higher Education*, 40, no. 1 (2021): 35–49.

such relationships; and the relative meekness of the Church on anti-racism issues—where are they, what have they done? I will not provide answers here for these challenges. I will say, however, that there have been exemplars in Catholic social living who also have been critical of their Church on these and other issues. It is essential to present stories of people who have responded to the tradition in word and deed, and who pushed the tradition—particularly laypeople. Note that CST is a living tradition, widely embraced by varying people through the centuries. We have a long list of saints and heroes, some of whom may have lived and worked in your community.[19]

Yet there is more. Students can learn that the marginalized and oppressed not only have a moral voice, but also that their experience can make them moral authorities. We need to learn about justice from people who suffer injustice. We need to learn about poverty from the poor. We need to learn about violence from the victims of violence. Although the poor only rarely are published, they are quoted and interviewed in the media. Find their narratives. Their voices are all around us but not often heard. Exposing these voices in the classroom may be the step that moves students from seeing the course as just another subject to be taken this semester and turns the class into something that gives direction to their lives next semester.

Explore the Conversation outside CST: What Matters in the Tradition also Matters to Others

Consider inviting other voices into the conversation, including voices that may reject conclusions of CST or agree with the conclusions but justify them on different grounds. This points to the vitality of the endeavor and, again, pushes the practice as an intellectual one. As I teach in Minnesota, many of my students are Lutheran, so statements from the ELCA offer comparative social theology in our class.[20] Last semester in order to invite students to engage with alternative constructions of human dignity, justice, and human rights, we read

---

[19] Here is a limited but basic list of people whose lives and writings can be part of a course: Dorothy Day, Dorothy Stang, St. Teresa of Calcutta, St. Oscar Romero, Cesar Chavez, Helen Prejean, the Maryknoll Martyrs, the Jesuit Martyrs of El Salvador, and Greg Boyle. See Daniel Cosacchi, "Formative Figures for Catholic Social Witness," *Journal of Moral Theology*, vol. 11, no. 2 (2022): 117–26, for more examples and discussion of teaching CST from the testimonies of individual lives. The list of Catholic organizations that can provide information here is rich indeed. I have relied heavily on Catholic Charities, Catholic Relief Services, and the Laudato Si' Movement (formerly the Global Catholic Climate Movement).

[20] See "Faith and Society," *Evangelical Lutheran Church in America*, www.elca.org/Faith/Faith-and-Society.

from Islamic studies[21] and secular political philosophy.[22] This encouraged students to work through the fundamental ideas behind their own starting principles and come to grips with how to articulate and defend the language of rights and dignity which they easily assume.

When I think of fundamental ideological challenges to CST, two positions dominate my imagination. The first is the notion that violence solves problems. CST is deeply suspicious that violence, at any level, can be used to defend dignity and establish justice. Some dedicated class time ought to be given in response to this idea. Sources on pacifism, the just war theory, and peacebuilding abound.[23] The second is systemic racism. In the past few years, many helpful books and articles on anti-racism have been written.[24] American Catholic bishops recently published two letters on race and racism.[25] The moment at hand calls those of us who are instructors of CST in the United States to respond to the "signs of the times,"[26] using the tradition in dialogue with other sources to challenge students to understand, on a fundamental level, the meaning of human dignity.[27] This ought to be reflected onto the tradition and, indeed, we might find parts of the tradition wanting.

---

[21] See for example Mohammad Hashim Kamali, "Human Dignity: An Islamic Perspective," *Malaysian Journal on Human Rights*, no. 2 (2007): 63–72. The article complements CST as it both defends human dignity and critiques Islamic and Western movements that reject this universal moral category in favor of a communal vision of dignity.

[22] See for example John Rawls, *A Theory of Justice* (Cambridge: Harvard University Press, 1971), 302–03, for his lexically ordered principles of justice for conversation between CTS and justice, and Alasdair MacIntyre, *After Virtue* (Notre Dame: University of Notre Dame Press, 2007), 68–70, for a rejection of the idea that there are "human" rights, in contrast to CST.

[23] This semester I will use Lisa Cahill, "Catholic Tradition on Peace, War, and Just Peace," in Eli McCarthy, ed., *A Just Peace Ethic Primer* (Washington, DC: Georgetown University Press, 2020), 35-64.

[24] Last semester I used Isabel Wilkerson, *Caste: The Origins of Our Discontents* (New York: Random House, 2020). This semester I will use Esau McCaulley, *Reading While Black: African American Biblical Interpretation as an Exercise in Hope* (Downers Grove: IVP Academic, 2020). I always use Martin Luther King, Jr., "Letter from a Birmingham Jail" (available in many places) and "Three Evils" (*May 10, 1967*), available in *The Atlantic*, www.theatlantic.com/magazine/archive/2018/02/martin-luther-king-hungry-club-forum/552533/.

[25] See the powerful "Pastoral Letter to the People of God in El Paso: Night Will be No More," by Bishop Mark Seitz, www.hopeborder.org/nightwillbenomore-eng and USCCB, *Open Wide Our Hearts: US Bishops Pastoral Letter on Racism*, www.usccb.org/issues-and-action/human-life-and-dignity/racism/upload/open-wide-our-hearts.pdf.

[26] Second Vatican Council, *Gaudium et Spes*, no. 4.

[27] Perhaps begin a discussion with three assertions: human diversity is a gift from our loving and generous God; human dignity is a fundamental value in Catholic moral tradition; the Catholic Church has long defined racism, whether expressed in personal actions/attitudes, organizational practices, or structural systems, as sinful.

One of the things we see in these conversations is that the terms used in Catholic social teaching may be the same as in secular or other religious discourses, but the meaning or implications of the terms in CST is distinctive. The Catholic notion of dignity is defined in response to our relational/social nature as well as our autonomy and agency. Most secular notions are limited to the latter. This is significant, as it directs the moral narrative of the tradition. The Catholic notion of dignity justifies economic rights as well as political rights (it is instructive to contrast this to the Bill of Rights or compare it to the U. N. Universal Declaration of Human Rights). It pushes the idea of the common good, in contrast to competing views, in relation to this full set of rights and the conditions by which they can be attained. It describes human flourishing as integral development and not simply as freedoms attained or as material development (although those are crucial). It claims responsibilities as well as rights and it links our flourishing to positive relations to others. CST is not simply a rights-based theory or worldview; it is a complex vision of the moral life.

Out of the Texts and into the World

I sometimes cringe when I hear people say that human dignity is the most important moral principle in Catholic social teaching. They are, of course, correct. Why cringe then? Because reducing human dignity to the abstract and academic status of a "principle" misses an absolutely critical dimension. Human dignity is a reality to be experienced, whether in yourself or another. It is not simply a moral principle to be declared. This is a life-directing point.

Can we design courses that create the conditions of possibility for students to encounter the dignity of others? Can we design opportunities where they come to know dignity in their heart as well as in their head? As Pope Francis says in *Fratelli Tutti*: "What is important is to create *processes* of encounter, processes that build a people that can accept differences. Let us arm our children [our students] with the weapons of dialogue! Let us teach them to fight the good fight of the culture of encounter!" (no. 217). The first step here is to create the space for this to occur *in the classroom*. We are, again, teaching Catholic social living.

In order to generate encounters with dignity beyond the classroom, consider direct engagement with the local community as a service-learning activity. Dividing a class into different experiences with different local partners may create an opportunity, when considered together, to appreciate another sense of the "social" in social justice— the many levels of action needed to address a public moral issue. This is merely a pitch; I will leave a discussion of the best practices of community engagement to others (although I would suggest that the instructor work alongside students in this).²⁸ Such experiences can easily be integrated with specific texts in the tradition. It is not just the experience that matters. As teachers of CST, we know that reflection and writing are essential to help students articulate their thoughts and feelings and, ultimately, their commitments. 🅼

Bernard Brady is Professor of Theology at the University of St. Thomas (MN), where he also serves as Associate Director of the Office for Mission and Director of the Murray Institute for Catholic Education. He is the author of *Essential Catholic Social Thought* and *Be Good & Do Good*, both published by Orbis Books, as well as *Christian Love* and *The Moral Bond of Community*, published by Georgetown University Press. He has published articles in the *Journal of Catholic Social Thought*, the *Journal of Catholic Higher Education*, the *Journal of Moral Theology*, the *Journal for Peace and Justice Studies*, and *The Thomist*.

---

[28] See Erin Brigham, *See, Judge, Act: Catholic Social Teaching and Service Learning* (Winona, MN: Anselm Academic, 2018) for one such discussion. Speakers from the community and case studies may also be helpful here. For case studies, see for example Lysaught, *Catholic Bioethics and Social Justice*.

Resisting Gnostic Spiritualism in the Catholic Social Teaching Classroom

Joyce A. Bautch

TEACHING CLASSES IN THE AREA OF CATHOLIC social teaching is not a consistent part of my course schedule, but I always welcome the opportunity whenever it comes along. With its unabashed objective to construct a world of equality and equity, grounded on nothing less than the sacred dignity of every human person, Catholic social teaching is especially appealing to students who recognize and value the essential importance of uniting personal belief with action. In my experience, college students have no tolerance for hypocrisy and as they quickly recognize, the message of Catholic social teaching is the church's resounding call to embrace and live a Christ-like existence of faithful integrity. In light of this reality, meaningful discussions about Catholic social teaching and its rich tradition of uniting orthodoxy (correct belief) and orthopraxy (correct practice) regularly give rise to enjoyable and memorable teaching and learning experiences. Thus, it is with fond recollection of my students' overall embrace of Catholic social teaching, as well as my own satisfaction introducing them to its heritage, that I am eager to accept this symposium's invitation for deeper personal reflection on my pedagogical experiences with Catholic social teaching.

Amid the many thoughts that emerge from my reflection, one particular realization stands apart and actually leads me to recall Pope Francis's 2015 address to the Fifth National Ecclesiastical Congress in Florence, Italy.[1] In his speech, Pope Francis cautions the Italian church not to replace "the humanism of the 'mind of Christ Jesus' (Phil 2:5)" with "abstract provisional sensations of the [human] spirit."[2] After he spends time considering temptations that can obstruct one's embrace of practical Christian humanism, the Pope extends special criticism for "any form of gnostic spiritualism" that rejects the mystery of the Incarnation and tries to create a false and theoretical understanding of Christianity. Ultimately, he warns, "Not putting into practice, not leading the Word into reality, means building on sand,

---

[1] Pope Francis, "Address to the Fifth Convention of the Italian Church," November 10, 2015, www.vatican.va/content/francesco/en/speeches/2015/november/documents/papa-francesco_20151110_firenze-convegno-chiesa-italiana.html.
[2] Francis, "Address to the Fifth Convention."

staying within pure idea and decaying into intimisms that bear no fruit, that render its dynamism barren."[3] When I examine my instructional experiences with Catholic social teaching, Pope Francis's message about gnostic spiritualism sounds particularly relevant.

I continue to encounter increasing numbers of college students entering my theology classroom with minimal faith formational experience, religious training, or comprehension of Catholic doctrine. If the starting point for a student's grasp of Catholic social teaching is absent any significant familiarity or depth of theological understanding, then attaining at least a functional level of theoretical comprehension often feels adequate, if not notable. In light of Pope Francis's admonition, however, reflection leads me to realize that settling for students' intellectual mastery of Catholic social teaching is settling for what may in fact be gnostic spiritualism. Rather than a theoretical grasp of Catholic social teaching, a much more fruitful, faithful, and worthwhile aim is to foster an affective understanding of the theological and spiritual truths that permeate Catholic social teaching.

To unpack my realization, this paper will progress in two steps. The first will provide a context for my reflection. Every theology professor has his or her own unique teaching situation and philosophy. To understand what I will share in this paper, it is only appropriate that I include some sort of framework for my ideas. A second important step is to capitalize on my reflection and describe some of the teaching tactics I use to discourage anything like gnostic spiritualism from seeping into my instruction or my students' understanding of Catholic social teaching.

My ability to reflect on how I approach Catholic social teaching in the classroom hinges on the essential fact that I enjoy the good fortune of teaching theology at a small Catholic liberal arts university. My formal training is in Catholic systematic theology, but inevitably some portion of my four-four teaching load necessitates that I design and deliver courses in areas outside of systematic theology and my areas of immediate interest. While I did not enter the field of theology and higher education intending to become a generalist, the curricular and staffing needs of my university's theology program make it necessary to accept and fulfill this role. After serving many years in this capacity, I do not resent the situation. In fact, experience has helped me realize that serving as a generalist actually extends a professional and personal incentive to keep my teaching as informed, interesting, and relevant as possible.

Typically, the courses I teach contain only a few students studying to earn a theology major or minor. Most students registered in my classes are not enrolled by choice but enter the course to complete a general education requirement. Based on what I observe and hear from

---

[3] Francis, "Address to the Fifth Convention."

friends and colleagues at other colleges and universities, my experience is not unique in this regard. Nor is the initial level of interest I may witness among my students. Whether it harks back to an unhelpful or uninspiring experience they may associate with worship, previous negative encounters with catechesis, private spiritual challenges or insecurity fueled by ignorance of Christian scripture, doctrine, and tradition, taking a required theology course with unfamiliar peers and an unknown professor is understandably intimidating for some students.[4]

To serve my students as effectively as possible, my teaching philosophy rests upon three educational goals. The first is to foster increased knowledge and awareness that theology has real-life implications and applications to any future life or career that they may envision. To meet this objective, it makes sense that I facilitate opportunities inviting and nourishing personal spiritual growth and development of faith. A second goal is to design theology courses that present material in as interesting and engaging manner as possible, upheld by activities and assessments expanding students' familiarity with the Catholic intellectual tradition. Finally, a third goal is to honor and extend the lasting impact of my own great teachers by always striving to teach with genuine Christ-like kindness, compelling academic rigor, and consistent personable fairness. In the spirit of Saint John Baptist de La Salle, the patron saint of all teachers, the disposition I have in mind is one of individualized loving care and encouragement. Together these goals and attitude increase the likelihood that my teaching creates the conditions in which students may ultimately open their minds and hearts to the guidance and action of the Holy Spirit.

My academic experiences with Catholic social teaching occur within this overall framework and philosophy. The first time I taught a course on Catholic social teaching was in the early years of my teaching career. As was the case then, I still find that a course on Catholic social teaching ordinarily begins on a positive note. When students first encounter the themes of Catholic social teaching and what they perceive to be a persistent call to build a just society and uphold the common good in a way that preserves equality and equity for all, class discussions and considerations generally proceed without much ado. It is easy to respect a faith-based organization that sets out to improve people's lives and the world we share. Occasionally students may deem parts of the tradition or particular themes curious (such as the matter of workers' rights or care for creation), but in large part, any potential hesitancy toward the content of Catholic social teaching dis-

---

[4] For helpful information and insight into today's traditional college student, see Ryan P. Burge, *The Nones: Where They Came From, Who They Are, and Where They Are Going* (Minneapolis: Fortress, 2021).

sipates rather quickly. As a systematic theologian tasked with designing a course on Catholic social teaching, it is difficult not to use these factors, as well as the expediency of clearly enumerated themes and objective details of historical development, to my advantage. All of it provides a sure amount of information and structure for planning a structured course on Catholic social teaching.

In light of Pope Francis's call against gnostic spiritualism, an honest appraisal of my past decisions to capitalize on the theoretical and historical underpinnings of Catholic social teaching for planning a course leads me to recognize the failings of such methodology. Catholic social teaching extends a challenge to construct a moral existence that truly honors the sacred worth and dignity of each human person. Educating students to learn definitions, facts, and abstract details about Catholic social teaching, apart from the enrichment of practical experiential learning and meaningful reflection, essentially robs them of a direct personal encounter with the transformational nature of both Catholic social teaching and Christian humanism.

The contrast between conceptual knowledge and evaluative knowledge that Richard M. Gula offers in his *Reason Informed by Faith* provides some clarifying language to explain. In his extended consideration about the sort of freedom and knowledge required for moral life, Gula considers notable differences between what conceptual knowledge allows one to comprehend versus what occurs in evaluative knowledge. Conceptual knowledge is "the kind of knowledge we have when we have the right information and have mastered the facts."[5] This type of understanding is "the least convincing kind of knowledge for achieving moral conversion."[6] In contrast to conceptual knowledge, there is evaluative knowledge, "a felt knowledge which we discover through personal involvement and reflection."[7] The potential impact of evaluative knowledge is profound and greater than that of conceptual knowledge because it fosters an understanding that "touches the deepest level of ourselves as persons."[8] In short, Gula's words lend direct support to the realization that nurturing students' proficiency in theoretical knowledge about Catholic social teaching is never a valid substitute for worthwhile affective learning experiences coupled with meaningful reflection and dialogue. This latter combination works best because it offers students a chance to consider how their face-to-face encounter with the sanctity of human life and dignity gives witness to the themes of Catholic social teaching and at the same

---

[5] Richard M. Gula, *Reason Informed by Faith: Foundations of Catholic Morality* (New York: Paulist, 1989), 83.
[6] Gula, *Reason Informed by Faith*, 84.
[7] Gula, *Reason Informed by Faith*, 85.
[8] Gula, *Reason Informed by Faith*, 85.

time provides vital pathways to reshape moral character, form convictions, and lead a Christ-centered ethical life.

How a professor chooses to impart affective learning experiences, reflection, and dialogue to instruct on Catholic social teaching is certainly going to vary. Honoring this fact is only appropriate and essential for individual effectiveness and success. In my own classroom, it is difficult to imagine leading a course on Catholic social teaching without requiring students to complete service-learning hours. To increase the odds that required service hours are as impactful as possible, it makes sense that I remain as directly involved as possible. For example, my involvement begins with individual student conversations to discuss and identify what type of activity and location sites could best align with a student's talents and personality. Through regularly written and recorded reflections and individual conference meetings, my engagement with every student's service-learning experience continues. Students know that they must distribute completion of their service hours throughout the semester. This detail ensures the ability to draw connections between their service work and almost all course readings, lectures, and cooperative learning activities. Regularly scheduled group discussions give an opportunity to hear what others are experiencing and learning from their local community involvement.

By implementing these rather simple tactics in the area of service learning and community engagement, I am choosing tactics likely to be quite common among college instructors. Nonetheless, they allow me to underscore the importance of reflective action and encourage awareness that volunteering uncritically, without careful social analysis or reflection, fails to grapple with the difficulty of enacting the social change Catholic social teaching demands.[9] There are structural injustices and systemic realities undergirding the situations of need I am asking students to witness, enter into, and serve. Careful and honest reflection and discussion about service-learning experiences are essential for identifying and evaluating how Catholic social teaching inspires and equips us to honor the innate dignity, rights, and responsibility of every human person, strive to live in solidarity, uplift the impoverished and vulnerable, and end injustice wherever it may appear in creation.

Lest it appear that my high regard for service-learning reflection is idealistic or naïve, I want to be clear that I am not trying to suggest that guided reflection about service learning automatically leads to evaluative knowledge or that it is a guaranteed panacea to gnostic spiritualism. Helping students reflect on their experiences is an important

---

[9] Susan Crawford Sullivan and Ron Pagnucco, *A Vision of Justice: Engaging Catholic Social Teaching on the College Campus* (Collegeville, MN: Liturgical Press, 2014), xvi–xvii.

tool for grasping the depths of Catholic social teaching and Christian humanism, but it may not always bear fruit. One obstacle, for example, is inability or unwillingness to extend sincere compassion and love. With this thought in mind, I always find it worthwhile to consider and discuss how compassion "is not a bending toward the underprivileged position; it is not a reaching out from on high to those who are less fortunate below; it is not a gesture of sympathy or pity. ... On the contrary, compassion means going directly to those people and places where suffering is most acute and building a home there."[10] To construct such empathy is to love our neighbor in solidarity—an essential factor in any pursuit of justice and peace. I encourage students to realize that this sort of dignifying compassion takes effort, noting that compassionate servanthood "does not just happen. We must be willing to let it occur, be willing to listen to the other, be willing to enter into the life of the other and experience the world through his or her eyes."[11]

In addition to considering and discussing helpful insights on compassion, I also incorporate two classroom exercises to encourage deeper appreciation for the meaning of solidarity. The first is an adaptation of a learning activity known as "The Stack of the Deck."[12] Usable in a variety of settings, this thought-provoking exercise prompts participants and observers to imagine multifaceted, long-term impacts and struggles associated with growing up in poverty. Its impact especially lies in how well it uncovers often overlooked factors contributing to what real-life options exist in young adult lives. Frequently in a follow-up discussion, I ask students to think of childhood friends whose lives were impacted by factors they did not have to face. It is a powerful recognition that fosters meaningful classroom conversation.

In another classroom exercise I ask students to consider and identify life advantages and disadvantages with hopes that they can see these realities and one another in a new light. In the class period before everyone voices their own personal examples of how they are advantaged and disadvantaged, I especially stress that no one should feel compelled to communicate what they are uncomfortable sharing aloud. On the day students share their examples, I begin by reiterating the courage of vulnerability and the importance of listening with respect and kindness. With each subsequent turn, the class gains an opportunity to see themselves and their classmates in a new light. It is in recognizing that everyone around us deals with their own nuanced

---

[10] Henri J. M. Nouwen, Donald P. McNeill, and Douglas A. Morrison, *Compassion: A Reflection on the Christian Life* (New York: Doubleday, 2006), 25.

[11] James P. Hanigan, *As I Have Loved You: The Challenge of Christian Ethics* (New York: Paulist, 1986).

[12] United States Conference of Catholic Bishops, "The Stack of the Deck," United States Conference of Catholic Bishops, 2011, www.usccb.org/offices/justice-peace-human-development/stack-deck-illustration-root-causes-poverty.

complexity of blessings and burdens that we may more fully understand the importance of solidarity. Before the exercise ends, I ask students to consider how they embrace the theme of solidarity in their acts of service, how solidarity is essential to seeking a peaceful and just society, and how solidarity may compare to looking upon oneself and one's neighbor through the eyes of Christ.

The prophetic call I perceive in Catholic social teaching is to construct a moral existence and a peaceful, just society that truly honor the sacred worth and dignity of each and every human person. Extended to all members of the church, it is a call to give witness to and incarnate the message and mission of Christ in the world. It is in recognizing and celebrating this life-giving and saving truth that my appreciation for Pope Francis's admonition against the use of gnostic spiritualism only deepens. To build any classroom consideration of Catholic social teaching on pure idea or theoretical knowledge is to deny students their opportunity to grow from affective experience, deepen their understanding through evaluative knowledge, and thereby potentially encounter the transformational fruits of Catholic social teaching. My hope is that by sharing these reflections, others may join me in attending to Pope Francis's message and always aim to introduce students to Catholic social teaching in a way that indeed leads the Word into reality. M

Joyce A. Bautch is Associate Professor of Theology at Saint Mary's University of Minnesota in Winona, Minnesota. She holds a PhD in Catholic systematic theology from Duquesne University.

Teaching Catholic Social Thought Online in the Philippines: From a Challenge to an Opportunity

Teofilo Giovan S. Pugeda III

THE ATENEO DE MANILA UNIVERSITY (AdMU) was established in 1859 by the Society of Jesus. It provides education from the elementary to the professional level.[1] AdMU consistently remains one of the top universities in the Philippines and the world.[2] Its distinguished alumni include Jose Rizal (Class of 1877), the national hero of the Philippines; Benigno Aquino III (Class of 1981), President of the Philippine Republic from 2010 to 2016; Maria Lourdes Sereno (Class of 1980), *de facto* Chief Justice of the Philippine Supreme Court from 2012 to 2018; and Cardinal Luis Antonio Tagle (Class of 1977), the Prefect for the Congregation for the Evangelization of Peoples who, right before his Vatican appointment, taught homiletics part-time in AdMU's federated institution, the Loyola School of Theology.[3] As a young Filipino lay moral theologian, I was accepted as a first-time teacher of Catholic Social Thought (CST) in AdMU. Problematically, I was accepted during a global pandemic. Not only did I have to teach for the first time under stressful circumstances, but I had to do so in an online setting and, compounding the situation, had to design my course with limited assistance.[4]

In this essay, I share my experiences as well as five pedagogical suggestions for teaching CST, which were the fruits of my reflection while teaching. These are that: CST pedagogy must [1] be animated by *magis* and *cura personalis*, [2] reflect the "mystery" of CST, [3] be social and egalitarian, [4] foster a spirit of encounter, and [5] be learner-centered. These five suggestions have relevance for both online and face-to-face pedagogy. Equally, I suggest, they have the potential to effectively respond to the needs of learners in poverty—a practice of CST via its pedagogy.

---

[1] AdMU is composed of an elementary, high school, college, law school, medical, and public health school, business school, and government school.
[2] AdMU was the top private university in the Philippines in the 2023 QS World University Rankings, see: www.topuniversities.com/university-rankings/world-university-rankings/2023.
[3] Cardinal Tagle took AB pre-divinity for his undergraduate course.
[4] I did, however, have much professional encouragement from my colleagues.

AdMU's Experience in Transitioning to Online Teaching

Due to the increase in Covid-19 cases, face-to-face classes in all levels throughout Metropolitan Manila were suspended beginning March 9, 2020, for what many thought would be a week or two at most. In retrospect, most face-to-face classes would not resume for nearly two years. On March 17, the main island of Luzon was placed on total lockdown. The Philippines reputedly had one of the world's longest lockdowns and one of the most stringent at times. Its regulations varied over the months according to the pandemic's development. The months of March and April 2020 fell under Enhanced Community Quarantine (ECQ), the strictest level.[5] Like all schools, AdMU was compelled to shift to online teaching when the ECQ was implemented. In this unfortunate state of affairs, some professors with years of teaching experience needed assistance in dealing with the digital world beyond email and basic software. Students were divided by their varying levels of internet connection, a considerable thing in a country beset by slow internet. Through the problems, online classes confusingly proceeded.

In a compassionate gesture, AdMU implemented a pass-all scheme for its eligible students at the beginning of April 2020. It was one of the first schools in the country to do so. According to the Vice-President of the Loyola Schools, Maria Luz C. Vilches:

> Giving a P [Pass] mark is the most humane way of dealing with student grades under the circumstances that we are in, where it is difficult and unfair to make a judgment of failure considering that students have not been given the benefit of a full semester to improve their performance.[6]

It also shortened its semester by a few weeks and even refunded some of its tuition. While all these measures soothed semestral worries, it did not yet address long-term concerns. It became apparent with the increase in infections that the campus would not be safe for face-to-face classes in the foreseeable future. In a difficult decision, AdMU decided to offer the academic year 2020–2021 completely online. In retrospect, Rapanta and colleagues rightly observed that "the rapid closing-off of face-to-face educational work, in response to the Covid-19 pandemic, gave teachers a strong sense of the difference between online teaching and their other modes of operation."[7]

---

[5] ECQs would be reimposed in Metropolitan Manila in April and August of 2021.

[6] For reference, the full memo is entitled "Remapping Academic Life in the Second Semester, SY 2019–2020." It can be found in the following link: drive.google.com/file/d/1C73bNCHdilFxmGVBAr9a2TQBs3or07cF/view.

[7] Chrysi Rapanta, Luca Botturi, Peter Goodyear, Lourdes Guàrdia, and Marguerite Koole, "Online University Teaching during and after the Covid-19 Crisis: Refocusing

The first order of business was to unify the online platform to be used for classes. AdMU launched the AteneoBlueCloud Canvas, adapted from the Canvas learning management system. In a university-wide memo issued on May 7, the then-president of AdMU, Fr. Jose Villarin, SJ, stated that:

> This coming school year [2020–2021], we are implementing innovative educational initiatives that are uniquely Jesuit and Atenean. We are delighted to announce AteneoBlueCloud (ABC), the vision behind all our new initiatives in online education, capturing Ateneo's distinctive approach called Adaptive Design for Learning to this innovative way of educating. AteneoBlueCloud will brand not only our virtual campus, but also the vibrant online community of learners and educators that we hope to build. It will be distinguished by the essential markers of Jesuit education, which is designed to transform the whole person into someone imbued with the spirit of *magis* and *cura personalis*. This means continuing to educate a person who can think critically, collaboratively, and creatively and, at the same time, serve and lead with competence and character.[8]

A close reading of the excerpt shows that AdMU's pedagogical intervention is animated by Ignatian spirituality. Explanations of two terms found in the excerpt are necessary to understand this, particularly for those unfamiliar with Ignatian spirituality. *Magis* is the Latin word for "more." In the context of Ignatian spirituality, it pertains to the conscious decision to achieve greater service for God, which is expressed in the motto of the Society of Jesus, *Ad Majorem Dei Gloriam* (for the greater glory of God). It does not mean being the best all the time, but rather seeking and offering the best out of every situation to God. Online learning presents many challenges to the students, but it can help them develop a sense of *magis* if properly guided by the teacher. In this regard, *cura personalis* are the Latin words for "care for the whole person." In the context of Ignatian spirituality, it pertains to the holistic formation of the person. It seeks to develop a person not just mentally, but physically and spiritually as well. Online learning presents many challenges for teachers in this regard. Teachers must not only teach students but also help them cope with the debilitating effects of prolonged online learning. Similarly, teachers must compensate for the absence of personal encounters by extending help often to the students. *Cura personalis* challenges teachers to carefully consider the unique circumstances of each student instead of just responding generically.

Teacher Presence and Learning Activity," *Postdigital Science and Education* 2, no. 9 (2020): 923–45, link.springer.com/article/10.1007/s42438-020-00155-y.

[8] For reference, the full memo can be found in the following link: drive.google.com/file/d/11tUrUUMxrd30UfnYLkWEqlp_NrTr82a-/view.

Brooding over these Latin phrases, my first suggestion is that *magis* and *cura personalis* must characterize a CST pedagogy. Precisely because CST begins with the idea that human society needs Gospel values does *magis* make sense for a CST pedagogy: it animates the notion that authentic *metanoia,* both individual and social, begins within, and extraordinary social injustices demand extraordinary social action. At the same time, CST may expose social injustices in ways unfamiliar to students. Importantly, these same social injustices may condition the environment from which some students come thereby striking a sensitive chord. More privileged students may feel ashamed at the disparity between themselves and marginalized sectors. *Cura personalis* in this way helps the student be empowered by CST rather than be disheartened by it. Bergman, however, proposes that "one of the primary tasks of Catholic social learning, as for Catholic education generally, is the fostering of healthy shame—or, as we are more likely to say, the formation of conscience."[9] It is important that educators of CST handle Bergman's proposal responsibly. Just as the implementation of CST requires principles properly adapted to the circumstances of the locale, so too, CST pedagogy must be properly adapted to the circumstances of students.

A stark change in the 2020–2021 academic year was the shift from a semestral system to a quarter one. Normally, there would be three semesters, an intersession (June–July), the first semester (August–December), and the second semester (January–May). Students would take an average of six classes or eighteen units per regular semester. But in the quarter system, the first and second semesters would each be divided into two parts for a total of four quarters. Each quarter would be eight weeks long. Students would now take an average of three classes or nine units per quarter. The premise behind this change was that it would be better for students to focus on a few classes over a contracted period than many classes over a long one. While this may be reasonable under the circumstances, there are pedagogical concerns about whether the contracted learning time compounded by online teaching is optimal for learning. This was a problem for CST courses offered by AdMU's theology department, where I was a new faculty member.[10]

My Experience Designing a CST Course

AdMU initially chose not to accept any more employees for the academic year 2020–2021 as a cost-cutting measure; it soon became clear that the influx of new students was greater than expected. As

---

[9] Roger Bergman, *Catholic Social Learning: Educating the Faith that Does Justice* (New York: Fordham University Press, 2011), 144.

[10] AdMU reverted to the semestral system for the academic year 2021–2022 after consultation with the university body.

such, AdMU began accepting new employees, and so I was accepted as lecturer at the theology department. Because of my specialization in moral theology, I was assigned to teach "TH 141: Theology of the Catholic Social Vision" to senior students during the fourth quarter (April–June), for the last time. AdMU underwent curriculum overhaul in 2017 where the course was rebranded as Theo 12 for sophomore students. By the academic year 2021–2022, the new curriculum took over entirely.

I had taken TH 141 in 2016, so I was familiar with the basic expectations of the course. In the spirit of academic freedom, I wanted to creatively craft my own take on it. Helpfully, AdMU's theology department had an online repository of materials to draw upon. Some were sample courses designed by other teachers free to be copied and changed as desired. In the sample courses I found online, one module was dedicated to Catholic social teaching and principles (Cst/Csp). For my part, I envisioned an online CST course that would focus on Cst/Csp. I would soon learn that designing an online CST course is a difficult but creative exercise. Citing Carr-Chellman and Duchastel, Rapata and colleagues state that "the essence of an online course is the organization of learning activities that enable the student to reach certain learning outcomes."[11] In their words, Rapata and colleagues add that:

> While there is no unique recipe, these activities or tasks should be based on a mix of design approaches (synchronous, asynchronous, online, offline), be described and communicated in an accurate and clear manner, have an adequate level of difficulty for students' capabilities and expectations, be related to authentic contexts to increase students' engagement and be accessible to everyone—taking into consideration the various practicalities that lie behind, for example, having a stable Internet connection, printing facilities or access to resources.[12]

The underlying learning outcome of my course was to enable my students to know how to use CST to assess different issues in the Philippines. I divided my course into six modules. Module 1 presented the historical development of Cst/Csp. Modules 2 to 5 were structured on the four basic Catholic social principles of human dignity, solidarity, subsidiarity, and the common good. Within each of them were topics I judged to be a good manifestation of the principle. For example, human rights were under human dignity, preferential option for the poor and the vulnerable under solidarity, the family under subsidiarity, and

---

[11] Rapanta, Botturi, Goodyear, Guàrdia, and Koole, "Online University Teaching during and after the Covid-19 Crisis," 937.
[12] Rapanta, Botturi, Goodyear, Guàrdia, and Koole, "Online University Teaching during and after the Covid-19 Crisis," 937.

Integral Ecology under the common good.[13] Catholic social teachings and Scripture contextualized the modules.

As I designed my course, I kept in mind that CST is distinct from secular social theories in that it comprises an element of "mystery." Far from being a vehicle for proselytism, CST can be an avenue for recognizing "the mystery within human existence,"[14] as Whittle describes Karl Rahner's attitude towards Catholic education.[15] Because CST contains an element of "mystery," my second suggestion is that CST pedagogy must reflect this. This may be done by recognizing the transcendental character of the Church's social teachings and principles throughout the course. Whittle suggests that educational presuppositions which deem rational development as the only consideration need to be reconsidered in light of Rahner's theology of mystery. Whittle states that "[Rahner's] theological insistence about the significance of certain kinds of mystery draws attention to an aspect of workings of reason that is typically overlooked in theories of education."[16] Hence, the common good, for example, is valued not just for its temporal benefits but also for its salvific orientation.

A module was to be released each Sunday. I chose not to release them all at the same time out of concern that students would go through them all in just a few days and would spend the rest of the semester without bothering to check the course again. My course content blended a variety of media composed of articles, images, and videos. For my requirements, I deviated from my colleagues' practice of assigning mostly typewritten papers. Instead, I wrote seven sets of reflective questions which the students were assigned to answer with at least 120 words each, substantiated by credible sources. I thought this set-up to be advantageous because the students did not have to upload a file and their answers were public to their peers for comment or critique. My questions were grounded in Philippine realities. Pope Paul VI's words are relevant here. He said that:

> It is up to Christian communities to analyze with objectivity the situation which is proper to their own country, to shed on it the light of the Gospel's unalterable words and to draw principles of reflection,

---

[13] To give a full outline, I placed human rights and dignity of work under human dignity; Christological dimensions, preferential option for the poor and the vulnerable, poverty and economic justice, liberation theology, social justice and evangelization, and mental health under solidarity; family and federalism under subsidiarity; integral ecology, business ethics, and participation under the common good.

[14] Sean Whittle, "Towards a Contemporary Philosophy of Catholic Education: Moving the Debate Forward," *International Studies in Catholic Education* 6, no. 1 (2014): 46–59, www.tandfonline.com/doi/abs/10.1080/19422539.2013.869953.

[15] What is referred to here is not necessarily education of Catholic doctrine, but education guided by Catholic values. Since teaching CST falls under both, Rahner's attitude applies fittingly.

[16] Whittle, "Towards a Contemporary Philosophy of Catholic Education," 55.

norms of judgement and directives for action from the social teaching of the Church. (*Octogesima Adveniens*, no. 4)

The use of reflective questions rather than clear-cut answers is supported by what Whitmore describes as the Aristotelian–Thomistic tradition of practical reason. By grounding the students' appreciation for CST, especially as described in the social documents, in Philippine realities, their answers manifest the *phronesis* of the Church's social teachings. As Whitmore states:

> Within this *exitus et reditus* context [i.e., humanity's destiny to return to God], the social teaching has all of the earmarks of practical reason: (1) its aim is to direct human activity or *praxis,* (2) regarding areas of life that are subject to change, (3) with less precision than theoretical reason, (4) and with the particular focus on which social arrangements facilitate and which hinder the practice of virtue.[17]

The public nature of their answers also fostered social and egalitarian learning. Whereas face-to-face teaching normally requires direct submission of requirements to the teacher with only him or her knowing the answer, online assignments provided a communal sense of learning. Students were encouraged to learn not only from the materials and me, but from each other. Thus, my third suggestion is that good CST pedagogy must be social and egalitarian just as the material promotes social and egalitarian concepts. While this can also be true for other humanities and social sciences courses, CST remains distinct because it is inherently oriented towards societal transformation according to the Gospel. In such a paradigm, social and egalitarian collaboration among students is not only optimal for the acquisition of data but also for mutual formation.

As a final requirement and further manifestation of *phronesis*, I asked my students to submit a two-page typewritten paper that reflected on a sectoral issue through any four topics found in the modules. Before the pandemic, TH 141 was paired with an immersion experience in which students would spend several days in a community. The community could be farming, fishing, indigenous, etc. The purpose of the immersion experience was to give students an encounter with people less privileged than themselves. During the pandemic, the immersion experience was transformed into an online talk and group-sharing. Out of concern that students would forget their virtual immersion experience by the end of the quarter, I ensured that their final requirement re-engaged with it. The paper was an exercise on the pas-

---

[17] Todd D. Whitmore, "Practicing the Common Good: The Pedagogical Implications of Catholic Social Teaching," *Teaching Theology and Religion* 3, no. 1 (2000): 4.

toral cycle of immersion experience, social analysis, theological reflection, and pastoral action, which constituted Module 6 of my course. In this way, the prophetic voices of the bishops who authored *Iustitia in Mundo* reverberate today, even if they did not anticipate the virtuality of the encounter. They wrote that education for justice is "a practical education: it comes through action, participation, and vital contact with the reality of injustice" (no. 53). In light of this, CST pedagogy must foster a spirit of encounter. Citing Rachel Jones, Hanchin reminds us that relations are the "constitutive and always embodied site of education understood as an ongoing and open-ended process."[18] With this in mind, Hanchin refers to Nel Noddings's identification of "encounter as integral to care animating relational pedagogy."[19]

In the context of this essay, this can be manifested in five relationships: [1] teacher and student, [2] student and transcendental, [3] student and fellow student, [4] student and world, and [5] student and self. The first relationship has a basis in my first suggestion on *magis* and *cura personalis*, the second in my second suggestion on the "mystery" of CST, and the third in my third suggestion on social and egalitarian learning. While a spirit of encounter should permeate all five relationships, it is especially important to structure the course to support encounters in the fourth relationship. CST should not be taught devoid of the voices of the economically vulnerable and it is less than ideal if their voices are filtered through media or spokespersons. Thus, my fourth suggestion is that CST pedagogy must foster a spirit of encounter by exerting every means to bring students into the world as understood by the economically vulnerable, so that they may speak directly to students. What Pope Francis stated in the context of inter-religious dialogue is also apt for inter-class dialogue:

> Each one of us is called to be an artisan of peace, uniting and not dividing, extinguishing hatred and not harboring it, opening the ways of dialogue and not raising new walls! We must dialogue, meet with one another to establish in the world the culture of dialogue, the culture of encounter.[20]

With regard to the fifth relationship, the student and self, my course was primarily asynchronous, but it had three online class meetings. The asynchronous set-up of my course was an attempt at pedagogical

---

[18] Timothy Hanchin, "Encounter and/as Pedagogy for Catholic Higher Education in Our Time," *Religious Education* 114, no. 5 (2019): 565–80, www.tandfonline.com/doi/abs/10.1080/00344087.2019.1631975.

[19] Hanchin, "Encounter and/as Pedagogy for Catholic Higher Education in Our Time," 573.

[20] Pope Francis, "Address to the Participants International Meeting for Peace by the Sant'Egidio Community," September 30, 2013, zenit.org/2013/09/30/pope-francis-address-to-the-participants-international-meeting-for-peace-by-the-sant-egidio/.

subsidiarity similar to that suggested by Whitmore.[21] Students were encouraged to acknowledge that they are primarily responsible for their education. As such, my fifth suggestion is that CST pedagogy must be learner-centered. As their lecturer, I provided support in their asynchronous learning enterprise rather than paternalistic instruction. It should be noted that this form of pedagogical subsidiarity does not apply equally well to all subjects. Some of AdMU's faculty and students found that the natural sciences and mathematics require more synchronous sessions than subjects in the humanities. Nevertheless, the pedagogical shift during the pandemic has challenged teachers' sense of purpose. In a post-pandemic era, I argue that teachers should take a more supportive role in the physical classroom instead of a paternalistic one. Students should take more responsibility for their learning in post-pandemic face-to-face classes similar to pandemic online classes.

Go and Atienza expound on this notion of pedagogical subsidiarity by presenting three roles of the student as an inquirer, meaning-maker, and creator. In turn, the teacher has the corresponding roles of designer, facilitator, and coach.[22] Citing Tapscott, Go and Atienza claim that "the way we behave as learners tends to resemble the way we act as members of the audience."[23] The pedagogical shift from teacher-centered to learner-centered demands that "teaching practices should suit an entire breed of students who have constant access to updated information delivered to them in a most interactive and portable way."[24] Simply put, face-to-face classes must appropriate the aspect of internet culture where the individual has more autonomy in learning. Online classes are best framed not in opposition to but in complement to face-to-face classes, and vice-versa.

MY EXPERIENCE TEACHING THE COURSE

AdMU decided to shorten the fourth quarter from eight to seven weeks to give ample time for teachers and students to rest. While principally good, it was ironically also stressful for many teachers to reconfigure their course schedules. Over the seven weeks, many of my students submitted their answers within six hours of the deadline, eight days after the release of the reflective questions. It was a matter of concern to me that some of their answers had no reference to CST. It seemed that their answers were made apart from the CST lessons and concepts. Nevertheless, the students generally exceeded the 120-word

---

[21] Whitmore, "Practicing the Common Good," 15.
[22] Johnny C. Go and Riza J. Atienza, *Learning by Refraction: A Practitioner's Guide to 21st-Century Ignatian Pedagogy* (Quezon City: Ateneo de Manila University Press, 2019), 31.
[23] Go and Atienza, *Learning by Refraction*, 13.
[24] Go and Atienza, *Learning by Refraction*, 14.

minimum by double the number of words signifying a desire to articulate well.

I provided individual formative comments for their answers in the encouragement of *magis* and as a sign of *cura personalis*. Every synchronous session began and ended with a prayer to cultivate a sense of "mystery." Some students also provided their feedback to their classmates' answers for social and egalitarian learning. They had virtual immersion with five marginalized sectors to foster a spirit of encounter. To gauge their learning, I released a suggestion survey midway through the course for any changes they desired in deference to the learner-centered nature of the course. One illuminating response was that, due to other commitments, a student preferred a more self-paced course rather than the more scheduled course I designed. What interested me was that the student was the only one among my twenty-three students to receive a perfect mark for the course. I assured the student that I would take into consideration the feedback for future course offerings. During the course, I received private messages from three students. They all informed me that a family member was sick which hindered their ability to optimally participate in the course. In the spirit once more of *cura personalis*, I emailed each of them reminding them of their deadlines lest they lag in the course.

Fortunately, my course ended well with all the students passing and their grades submitted on time. I realized afterward that as a possible integrating exercise on the first to fifth suggestions for future course offerings, the students, aided by personal prayer and discernment, could collaborate with the economically vulnerable in crafting CST-based policies for their communities, with the teacher and fellow students helping refine the policies. These policies could be drafted into a set of recommendations to be forwarded to the local government for consideration in implementing existing legislation. Happily, my first-time teaching CST sparked further creativity in me.

Concluding Thoughts

My aspiration in becoming a teacher of CST was to make a visible impact on my students. With the onset of online teaching, it seemed I was going to be disappointed. As I taught CST online over seven weeks, my aspiration was emboldened though modified to consider the conditions of online teaching. In my opinion, teaching CST has become all the more imperative given the injustices in the Philippines worsened by the pandemic. Millions of Filipinos were left jobless, thereby contributing to the already dire economic gaps, and the number of human rights abuses increased. By teaching CST online in a predominantly Catholic country constantly striving for justice, I hope to have inspired university students to graduate with the firm resolution to respond to the "signs of the times." Teaching CST online has also led me to constructive ends. While a challenge in terms of designing, I recognized it as an opportunity to develop a CST pedagogy.

As suggested in this essay, CST pedagogy must [1] be animated by *magis* and *cura personalis*, [2] reflect the "mystery" of CST, [3] be social and egalitarian, [4] foster a spirit of encounter, and [5] be learner-centered. These five suggestions underlie the case that students learn CST best by experiencing it pedagogically.[25] Hence, I invite others to consider these five suggestions when teaching CST, both face-to-face and online, and adapt them according to local circumstances. In this regard, Go and Atienza recommend *tantum quantum*, which is Latin for "in as much as" or "insofar as." According to them, "for St. Ignatius of Loyola, *tantum quantum* is an invitation to discern what is helpful and to make the most of it, while feeling completely free to discard the rest."[26]

The five suggestions were the fruits of my reflection while teaching during a global health crisis. While the Covid-19 pandemic will eventually end, the pandemic of poverty the Philippines is mired in will persist much longer. Poverty constitutes a great hindrance to learning. As such, the five suggestions proffered in this essay have the potential to effectively respond to the needs of learners in poverty. I encourage their pedagogical adaptation in the poverty context. As an example, social and egalitarian learning of CST may encourage sharing of limited resources among learners in poverty as an actual practice of CST. Finally, since the Philippines extended online learning for the academic year 2021–2022, I invite further research to uncover the long-term pedagogical implications of online learning in the country. The government did allow medical and allied courses to conduct limited face-to-face classes in early 2021 and limited face-to-face undergraduate classes in February 2022. Moving on, I hope to teach for the first time in a physical classroom by August 2022. I am eager to see what new insights I can gain from that experience. For now, I end with another quote by Pope Francis:

> Teaching is a *beautiful profession* ... because it allows us to see the people who are entrusted to our care grow day after day. It is a little like being parents, at least spiritually. It is a great responsibility! Teaching is a serious commitment that only a mature and well-balanced person can undertake. Such a commitment can be intimidating but remember that no teacher is ever alone: they always share their

---

[25] As a sixth suggestion, I propose that CST pedagogy must be interdisciplinary, in recognition of the valuable aid that the social sciences give towards a fuller moral assessment of social issues, but I will leave this for another essay.

[26] Go and Atienza, *Learning by Refraction,* 150.

work with other colleagues and the entire educational community to which they belong.[27]

Teofilo Giovan S. Pugeda III is a lecturer at the theology department of the Ateneo de Manila University in Quezon City, Philippines. He earned his Master of Arts in Theological Studies with concentration in moral theology from the same institution.

---

[27] Pope Francis, "Address of His Holiness Pope Francis to Members of the Italian Union of Catholic School Teachers, Managers, Educators and Trainers," March 14, 2015, www.vatican.va/content/francesco/en/speeches/2015/march/documents/papa-francesco_20150314_uciim.html.

Formative Figures for Catholic Social Witness

Daniel Cosacchi

WHEN THE INAUGURAL ISSUE OF THE *Journal of Moral Theology* was published, the editors selected as the theme "Formative Figures of Contemporary American Catholic Moral Theology."[1] At that time, I was a doctoral student serving as teaching assistant, but I already had a distinct sense that undergraduate students were drawn to interesting and passionate individuals. I could see these students being put off by the language of papal encyclicals but drawn into the life and work of engaging people such as Dorothy Day, Daniel Berrigan, or Thomas Merton. As Pope Paul VI remarked, "Modern man [sic] listens more willingly to witnesses than to teachers, and if he does listen to teachers, it is because they are witnesses" (*Evangelii Nuntiandi*, no. 42).[2]

How might instructors best translate Catholic social teaching to Catholic social learning? In my experience, student-led deep dives into the lives and witness of dynamic, richly human figures who have taken the principles of CST off the page of the encyclical and into the "real world" have proven especially effective. By encouraging students in my "Catholic Social Teaching" courses to select a major figure who has practiced Catholic social living through their own witness, I aim to give students more ownership over some units of the course.[3] While

---

[1] For their explanation of this approach, see David Cloutier and William C. Mattison III, "A Note from the Issue Editors," *Journal of Moral Theology* 1, no. 1 (2012): 22. This issue had essays examining the influence of Bernard Häring, Servais Pinckaers, John Courtney Murray, James Gustafson, Pope John Paul II, and Stanley Hauerwas on American Catholic moral theology. Of particular interest for an evaluation of CST would be Murray. For more on him, see David Hollenbach, SJ, "Religious Freedom, Morality, and Law: John Courtney Murray Today," in the aforementioned issue, 69–91.

[2] There has been an ongoing pedagogical debate regarding the best approach for teaching novices in a field, such as undergraduate students in a theology or religious studies course. See Pamela J. Hinds, Michael Patterson, and Jeffrey Pfeffer, "Bothered by Abstraction: The Effect of Expertise on Knowledge Transfer and Subsequent Novice Performance," *Journal of Applied Psychology* 86, no. 6 (2001): 1232–43, and Paul A. Kirschner, "Epistemology or Pedagogy, That Is the Question," in Sigmund Tobias and Thomas M. Duffy, *Constructivist Instruction: Success or Failure?* (New York: Routledge, 2009), 144–57. Neither of these studies concludes that one or the other approach ought to be used exclusively, but that each is helpful.

[3] The major text I have used when teaching this "Catholic Social Teaching" course is Bernard V. Brady, *Essential Catholic Social Thought*, 2nd ed. (Maryknoll, NY: Orbis

some students may not be interested in economic theory, for example, almost all of them are interested in making a living wage and working in safe conditions; therefore, they are drawn to the witness of John Ryan, Cesar Chavez, Jessie Lopez de la Cruz, and Jerzy Popiełuszko. While many of my students have not really given much thought to serving in the military, they are interested in the Vietnam-era opposition to the draft, because it would have affected their age peers; therefore, they often find the witness of the Catonsville Nine to be compelling. While my students may not know anyone on death row, the desperately high stakes of anti-death penalty activism came alive for them through our study of Sister Helen Prejean—it didn't hurt that *Dead Man Walking* is an Oscar-winning film either.[4] In this essay I argue that teaching Catholic social thought through the lens of formative figures is one way to make the principles espoused in social encyclicals affectively compelling to our students' lives so that these students can see their own lives as formative models for others. Moreover, research on novice-learning demonstrates that novices learn better by complementing abstract concepts with concrete examples.[5] I will make this point through the classic model prescribed by one of these formative figures, Joseph Cardijn:[6] the see-judge-act methodology.[7]

Throughout this essay, I will return to the theme of conversion, because it necessarily combines the three parts of the model I am employing. Conversion always requires passion. One of the areas many of my students and I have been most interested in learning about recently has been CST's largely inadequate treatment of racial justice. As Bryan Massingale, himself a formative figure in CST, has lamented, "American Catholic social teaching on race suffers from a *lack of passion*. ... It is difficult *not* to conclude that Catholic engagement with racism is a matter of low institutional commitment, priority, and importance. If 'passion' connotes commitment, involvement, and fervor, the Catholic stance on racism, in contrast, can be characterized

---

Books, 2017). For a comprehensive list of CST figures ("Significant Contributors to the Tradition"), see 15–22. For the term "Catholic social living," see Bernard V. Brady, "From Catholic Social Thought to Catholic Social Living: A Narrative of the Tradition," *Journal of Catholic Social Thought* 15, no. 2 (2018): 317–52.

[4] One of these class sessions included a personal visit to the class by Prejean. Such a perk is another great reason to study formative figures in the tradition, especially contemporary ones who might be available in person or via videoconference.

[5] See, e.g., Hinds, Patterson, and Pfeffer, "Bothered by Abstraction," 1242.

[6] See Kevin Ahern, *Structures of Grace: Catholic Organizations Serving the Global Common Good* (Maryknoll, NY: Orbis Books, 2015), 66–70.

[7] Another interesting interpretation for this methodology is presented in Clodovis Boff, "Methodology of the Theology of Liberation," in *Systematic Theology: Perspectives from Liberation Theology*, ed. Jon Sobrino and Ignacio Ellacuría (Maryknoll, NY: Orbis Books, 1996), 11–21. Boff replaces the words "see," "judge," and "act" with "socioanalytic mediation," "hermeneutic mediation," and "practical mediation."

as tepid, lukewarm, and half-hearted."[8] In the very next section of the chapter, Massingale cites from a slave spiritual sung by Sister Thea Bowman during her address to the United States Catholic bishops in 1989, shortly before her death.[9] The words of "Sometimes I Feel Like a Motherless Child" elicit emotion in all of us when we read them on the page. But my students and I still don't grasp the larger picture until we watch footage of Bowman singing to a group of predominantly white clerics.[10] There is something about witnessing Bowman's lived, embodied passion for justice that leads us to experience something more than reading the beautiful words that Bowman uttered. We move from empathy to compassion, which "moves the will to justice."[11]

SEE: THE WITNESS OF PASSIONATE LIVES

We all look upon things on a daily basis: family and friends, television, books, social media, street signs. What do we actually *see* when we look at these things? Viewing something on the surface level is insufficient, by itself, for a revolutionary response to social injustice. Nonetheless, it is a necessary first step in this process. On this point, one of the most interesting and dramatic CST figures is Saint Óscar Romero of San Salvador. Students are able to read his writings,[12] learn about his life,[13] and even view film of his ministry,[14] as well as hear the bullet being shot and ultimately ending his saintly life.[15] As with Bowman, Romero presents a beautiful message for us to see. We can each have our eyes opened by a harsh reality arising in our lives. Romero understood what we can all recognize in seeking to live a more faithful life. Part of the beauty of Romero's life resides in the fact that his own conversion experience is something to which many of my students and I can relate. As Clodovis Boff writes, "If faith is to be efficacious, just as with Christian love, it must have its eyes open to the historical reality of which it seeks to be the leaven."[16]

---

[8] Bryan N. Massingale, *Racial Justice and the Catholic Church* (Maryknoll, NY: Orbis Books, 2010), 77.
[9] See Massingale, *Racial Justice*, 78.
[10] For footage of the entire address, see www.youtube.com/watch?v=uOV0nQkjuoA&t=156s
[11] Massingale, *Racial Justice*, 116.
[12] See Oscar Romero, *Voice of the Voiceless*, trans. Michael J. Walsh (Maryknoll, NY: Orbis Books, 1985).
[13] See James R. Brockman, *Romero: A Life: The Essential Biography of a Modern Martyr and Christian Hero* (Maryknoll, NY: Orbis Books, 1989), and María López Vigil, *Oscar Romero: Memories in Mosaic*, trans. Kathy Ogle (Washington, DC: EPICA, 2000).
[14] *Monseñor: The Last Journey of Oscar Romero*, directed by Ana Carrigan and Juliet Weber (First Run Features, 2010). DVD.
[15] www.romerotrust.org.uk/homilies-and-writings/homilies/final-homily-archbishop-romero.
[16] Boff, "Methodology of the Theology of Liberation," 11.

One thing that sets apart beautiful messages is that the messenger, although imperfect, has an uncanny ability to synthesize the reality of the situation in which they live and make it intelligible for their audience. Just as Bowman was able to make racism in the church accessible for the bishops to whom she spoke, Romero was able to make the injustices in El Salvador a part of the visible theological reality to his congregation, which was most of the country. This was a result of Romero's conversion, which is a poignant and controversial topic.[17] Even though the term "conversion" is fraught with epistemological baggage often tied up with changing from affiliation to one religious tradition into another, it ought to be a fundamental part of any authentic religious experience. In categorizing Romero's life as prophetic, Jon Sobrino saw Romero as constantly calling others to conversion in their own lives.[18] Michael Lee explains this type of conversion as "seeing anew."[19] What we see is always the reality confronting us in the world.

Part of seeing the injustice in the world is knowing where the systemic problem is contained. In Romero's case, his ability to interpret the gospel in light of what was happening in El Salvador was poignant. In a warning from Romero's Fourth Pastoral Letter that is just as timely today as it was in 1979, he writes:

> With respect to the classes that have social, political, and economic power, the church calls upon them, before all else, to be converted, to remember their very grave responsibility to overcome disorder and violence not by means of repression but through justice and the participation of ordinary people.[20]

At first, my students think that Romero's situation was especially unique because he wrote those words in the early stages of the Salvadoran Civil War that resulted in untold death and destruction. It was, we are sometimes tempted to think, a different time and place! We are too easily lured into thinking that our own experience is so different from what Romero saw. In fact, his is an ongoing call to conversion for all of us, all of the time. Such a clarion call takes on added urgency for citizens of the richest nation in the world at a time of unparalleled

---

[17] The best account of Romero's conversion is found in Michael E. Lee, *Revolutionary Saint: The Theological Legacy of Óscar Romero* (Maryknoll, NY: Orbis Books, 2018), 44–85. For other treatments, see Jon Sobrino, *Archbishop Romero: Memories and Reflections*, rev. ed. (Maryknoll, NY: Orbis Books, 2016), 14–25; Ignacio Ellacuría, "Monseñor Romero: One Sent by God to Save His People," trans. Michael E. Lee, in Ignacio Ellacuría, *Essays on History, Liberation, and Salvation*, ed. Michael E. Lee (Maryknoll, NY: Orbis Books, 2013), 287–90.

[18] See Sobrino, *Archbishop Romero*, 113.

[19] Lee, *Revolutionary Saint*, 69–76.

[20] Romero, *Voice of the Voiceless*, 141.

wealth. When I remind my students that we are among the most privileged because we have a college education, Romero's prophetic call becomes all the more serious.

Even though many of my students have been slower to appreciate the encyclical tradition than the figure tradition, because they are drawn to Pope Francis, *Laudato Si'* has been well received in the classroom. Like Romero's own preaching, in *Laudato Si'* Francis calls the entire world to undergo a conversion, specifically an "ecological conversion" (*Laudato Si'*, nos. 216–21).[21] Despite formal and often inaccessible language students sometimes have trouble engaging, encyclicals have the potential to move people to conversion. Part of what makes Francis's call to ecological conversion so compelling is that he too utilizes a formative figure whose own personal conversion narrative is among the most dramatic and widely known, namely Saint Francis of Assisi (*Laudato Si'*, no. 218). As Elizabeth Johnson wrote a few years before Francis promulgated *Laudato Si'*, this type of conversion requires intellectual, emotional, and ethical paradigm shifts in every individual, and the global community together:

> In sum, ecological conversion means falling in love with the Earth as an inherently valuable, living community in which we participate, and bending every effort to be creatively faithful to its well-being, in tune with the living God who brought it into being and cherishes it with unconditional love.[22]

When we really *see* the reality surrounding us, we can fall in love with the idea of bringing about justice. The formative figures, in their concrete realities, can help students and instructors *see* in a way that abstract and formal encyclical language sometimes cannot. The next step, though, is discerning how the world needs that love to be spread here and now in our precise contexts.

JUDGE: INTERPRETING THE PRINCIPLES TODAY

The second step in the model is to judge, or what Boff calls the "hermeneutical mediation." To frame this mediation, he poses this question: "What does the word of God say about this situation?"[23] In this step of the theological process, my students get a taste for how scripture has responded to particular questions throughout salvation

---

[21] Francis notes that Pope John Paul II first introduced this phrase in his General Audience catechesis. See John Paul II, "General Audience," January 17, 2001, www.vatican.va/content/john-paul-ii/en/audiences/2001/documents/hf_jp-ii_aud_20010117.html.

[22] Elizabeth A. Johnson, *Ask the Beasts: Darwin and the God of Love* (London: Bloomsbury Academic, 2014), 259.

[23] Boff, "Methodology of the Theology of Liberation," 15.

history. They also see how certain individuals have interpreted scripture in response to injustices of their own day. The students see that in so responding to the Bible, these formative figures are making a judgment. This type of discernment—legitimate *judgment*—is the type of learning that we want our students to do. Often, when listening to my students discussing this or that major figure in the Catholic social tradition, they move from objectivity to awe. As they progress, they are sometimes overcome by emotion, as with their discussion of the "martyr of the Amazon," Sister Dorothy Stang.[24] When students learn about the precious lives and deaths of those committed to justice for the poor and the earth itself, they are often moved. In turn, they begin judging their own lives and those of their peers, and even those in leadership positions in the church and society today. Most of all, they *judge* what injustices surround them on a daily basis here and now. As we all know, there is no shortage of such tragic realities in our world today. What does God's word say about them? How would these major figures act? The students are left to make a judgment for themselves.

What is education for? Most professors have learned that education is for falling in love. First, when we are in school ourselves, it is for falling in love with our discipline. Much like learning something new and wonderful about a romantic partner or close friend, reading a beautiful text changes our view of the world. It is no different with CST. We have fallen in love with principles, popes, and even encyclical letters. They have shaped our lives in the years since we first discovered them. Equally important, however, we professors must fall in love with our students. When we love something, we always want to share it. When we love someone, we always want to share what we feel is most important with that person. In an essay dealing with how to teach war and peace to undergraduates, William French explains: "My aim is to fill the students with awe regarding the rapidity of humanity's expanding firepower and weapons capabilities."[25] Having taught lessons on war and peace in our CST courses, how can we not be filled with awe when discussing these life and death issues? When we teach any course, one of our main objectives for the semester is to curate opportunities for awe. Successful instructors can make the words of St. Luke their own at the end of the semester: "Awe came upon everyone" (Acts 2:43).[26]

If my students are emblematic of most traditional undergraduates today, then their lives are saturated by news and entertainment media.

---

[24] See Roseanne Murphy, *Martyr of the Amazon: The Life of Sister Dorothy Stang* (Maryknoll, NY: Orbis Books, 2007).

[25] William French, "Teaching the Just War Tradition," in Brian K. Pennington, ed., *Teaching Religion and Violence* (New York: Oxford University Press, 2012), 302.

[26] Translation from the NRSV. For a particularly helpful application of this passage, see Gregory Boyle, *Barking to the Choir: The Power of Radical Kinship* (New York: Simon and Schuster, 2017), 51–72.

Speaking from my own experience, sometimes this relationship with electronic devices can numb us to awe-filled experiences. This reality has led me to think about the best ways for my students to judge the injustices of the world today. I have seen my students flourish in producing their own podcasts about perennial issues in CST, using academic research skills in their preparation but presenting in a fresh, nontraditional format that helps them literally join in the ongoing discourse about these topics. Even if Pope Leo XIII did not know what a podcast was, today my students are debating the relative merits of labor strikes with each other in 15–20-minute episodes. I also invite them to think creatively about creating a context for their work: they devise a name for their program, imagine themselves employed by major Catholic or secular news outlets, and even sometimes compose their own theme music to accompany the discussion. As any instructor can attest, encouraging creativity and ownership is foundational to the success of a project because it helps students tap into their own potential, interests, and strengths. More importantly, it moves what may have originally been a topic of interest to one of awe. As for me, I am often in awe of the irony surrounding what I hear when I evaluate these podcasts. Using the same medium—radio—as Pope Pius XII used at Christmas 1956 to communicate to Catholics that they were not allowed to be conscientious objectors to warfare,[27] my students today are examining the heroic witness of Blessed Franz Jägerstätter who refused to serve in the Nazi army and paid with his life.[28] What would they have done in Jägerstätter's position?

Naturally, we also read excerpts from the classic CST documents from magisterial sources: popes, the synod of bishops, and national episcopal conferences.[29] Through their study of formative figures the students are uniquely empowered to judge for themselves how best to integrate CST into the world today. As part of their final assignment for the semester, my students draft an encyclical or pastoral letter on a topic dealing with a CST principle. While many of these begin by using the tried-and-true style of the papal encyclical, the letters often take on a life of their own, displaying the particular passion that students have developed for an issue over the course of the semester. In other words, they heed Massingale's advice noted above, contributing

---

[27] See Todd D. Whitmore, "The Reception of Catholic Approaches to Peace and War in the United States," in Kenneth R. Himes, ed., *Modern Catholic Social Teaching: Commentaries and Interpretations*, 2nd ed. (Washington, DC: Georgetown University Press, 2018), 580.

[28] See Gordon Zahn, *In Solitary Witness: The Life and Death of Franz Jägerstätter* (New York: Henry Holt, 1964).

[29] The best resources are David J. O'Brien and Thomas A. Shannon, eds., *Catholic Social Thought: Encyclicals and Documents from Pope Leo XIII to Pope Francis*, 3rd rev. ed. (Maryknoll, NY: Orbis Books, 2016) and www.vatican.va.

their voices to the sometimes passion-less tradition of CST and energizing it by their own study, engagement, and witness.

ACT: SOLIDARITY IS A VERB. IN OTHER WORDS, DO IT!

On November 16, 1989, six Jesuit priests, their housekeeper, and her daughter, were brutally murdered by the Salvadoran military in their homes as they slept.[30] When we study this massacre, my students are shocked. I have often taught this lesson on a campus with Jesuit priests living among the students themselves. The students, rightly, cannot imagine such a fate befalling their professors, chaplains, and friends. They have a very particular vision of what it means to be a student at a Jesuit and Catholic university. Yet, Ignacio Ellacuría's vision of such a university was precisely what got him killed. This is one of the greatest contextual challenges I have encountered in teaching CST: our reality in the United States is sometimes difficult for my students (and me) to compare with the reality of other time periods or places, for example, the Salvadoran Civil War.

When my students and I read together Ellacuría's 1982 Commencement Address at Santa Clara University, "The Task of a Christian University," we are all stunned.[31] Ellacuría explained that the university, and especially the Christian university, ought to have two central concerns: the intellectual life and the social reality. In my day-to-day work as a professor, I know that I often spend too much time focusing on the first of these issues: reading books and essays, correcting exams, fielding students' questions during office hours, planning lessons. I do my best work when I recall that the university ought to serve the social reality we experience. In particular, the preferential option for the poor is a concept that my students sometimes struggle to grasp. Coincidentally, a providential pedagogical example presented itself the very day I taught this lesson plan in Spring 2021. My family and I were awakened in the middle of the night by the fire alarms blaring in our apartment. My students imagined their own families and homes in a similar predicament at this point. "Now imagine," I asked them, "if the firefighters arrived and started dousing your neighbor's house with water instead of your own." Immediately, to a person, the students understood what preferential option for the poor looks like: God loves everyone, but there are always people who take a priority based on their particular need.

---

[30] See Teresa Whitfield, *Paying the Price: Ignacio Ellacuría and the Murdered Jesuits of El Salvador* (Philadelphia: Temple University Press, 1994); Robert Lassalle-Klein, *Blood and Ink: Ignacio Ellacuría, Jon Sobrino, and the Jesuit Martyrs of the University of Central America* (Maryknoll, NY: Orbis Books, 2014); and Jon Sobrino, Ignacio Ellacuría et al., *Companions of Jesus: The Jesuit Martyrs of El Salvador* (Maryknoll, NY: Orbis Books, 1990).
[31] See Sobrino, Ellacuría, et al., *Companions of Jesus*, 147–51.

But how does the university show its priorities? How does it *act*? By providing its specialized gifts and talents with those who need what the university can offer. As Ellacuría remarks in his commencement address,

> A Christian university must take into account the gospel preference for the poor. This does not mean that only the poor study at the university; it does not mean that the university should abdicate its mission of academic excellence—excellence needed in order to solve complex social problems. It does mean that the university should be present intellectually where it is needed: to provide science for those who have no science; to provide skills for the unskilled; to be a voice for those who have no voice; to give intellectual support for those who do not possess the academic qualifications to promote and legitimate their rights.[32]

To continue in the same vein as Ellacuría, the university ought to act in solidarity with those who have no one acting in solidarity with them. Many of my students aspire to careers which will earn them a lot of money over their lifetimes. I ask them: "Money for what ends?" After those Jesuits and their lay companions were murdered, the Jesuits asked for volunteers to replace them. One of these substitutes, Dean Brackley, poses the question like this: "What about pursuing higher education in a world of hunger? If we have that opportunity, then studying means storing up cultural capital to be administered later on behalf of those who need us."[33] Or to paraphrase Daniel Berrigan: "Solidarity is a verb, in other words, do it!"[34]

Especially as they near their final days on campus, living only a few minutes from their closest friends, my students become aware that college is not the place to which they were going, but the place from which they will be called to make a difference in the world. My students become moved when they learn of another group of Salvadoran martyrs, this time originating from their own homeland: the United States. Each semester, when we discuss the four American missionaries—Maryknoll Sisters Maura Clarke and Ita Ford, laywoman Jean Donovan, and Ursuline Sister Dorothy Kazel—students are keenly aware of what got these women killed: they underwent the first two of Boff's mediations and ultimately decided to act. In describing this third step as essential in liberation theology, Boff is clear about the ramifications: "It emerges from action and leads to action, and the round trip is steeped and wrapped in the atmosphere of faith from start

---

[32] Sobrino, Ellacuría, et al., *Companions of Jesus*, 150.
[33] Dean Brackley, *The Call to Discernment in Troubled Times: New Perspectives on the Transformative Wisdom of Ignatius of Loyola* (New York: Crossroad, 2004), 101.
[34] See Daniel Berrigan, *Testimony: The Word Made Fresh* (Maryknoll, NY: Orbis Books, 2004), 3.

to finish."[35] After we discuss these events, I distribute to the students a graphic design by Sister Jean Morningstar of each of these martyrs crucified on the same cross. Under the image, it reads, "Image of God, Image of Christ." These words bring home to the students just what is most essential in Christian discipleship on the social level: it takes concrete action.

CONCLUSION

Students come to our classrooms full of potential and, often, not as full of background knowledge of or interest in CST. It becomes our immense privilege as their instructors to shape the ways in which these young people will begin to engage with the tradition in a meaningful way. We ought to rely on *both* our own expertise of the encyclicals and the principles they espouse, *and* the students' own research and interest in formative figures. The encyclical texts are surely sources of clarification and encouragement in a world marred by sin, injustice, and division. Those words become alive when students see how they have been understood, interpreted, and ultimately lived by some of the most significant figures in the Catholic tradition. These figures present the instructors of these courses with an opportunity to live up to our vocation as authentic teachers, who will witness with our very lives, as Pope Paul VI encouraged us to do. All of the figures mentioned in the preceding sections of this essay are ripe for further study by our students and us. Many of us had our lives changed by professors introducing their lives to us. By preparing lesson plans on these figures, we can transform our classrooms into laboratories for Christian intellectual development and discipleship. In preparing presentations on their remarkable lives, our students might find in themselves something that compels them to transform the world—what a noble thing.

Daniel Cosacchi is Vice President for Mission and Ministry at the University of Scranton. Previously, he taught in the religious studies departments at Marywood University and Fairfield University. He is co-editor of *The Berrigan Letters: Personal Correspondence between Daniel and Philip Berrigan* (Orbis Books, 2016), and his forthcoming book is *Great American Prophets: Pope Francis's Models of Christian Life* (Paulist, 2022). He received the doctorate in ethics and theology from Loyola University, Chicago in 2016.

---

[35] Boff, "Methodology of the Theology of Liberation," 20.

Solidarity, Praxis, and Discernment: Formation at the Catholic Worker

Casey Mullaney

WHEN THE CATHOLIC WORKER IS MENTIONED in the context of Church history or twentieth-century social movements, it is typically as a lay organization caring for the homeless and an auxiliary to the peace movement. While the performance of works of mercy and advocacy for peace are significant parts of the Catholic Worker vocation, movement founders Dorothy Day and Peter Maurin also understood the Worker as a place of learning and formation.

In a 1970 column in *The Catholic Worker,* Day wrote "'What is it all about, this Catholic Worker movement?'—So many ask us this question … I usually try to explain it in simple terms. We are a school not only for the students, the young, who come to us, but for all of us. We are also a house of hospitality, for worker, for scholar, for young and for old."[1] Even before the founding of the first house of hospitality, the Catholic Worker movement had been invested in education. The labor movements where Day received her political formation and the earliest texts of the Catholic social tradition all articulated the capabilities of the poor and working classes for intellectual development and self-determination. These convictions inspired Peter Maurin's program of "round-table discussions for the clarification of thought," a practice which continues in Catholic Worker communities to this day.[2]

In our community, St. Peter Claver Catholic Worker in South Bend, Indiana, these discussions typically take place in the evening after a big potluck dinner. Once the dishes are cleared away and the

---

[1] Dorothy Day, "On Pilgrimage—Our Spring Appeal," *The Catholic Worker*, May 1970, 1, 2, 11.
[2] The Catholic Worker movement was founded by Dorothy Day and Peter Maurin in New York City on May 1st, 1933. The pair began by publishing a newspaper addressed primarily to unemployed laborers, outlining the social doctrine of the Catholic Church, which Day and Maurin saw as a solution and theoretical framework for addressing the rampant poverty and homelessness during the Great Depression. Day opened the first Catholic Worker "house of hospitality" soon after this, offering meals and overnight housing to the poor of New York.

kettle is put on for tea, someone passes around reading material—copies of a recent article from another community's newsletter, selections from a book on a relevant social issue, or a short text on theology or political theory. The conversation that follows is inevitably lively; the informal setting helps level distinctions in status or level of education, and the mix of community residents, guests experiencing homelessness, college volunteers, and other friends allows for questioning, side-tracking, tangential remarks, and a certain amount of serious and genuine reflection. These conversations are an education in solidarity, both in form and content. As an event, "clarification of thought" is an opportunity for members of the community to connect theory to practice and forge intellectual and affective links between the foundational values of the Catholic social tradition and the events and experiences of their own lives.

The work of Russian philosopher Peter Kropotkin inspired Maurin to encourage workers and scholars to share each other's lives; communities where "workers could become scholars and scholars become workers" would overcome intellectual elitism by developing relationships across class lines and enable each person to develop their physical and intellectual capabilities regardless of the type of labor they performed.[3] The roundtable discussions and clarification of thought grew out of these anarchist principles; outside of the Catholic Worker, I have encountered few other settings where undergraduate students, homemakers, and people experiencing homelessness gather together for a meal and contribute their insights and life experiences to the discussion of a text. Clarification of thought is a long-term process, one that continues through the praxis of reflecting on readings and discussions in light of the daily tasks and interpersonal interactions that take place in our men's and women's residences and our drop-in center, where our unhoused neighbors can come to have breakfast and do a load of laundry or take a shower. I have noticed that it is our younger volunteers—the middle-school to post-college age bracket—who are most drawn to these deep, introspective conversations held across a weedy garden bed or a dishpan full of coffee cups. As educators in the Catholic social tradition, we can look to the 1979 Puebla conference and recognize these as opportunities to enact the "preferential option for young people" and enter into these conversations with the seriousness and sincerity they demand. Our students are also interlocutors.

The Catholic Worker is a movement dedicated to hospitality; I have found these informal exchanges with young volunteers to be sites where I am most aware that I am both offering and receiving openness

---

[3] Jim Consedine, "Anarchism and the Catholic Worker," *The Common Good*, December 2010, edition 55, wp.catholicworker.org.nz/the-common-good/anarchism-and-the-catholic-worker/.

and welcome. By taking young people seriously in acts of conversational hospitality we can give them a great gift: stability and the opportunity to put down deep roots in a rich intellectual and spiritual tradition. In the life of the St. Peter Claver Catholic Worker community, I have spent a significant amount of the past six years shepherding and working alongside student volunteers. Students have a long history of participation in the Worker movement, not only in our community, but in many of the Catholic Worker houses and farm communities around the country. In the year before her death, Day wrote about them with gratitude in her column for the *Catholic Worker* newspaper, "On Pilgrimage." "There are a goodly number of students with us who 'have the house' on certain days or hours, and what a good example they set for others," she wrote. "They have what Peter Maurin called 'a philosophy of work.'"[4]

After a semester, a summer, or a year or two in and around our community, what I hope students and volunteers take away is an orientation towards bone-deep solidarity and responsibility to other human beings, other creatures, and the Earth. The young people drawn to the Worker, and I think to other environments where they will encounter the Catholic social tradition, have an intuitive sense of the urgency and vitality of the Gospel. They are seeking a counter-witness to the "throwaway culture" Pope Francis speaks of in *Evangelii Gaudium*, where "everything comes under the laws of competition and the survival of the fittest, where the powerful feed upon the powerless," and where "masses of people find themselves excluded and marginalized: without work, without possibilities, without any means of escape" (no. 53). The Church and the world are in aching need of the intelligence, wisdom, energy, and fresh perspective young people bring to these conversations. In turn, what they require from educators and others charged with their formation are a sense of coherency and authenticity, a willingness to respond to challenging inquiries, and communities in which young people can test out the ideals of Catholic social teaching and make a meaningful contribution from their own gifts and inner resources. The texts of the Catholic social tradition are broad and contain few specific prescriptions for policy or individual action. To be fully integrated into their formation, our students must have a space to put these ideals into practice.

In my experience as a guide and educator in the Catholic social tradition, it is the move from dialogue, conversation, and reflection to action that students find most compelling. Those who are young right now understand that we do not have time to wait; we must act. We do not have time to wait and see what happens to our planet's climate, we do not have time to let anti-Black racism gradually "fade away," and we do not have time for a small percentage of the world's wealth to

---

[4] Dorothy Day, "On Pilgrimage," *The Catholic Worker*, June 1979, 2, 6.

trickle down to the millions of children living today in extreme poverty around the world. John Paul II anticipated the type of reactionary resistance this urgency often generates, and stated clearly that "anyone wishing to renounce the difficult yet noble task of improving the lot of man in his totality, and of all people, with the excuse that the struggle is difficult and that constant effort is required, or simply because of the experience of defeat and the need to begin again, that person would be betraying the will of God the Creator" (*Sollicitudo Rei Socialis,* no. 30). The young people who come to volunteer at the Worker know this already. They are asking what they can do, and in this readiness to act, I see the kind of responsibility we at the Catholic Worker identify with as holiness.

The political ethic and interpersonal posture of the Catholic Worker is one which preserves the priority of the image of God in each and every human being. This ethic also prioritizes personal responsibility and interdependence. In 1987, this is how Pope John Paul II spoke about solidarity in *Sollicitudo Rei Socialis,* which builds on the claims of *Populorum Progressio* (1967), the first papal document to affirm "that the social question has acquired a worldwide dimension" obligating us to act (no. 9). In *Sollicitudo Rei Socialis,* John Paul II expands upon the obligations identified in *Populorum Progressio* and claims that the most significant contribution of his predecessor's encyclical was not in its naming of the global nature of social concerns, but in impressing upon the Church their moral dimension.

Looking back at the world of 1967 from twenty years' distance, *Sollicitudo Rei Socialis* sees that the promises of global development did not come to fruition. From our own standpoint, well into the twenty-first century, the vast disparities of wealth and opportunity between the rich and the poor have only increased, and although this encyclical focuses on relationships of solidarity across national boundaries and between nations and peoples of different countries, *Sollicitudo Rei Socialis* is able to shed helpful light on the American context and the need for work based on cross-class and interracial solidarity here today.

On a domestic scale, the question of solidarity that John Paul II addresses in *Sollicitudo Rei Socialis* is very much alive in our dealings with guests, neighbors, city officials, and volunteers at St. Peter Claver Catholic Worker; considering solidarity in the context of our community has been an immensely helpful process of discernment for many of us. Today, with near-constant and unlimited access to the internet, we are even more aware of world issues and the interconnectedness of various social struggles; however, the moral evaluation of these realities remains challenging. *Sollicitudo Rei Socialis* is helpful in that following *Populorum Progressio*, it clarifies a duty to act. As John Paul II writes, all of us "have the moral obligation, according to the degree of each one's responsibility, to take into consideration, in personal decisions and decisions of government, this relationship of universality, this interdependence which exists between their conduct and the poverty and underdevelopment of so many millions of people. Pope Paul's encyclical translates more succinctly the moral obligation as the 'duty of solidarity'" (no. 9). Beyond simply asserting that solidarity is in fact a duty, this statement also identifies degrees of responsibility; all of us share in the vocation of labor for the common good, but those who are in positions of greater privilege and influence are obliged to use that outsized share of power to ensure that those not so positioned are able to meet their own needs.

In *Sollicitudo Rei Socialis,* human relationships and the world of work and imagination are the raw materials which can potentially facilitate an encounter with the holy. Labor, struggle, and human efforts to construct a just social order are graced sites where through discernment we might come to better understand how generously God desires to provide for all Creation. These are the things we are attempting to understand better through our efforts at community-building and hospitality at the Catholic Worker. In this context, interdependence is a moral category, and it is within this framework that John Paul II explains in very practical terms what he means by our vocation to lives of solidarity:

> When interdependence becomes recognized in this way, the correlative response as a moral and social attitude, as a "virtue" is solidarity. This then is not a feeling of vague compassion or shallow distress at the misfortunes of so many people, both near and far. On the contrary, it is a firm and persevering determination to commit oneself to the common good; that is to say the good of all and of each individual, because we are all really responsible for all. (no. 38)

Pope Francis, in *Evangelii Gaudium,* speaks of the "habits" of solidarity. He writes that

> solidarity must be lived as the decision to restore to the poor what belongs to them. These convictions and habits of solidarity, when they are put into practice, open the way to other structural transformations and make them possible. Changing structures without generating new convictions and attitudes will only ensure that those same structures will become, sooner or later, corrupt, oppressive, and ineffectual. (no. 189)

In the thought of St. Thomas Aquinas, a habit is a stable quality or disposition in an acting subject.[5] We might ask then what the habits of solidarity look like in practice. In the famous photograph of Day's last

---

[5] *Summa Theologiae* I-II, q. 49, a. 2.

arrest, taken at a United Farm Workers picket in 1973, Day sits with her knees crossed and hands folded. She is wearing sensible shoes, dark stockings, and a plain dress. Her face is lined under her sunhat, and her mouth is set and firm. This image of physical frailty and spiritual vigor is effective on its own, but this photograph is particularly instructive because it also confronts the viewer with the horizon of risk strikers faced that day; the elderly Day is framed by two large, male police officers with a gun and a billy-club prominently displayed on each hip.

Thanks to the ubiquity of cell phone cameras, during the Black Lives Matter protests in the summer of 2020 millions of people around the world saw a nearly identical version of this confrontation play out on the streets of Buffalo, New York, when seventy-five-year-old Martin Gugino was knocked unconscious by police officers in riot gear. In the video, Gugino approaches a line of heavily armed police officers and engages two of them in a brief conversation. He gestures with his cell phone, and suddenly the officers he is speaking with reach out and shove him backwards. Gugino stumbles, but is unable to catch himself, and his body crumples to the ground with the force of the police officer's violent thrust. The video cuts away as blood pools around Gugino's head and police prevent other protestors from rushing to his aid. A member of our Catholic Worker community told me that as soon as she saw the video, she recognized the man whose skull hit the concrete with a sickening thud as a fellow Worker.

There is a particular gait she recognized, embodied language in Gugino's open shoulders, visible but lowered hands, emphatic, understated gestures, and purposeful eye contact. To the careful observer, these are the trained, bodily disciplines of de-escalation, practiced to the point of connaturalization and habituation. Within the context of the United Farmworkers' strike and the Black Lives Matter protests, the physical stance taken by Day and Gugino is one of solidarity. Day and Gugino are both white, well-educated, and Catholic, members of a previously-minoritized Christian denomination that by the 1970's had clawed its way to respectability. Both possessed privileges they could have used to insulate themselves from the injustices experienced by the poor and especially by people of color; however, recognition of their shared membership in the Body of Christ with those facing oppression compelled them to take up these struggles for justice as their own, putting their bodies on the line in confrontation with the State. For people of privilege, solidarity involves taking up responsibility and willingly taking on a portion of the danger and risk that those lacking privilege live with under duress.

Solidarity is a duty and responsibility, but in our experience at St. Peter Claver house, it is also a joy, even in the moments when it demands sacrifice and willing acceptance of risk. "It is a wonderful thing to be God's faithful people. We achieve fulfilment when we break down walls and our heart is filled with faces and names!" writes Pope Francis in *Evangelii Gaudium* (no. 274). In this exhortation, Francis emphasizes the role of solidarity in the spaces of urban encounter where the Catholic Worker movement is most deeply rooted. While far too many of our neighbors experience the city as a site of racism, violence, and exclusion, the city also is a model through which the Christian imagination understands the fulfillment of God's kingdom.

Cities are places of conflict as well as communion; as Francis writes,

> The Gospel tells us constantly to run the risk of a face-to-face encounter with others, with their physical presence which challenges us, with their pain and their pleas, with their joy which infects us in our close and continuous interaction. True faith in the incarnate Son of God is inseparable from self-giving, from membership in the community, from service, from reconciliation with others. The Son of God, by becoming flesh, summoned us to the revolution of tenderness. (no. 88)

In *Evangelii Gaudium,* the affective and interpersonal dimensions of solidarity are most fully developed. The experiences of "close and continuous" interaction with others in the defining moments of their lives creates in us the desire to commit ourselves to the flourishing of particular individuals and communities and from there, to that of the human family and all of creation. These opportunities for encounter, reflection, and action occur in a continuing spiral when we accept what Francis calls "the social aspect of the Gospel" (no. 88); lay movements such as the Catholic Worker can provide students and practitioners of the Catholic social tradition space and conversation partners with whom to deepen their understanding of the spiritual dimension and significance of these encounters.

Solidarity, the option for the poor, and the dignity of the human person are all intellectual and moral commitments, but the fullest understanding of these principles requires an embodied stance. Learning to take up a stance of responsibility, becoming capable of the type of witness Day and Gugino offer takes practice. What the Catholic Worker and communities like it can offer to students of the Catholic social tradition is an opportunity to become literate in the bodily and emotional disciplines enabling us to affirm the commitments of CST with our whole lives. This type of practice literally shapes the way we move in the world. In the video from the Black Lives Matter protests, it is clear that these bodily disciplines are not legible to the police officers Gugino engages; however, reflecting from the perspective of the Catholic social tradition, they are a form of embodied speech. I have seen members of my own Catholic Worker community, men and women starting in their late teens and early twenties, use these same bodily disciplines of engagement and nonviolent de-escalation to calm agitated guests at our drop-in center or break up physical altercations in our parking lot. My friends practice a creative *askesis* of nonviolence to de-escalate these tense situations, injecting humor and warmth where there is anger and hostility. This *askesis* mirrors the humanity of both aggressor and victim and presents a reimagined relationship to violent control.

John Paul II writes:

> In the light of faith, solidarity seeks to go beyond itself, to take on the specifically Christian dimension of total gratuity, forgiveness, and reconciliation. One's neighbor is then not only a human being with his or her own rights and a fundamental equality with everyone else, but becomes the living image of God the Father, redeemed by the blood of Jesus Christ and placed under the permanent action of the Holy Spirit." (*Sollicitudo Rei Socialis*, no. 39)

As Catholic Workers, my neighbors put their bodies between people who mean violence and those upon whom they would inflict it. They are habituated to solidarity; this virtue has become part of who they are and how they move through the world. The capacity to stand unarmed before a line of police officers in riot gear is seeded and grown at the soup kitchen, in the daily tasks of offering hospitality.

Solidarity as articulated and practiced at the Catholic Worker is a stance capable of encompassing both dramatic clashes with state-sanctioned violence and everyday interpersonal interactions, each one an opportunity to treat the other as a holy being. Francis writes,

> If we are to share our lives with others and generously give of ourselves, we also have to realize that every person is worthy of our giving ... because they are God's handiwork, his creation. God created that person in his image, and he or she reflects something of God's glory. Every human being is the object of God's infinite tenderness, and he himself is present in their lives. Jesus offered his precious blood on the cross for that person. Appearances notwithstanding, every person is immensely holy and deserves our love. (no. 274)

The crises of racism, climate change, and the COVID-19 pandemic have in recent years revealed the fragility and inadequacy of institutional safety nets and in many communities have reignited interest in the disciplines of solidarity: protest, mutual aid, and creative re-envisioning of a just and holy social order. This is the work of bringing about God's kingdom. Study and conversation, as they take place during community "clarifications of thought," can join with these practical disciplines to refine and deepen Christian social praxis.

A lay movement like the Catholic Worker can perhaps push magisterial Catholic social teaching further and enrich our theoretical and lived understanding of solidarity by providing a "learning laboratory" of sorts: multigenerational and cross-class communities in which students can enact, reflect on, and further challenge what the popes have taught in the texts of the Catholic social tradition. The holiness of the Catholic Worker ethos is the practice of treating every individual as a holy being. John Paul II's call for radical awareness of the sanctity and dignity of each human person likewise states,

> Solidarity helps us to see the "other"—whether a person, people, or nation—not just as some kind of instrument, with a work capacity and physical strength to be exploited at low cost and then discarded when no longer useful, but as our "neighbor," a "helper" (cf. Gen 2:18–20), to be made a sharer, on par with ourselves, in the banquet of life to which all are equally invited by God. Hence the importance of reawakening the religious awareness of individuals and peoples. (*Sollicitudo Rei Socialis*, no. 39)

Solidarity, as John Paul II describes it, is the fruit of praxis, in which careful reflection and discernment informed by practical experience enable the practitioner to fully realize and embody this posture of attentiveness to God's presence and action. At the Catholic Worker, my hope is that students—and every one of us—will take advantage of the many opportunities for encounters with neighbors, helpers, and other holy beings to sharpen their vision and integrate into their daily consciousness this "religious awareness" of the image of God in everyone they meet. M

Casey Mullaney is a summer 2022 graduate of the doctoral program in moral theology at the University of Notre Dame. Her research uses ethnographic methods to pose theological questions about embodiment, labor, and ritual formation. She is also a member of the St. Peter Claver Catholic Worker community in South Bend, Indiana, where she cooks, cares for neighbors, and organizes youth and student programming.

"Are We Theologians?": A Practical Theology Approach to Catholic Social Teaching with Women Religious in East Africa

Sarah C. DeMarais

AT HER ORIENTATION TO STUDY WITH THE LOYOLA Institute for Ministry, a Kenyan sister abruptly asked me: "Tell me, are we theologians?" Surprised, I responded: "Yes, you will be doing theology in these courses. You are theologians." I was awed when the room, full of East African Catholic sisters, broke out into cheers: "Wow, we are theologians!"

The sisters' enthusiasm for theological study highlights the reality that women and girls in East Africa face limited access to educational opportunities,[1] including theological education. Yet even with obstacles to formal education, Catholic women religious are powerful agents of the Catholic social tradition, advancing peace, justice, and development through their ministries. Though sisters "operate within Catholic social teaching's frame of integral human development," the impact of their ministries can be "easily overlooked as charity."[2] In East Africa,[3] sisters themselves do not always make explicit connections between their ministries and the social teaching of the Church.[4]

---

[1] For example, about 60 percent of sisters in Tanzania have not completed secondary school: See Melanie Lidman, "Lack of Education among Sisters a Challenge for Tanzanian Formators," *Global Sisters Report*, April 11, 2016, www.globalsistersreport.org/news/spirituality/lack-education-among-sisters-challenge-tanzania-formators-39131.

[2] Meghan J. Clark, "Charity, Justice, and Development in Practice: A Case Study of the Daughters of Charity in East Africa," *Journal of Moral Theology* 9, no. 2 (2020): 2, 6.

[3] The boundaries of what is considered East or Eastern Africa are disputed. The participants in the projects described here are primarily from Kenya and Tanzania, and also Uganda, South Sudan, Malawi, and Zambia.

[4] Catherine Sexton and Maria Calderón Muñoz, *Religious Life for Women in East and Central Africa: A Sustainable Future*, Conrad N. Hilton Foundation, 2020, www.hiltonfoundation.org/wp-content/uploads/2020/08/Religious-Life-for-Women-in-East-and-Central-Africa%E2%80%94A-Sustainable-Future.pdf.

The Catholic bishops of Africa called in 2009 for mandatory ongoing formation for women religious in social doctrine.[5] However, East African sisters share with me that Catholic social teaching is minimally included in their formation programs, if at all. When women's congregations do have formation in CST, they may pay a priest to visit for a brief lecture.[6] While this approach could impart some doctrinal information, it hardly prepares sisters for ongoing discernment of how the Church's social tradition intersects with their congregational charism and mission. Sisters work closely with poor and marginalized people, confront serious social issues, and deserve access to tools to discern how best to bring about justice and the common good in their unique contexts.

I describe in this essay a project aimed at empowering East African sisters as practical theologians and agents of the Catholic social tradition. The Loyola Institute for Ministry (LIM) of Loyola University New Orleans, a Catholic and Jesuit university, offers degrees and certificates in pastoral studies and religious education. To date, forty-one East African sisters have earned LIM's online Certificate in Catholic Social Teaching. I discuss how we at LIM teach CST through a unique and inculturated method of practical theology, and how our students have subsequently engaged with, applied, and shared CST in their ministries. Ultimately, the education of a relatively small number of sisters has built the capacity of their congregations for more vibrantly living their charism and mission, and for pursuing partnerships for the common good. I hope this program description will inspire further pedagogies of CST that privilege practical and contextual theologies, thereby empowering local praxis in the service of human development.

LIM's Method of Practical Theology

Practical theology takes place in community and "is directed towards individual and social transformation in Christ."[7] LIM's distinctive approach to practical theology is inspired by the work of David Tracy and Bernard Lonergan. LIM's approach follows Tracy's "revisionist model" of theology, which insists on "critical correlation" of theology's two sources, "common human experience and language"

---

[5] II Special Assembly for Africa of the Synod of Bishops, "Final List of Propositions," 2009, no. 18, www.vatican.va/roman_curia/synod/documents/rc_synod_doc_20091023_elenco-prop-finali_en.html.

[6] This is based on anecdotal reports from our students. We are currently collecting additional data about CST and formation programs in East Africa and assisting formators to revise formation curricula to address CST.

[7] Association of Graduate Programs in Ministry's 1992 position statement, quoted in Barbara J. Fleischer and Tracey Lamont, "Practical Theology and Ministry Praxis," in *Introduction to Practical Theology,* ed. B. J. Fleischer and T. Lamont (New Orleans: Loyola Institute for Ministry, 2020), 15.

and "the meanings present in the Christian fact."[8] To this end of dialogue between experience and tradition, LIM developed a process of practical theological reflection that derives from Lonergan's four-step method of experiencing, judging, understanding, and deciding.[9] Specifically, it involves 1) identifying a ministry situation, a "concern," on which to reflect, 2) articulating an initial understanding or interpretation of that concern by means of one's own questions, 3) testing that initial understanding through questions raised by research into five contexts of ministry (cultural, personal, institutional, Christian tradition, and creation[10]), and 4) deciding a future course of action based on new insights. LIM's method for reflection on ministerial praxis is recursive since the action in step four becomes a new subject for further reflection and testing. LIM learning communities thus bring the Christian tradition, including Catholic social teaching, into mutually interpretive conversation with students' diverse and contextual experiences and concerns.

LIM's CERTIFICATE IN CATHOLIC SOCIAL TEACHING

Loyola University New Orleans has been awarded three grants to date through the Conrad N. Hilton Foundation's Catholic Sisters Initiative. The Initiative "aims to increase the capacity of sisters to meaningfully address poverty, and elevate their voice and influence as moral leaders of change in the global effort to relieve human suffering and restore human dignity."[11] In partnership with the Hilton Foundation, LIM has facilitated online theological education for Catholic sisters in East and West Africa, Asia, and North America through three projects since 2014: "Communicating Charism," "Catholic Sisters in Partnership for Sustainability," and "Living Charisms for Sustainable

---

[8] David Tracy, *Blessed Rage for Order* (New York: Seabury, 1975), 43.
[9] Bernard Lonergan, *Method in Theology* (New York: Herder & Herder, 1972), 14. For a fuller exploration of the development of LIM's method, including the influence of Tracy and Lonergan and contributions of Charles Winters and former LIM Director Bernard Lee, see Barbara J. Fleischer, "A Theological Method for Adult Education Rooted in the Works of Tracy and Lonergan," *Religious Education* 95, no. 1 (2000): 23–37.
[10] The creation context (natural world, ecological, or cosmological context) was the latest addition to LIM's method, inspired by LIM faculty Kathleen O'Gorman. Creation can be understood as a meta-context "that makes possible all subsequent contexts." See Kathleen O'Gorman, "The Cosmological and Ecological Contexts of Ministry," in *Introduction to Practical Theology*, 234.
[11] Conrad N. Hilton Foundation, "Catholic Sisters," www.hiltonfoundation.org/programs/catholic-sisters.

Human Development."[12] In the latter two, Catholic sisters in East Africa have studied online for LIM's Certificate in Catholic Social Teaching.[13]

Students can earn this four-course certificate at the undergraduate or graduate level. The curriculum is designed so that a student with little prior formal theological education can develop skills for practical theological reflection and achieve a foundational understanding of CST. Students' increased knowledge of CST comes to enrich their theological reflection, prompting deeper understandings of the needs of those with whom they minister and the contexts in which ministry takes place. To empower students to pursue opportunities for partnership within and beyond the Church, the courses explore how CST intersects with secular approaches to development, including the United Nations Sustainable Development Goals (SDGs).[14] Students ultimately share their learnings with others and mobilize collective action for development. Below I describe the certificate courses and highlight some aspects of their design and delivery, including inculturation for East African contexts and the integration of Ignatian spirituality.

Course Sequence & Projects

The project "Catholic Sisters in Partnership for Sustainability" started with in-person, three-day orientation workshops that I led in Kenya and Tanzania in March 2018. I offered brief introductions to some sources, history, and themes of CST and the UN SDGs. Sisters participated in small- and large-group discussions to make initial connections between CST, the SDGs, and the needs of people in their own communities. Sisters led us in prayer that illustrated their distinctive congregational charisms. After orientation, students completed the following courses:

---

[12] See the project websites for more information, including participating congregations: cnh.loyno.edu/lim/communicating-charism, cnh.loyno.edu/lim/sisters-and-sustainability and cnh.loyno.edu/lim/charism-and-cst.
[13] I focus in this essay primarily on how the certificate program was delivered in "Catholic Sisters in Partnership for Sustainability," which has been completed and evaluated. Following our learnings from that project, "Living Charisms for Sustainable Human Development" (still in progress) advances integral human development and trauma-informed care for vulnerable youth and aims to transform congregational cultures (through, among other efforts, students revising formation curricula and leading retreats incorporating CST).
[14] The 17 UN SDGs comprise the 2030 Agenda for Sustainable Development, adopted by UN Member States in 2015 as a "blueprint for peace and prosperity for people and the planet" (United Nations, sdgs.un.org/goals). The final goal is partnership to achieve sustainable development. For a Catholic moral vision for the agenda, see Meghan J. Clark, "Seeking Solidarity for Development: Insights from Catholic Social Thought for Implementing the UN Agenda," *Journal of Catholic Social Thought* 13, no. 2 (2016): 311–28.

- *Introduction to Practical Theology* introduced students to LIM's method of practical theological reflection, including analysis of cultural, personal, institutional, Christian tradition, and creation contexts of ministry. Students applied the method to decide how to respond to a self-selected "concern" in their own ministries.
- *Jesus and the Christian Tradition* led students to explore the life of Jesus and the Christian tradition, with particular emphasis on theologies of grace and African Christologies. Students refined their skills for contextual analysis in practical theological reflection.
- *CST and Sustainable Development* included a deeper study of CST, using Thomas Massaro, SJ's *Living Justice*[15] and Pope Francis's *Laudato Si'* as major texts. Students reflected on how CST connects to their ministries and congregational charism and mission, and the UN SDGs. Students developed skills for communicating about CST and partnering with ministry stakeholders and secular organizations pursuing development goals.
- In the fourth course, *Praxis—Developing Partnerships for Ministry*, students completed two major capstone projects. Each developed and led a workshop for ministry stakeholders with the goal of empowering them as agents of sustainable development. Workshops involved students introducing participants to CST and the SDGs (creating educational materials in local languages as needed), then applying their practical theological reflection skills to guide discernment of community needs, identifying and implementing at least one tangible action in support of sustainable development. For the second capstone project, students established a new organizational partnership to advance their ministry for sustainable development.

Online Pedagogy

Each course was taught by LIM faculty asynchronously on the Blackboard online learning platform. I served as Teaching Assistant, providing particular support for academic theological writing. The courses included weekly modules with distinct learning goals and assignments, including a discussion board. Students wrote in response to one or two discussion questions and replied to their peers. Faculty served as co-participants in the online discussion boards, supporting and challenging students. Students also submitted written assignments for feedback, including longer papers, short essay responses, and spiritual reflections.

---

[15] Thomas Massaro, *Living Justice: Catholic Social Teaching in Action* (London: Rowman & Littlefield, 2016).

Inconsistent electricity and internet access were obstacles to online participation, particularly for students in rural areas. With grant funding, we were able to provide students laptops and flash drives with course texts and videos.[16] The flash drives mitigated bandwidth demands, but students still needed to access Blackboard regularly to participate in discussions and submit assignments. In addition to technical challenges, students faced competing demands on their time, including full-time ministries, congregational commitments (such as retreats), and health issues. Faculty offered flexible deadlines, patience, and considerable support for students to help them achieve learning outcomes, particularly in the Praxis capstone course.

In addition to Blackboard and email, I communicated with students through WhatsApp (a chat program more readily accessible in low-bandwidth environments). Outside of coursework, students used WhatsApp groups to share encouragement, prayers, and videos, furthering our online learning community.

Inculturation

Inculturation, the taking root of the Gospel in particular contexts, reflects the wisdom of the Incarnation (*Ecclesia in Africa*, no. 60). God communicated the Word not in the abstract but in the person of a first-century Galilean Jew and so invites those who would convey the Gospel today to attend to the particular, local, and embodied. For the past forty years, LIM has offered its face-to-face extension ("LIMEX") community learning model in North and Central America, Africa, and Europe. Outside of North America, it partners with sponsoring agencies to adapt the program, its courses, and materials to local realities. LIM's theological curriculum has been and continues to be shaped by this global learning community, wherein small groups engage with and inculturate materials for their distinctive contexts. LIM's method of practical theological reflection, described above, is itself readily adaptable to geographically and culturally diverse contexts in its respect for particularity. The method is student-driven, tasking students with identifying, analyzing, and responding to unique contextual needs. The method gives explicit attention to particular sociocultural, political, historical, and institutional contexts, placing these realities in dialogue with the Christian tradition. To aid their analysis of a ministry concern, for example, students interview "wise practitioners" closely involved with the situation, "to hear what they consider the significant symbols, stories, ethos, and worldview of the people [with whom one ministers] and the life chances, mediating structures, and

---

[16] Funding from the Hilton Foundation also fully covered student tuition, and fees for the certificate program, and accommodation for the orientation meetings.

social control at their disposal."[17] This activity encourages students to honor local wisdom and ways of knowing in the spirit of the CST principle of subsidiarity.

Rather than maintain an uncritical Eurocentrism, this project pays attention to differences in social location and the implications of those for theology. To support East African students in their growth as practical theologians engaging with local concerns, the curriculum of LIM's Certificate in CST includes texts by and videos featuring African theologians, ministers, and activists.[18] Some of the videos were created by LIM through our partnerships with communities in West and East Africa.

Building on this engagement with diverse texts and media, course activities empowered students to connect critically with their local contexts and experiences. For example, students compared their own sociocultural and political contexts with those of first-century Galilee, translated "grace" into their first languages, and shared culturally relevant images of Jesus. A student from Malawi reflected that Jesus is an "intimate friend" for African women: Jesus is "ever with them, restoring their energies when they fetch water from faraway rivers and wells. ... In times of lack of food, clothing and water, Jesus suffers with them while reaffirming their hopes that all shall be well someday."[19]

In their final projects, students created their own inculturated materials for sharing CST within their communities. For example, a Kenyan student translated the themes of CST into Kiswahili.[20] At its best, inculturation both inspires students to draw on positive cultural values and empowers critique of traditions that are antithetical to human dignity.[21] Inspired by CST and in their ministries, for example, students have challenged destructive practices like child marriage and female

---

[17] Michael A. Cowan, "The Sociocultural Context of Ministry," in *Introduction to Practical Theology*, 146.

[18] African theologians whose scholarship enriched our students' learning in this project include Teresia Hinga, Stan Chu Ilo, Emmanuel Katongole, Laurenti Magesa, Anne Nasimiyu-Wasike, Paulinus I. Odozor, Mercy Amba Oduyoye, Teresa Okure, and Agbonkhianmeghe E. Orobator.

[19] Sr. Diana Malikebu, 2021. Shared with permission. This reflection was inspired by Anne Nasimiyu-Wasike, "Christology and an African Woman's Experience," in *Faces of Jesus in Africa*, ed. R. J. Schreiter (New York: Orbis Books, 1991), 70–81.

[20] Sr. Jane Frances Mulongo, IBVM, translated into Kiswahili documents (originally from Catholic Relief Services, with permission) for adults (cnh.loyno.edu/sites/default/files/images/cst_poster_adult_swahili_loyola_final.pdf) and children (cnh.loyno.edu/sites/default/files/images/cst_poster_children_swahili_loyola_final.pdf).

[21] For a discussion of the liberative potential of inculturation in Africa, see J. J. Carney, "Inculturating through the Lens of Liberation: John Mary Waliggo and the Renewal of Catholic Tradition in Africa," *Journal of Moral Theology* 10, no. 2 (2021): 194–211.

genital mutilation.[22] Conscious of our own location as an educational organization based in North America, LIM learns with students by continually soliciting feedback to discern the relevance of course materials, pedagogical approaches, and assignments. Our hope is that students will whole-heartedly engage both the Christian tradition (particularly CST) and their own cultural values and practices towards just praxis.

Ignatian Spiritual Formation

All courses in the program integrate spiritual formation in the Ignatian tradition. LIM's approach to spiritual formation, as developed by Jerry Fagin, SJ, and inspired by St. Ignatius Loyola's *Spiritual Exercises*, invites students "to foster their relationship with God by internalizing the basic Christian themes ... of God's love, conversion, the call to discipleship, a personal relationship with Jesus and a sharing in the Paschal Mystery."[23]

Each course focuses on particular "graces" and offers resources for praying with Scripture, journaling, faith sharing, and praying the examen of consciousness. For example, in the course "Jesus and the Christian Tradition," students are invited to pray for the grace to "know, love, and serve Jesus," and are taught how to practice imaginative prayer with Gospel stories. In the Praxis course, students pray for the grace "to rejoice with Jesus and experience a sense of mission" by imagining the Resurrected Jesus's appearance to His mother. Twice each course, students submit a written reflection on their experiences with the spiritual formation program.

Feedback from the sisters indicated that they highly valued the integration of spiritual development in the courses. Some noted that Ignatian spiritual practices deepened their engagement with their congregation's own charism and spiritual traditions, and some have shared new practices with their communities through retreats and communal prayer.

PROJECT OUTCOMES

Inspired by their study of CST, sisters mobilized their communities to act for integral human development. Each action was collaborative and a testament to the transformative power of the sisters' leadership. By the end of the project "Catholic Sisters in Partnership for Sustainability," sisters had led workshops educating nearly 700 people about

---

[22] The Loreto Sisters' Termination of FGM program is featured in the film series *As I Have Done* (2019), produced by Salt + Light Media in partnership with the Loyola Institute for Ministry and funded by the Conrad N. Hilton Foundation: slmedia.org/s/y2UxdMT9/as-i-have-done.

[23] Jerry Fagin, *Loyola Institute for Ministry Spiritual Formation Program* (New Orleans: Loyola Institute for Ministry, 2010).

CST and development and guiding communal discernment on how to promote sustainable development locally.[24] The many fruits of the students' workshops and partnerships include the following: sisters and their collaborators developed and implemented a diocese-wide child protection policy, established a safe library for conflict-affected youth, built a surgical unit for Caesarean deliveries, repaired a road to improve access to a health center, organized at least six tree planting projects, advocated against domestic violence through writing and performing songs, trained single mothers in poultry farming, and organized parents in a slum for entrepreneurship training. This sampling of projects illustrates how a practical theological approach that honors experience and contextuality empowers students to discern and respond to community needs in light of the Catholic social tradition.

These community-level benefits were made possible by the students' own growth, as they learned how to promote development that honors human dignity and encourages participation and justice. A project evaluator found that students reported extremely high satisfaction with the program, increased knowledge and understanding of CST and SDGs, increased commitment and self-confidence for acting on their principles, and increased leadership skills.[25] Sisters beautifully described their spiritual growth; one wrote: "The course has been an eye-opener to me: I can take responsibility. ... I have grown in the freedom to see and respond to needs not just in my ministry but around me."[26]

Though we hoped students would be personally inspired by CST and grow in Ignatian freedom towards courageous action for human flourishing, we did not fully anticipate their enthusiasm for sharing knowledge of CST. Some have continued to lead community workshops, and formators have integrated CST into their programs.[27] The successes of this project affirm our practical theology approach and demonstrate that educating sisters in CST, collaborative and practical theological reflection, a spirituality of discernment, and skills for leadership benefits sisters, their congregations, the poor and marginalized, and the natural world.

---

[24] Additionally, in our current project to date ("Living Charisms for Sustainable Human Development"), sisters have led workshops engaging 470 young people in development efforts inspired by CST.
[25] Stephen W. Mumford, *Evaluation of Loyola Institute for Ministry's "Catholic Sisters in Partnership for Sustainability": Final report*. Loyola Institute for Ministry, 2019.
[26] Sr. Eunice Ndabih, IBVM, 2020. Shared with permission.
[27] Following students' enthusiasm and wisdom, we recruited more formators to study in the second iteration of the Certificate in CST and formalized curricula revision as a course requirement. Seven congregations have since integrated CST into novitiate and/or juniorate formation.

CONCLUSION

Through accompaniment of students in this project, I have grown to better understand the complexity of sisters' positions in Church and society. East African sisters often find themselves with limited resources and in locations of unequal power. With creativity and perseverance, they demonstrate innovative leadership even in unjust situations. Sisters are moral leaders working collaboratively to advance justice and integral human development.

The student who wondered whether she was a theologian has since learned a method of practical theology and grown to understand and love Catholic social teaching. She can now do practical theology in service of her community and the Gospel. Inculturated and practical theological education that incorporates Ignatian spiritual formation has equipped these students for changemaking. Sisters' impactful community engagement work, in solidarity with poor and marginalized persons and with the natural world, then prompts further theological reflection, in a recursive cycle that deepens love and justice. As illustrated by the following essays (below, 146-65), LIM's students are joyfully sharing and living out what they have learned about Catholic social teaching, showing fidelity to the Church's social mission through love for Christ in the poor. Ⓜ

Sarah DeMarais, MS, MEd, is Associate Project Director at the Loyola Institute for Ministry and facilitates theological education for Catholic sisters in Africa. She holds a Master of Education and Bachelor of Theology and Peace Studies from the University of Notre Dame, and a Master of Science in Clinical Mental Health Counseling from Loyola University New Orleans. She has assisted with development projects in Uganda, taught, provided therapy, and directed a nonprofit residential program for adolescents. Sarah's writing has been published in *Journal of Counselor Practice* and *Louisiana Journal of Counseling*. She recently developed and taught the graduate theology course "Trauma-Informed Care for Vulnerable Youth," in which Catholic sisters in East Africa discerned how to improve youth-serving ministries in light of Catholic social thought on trauma and integral human development.

Pedagogical Reflections by East African Women Religious Alumnae of the Loyola Institute for Ministry

Srs. Charity Bbalo, Lucy Kimaro, and Jane Frances Mulongo

CATHOLIC SOCIAL TEACHING INSPIRES Women to Care for the Environment
Sr. Charity Bbalo, RSHS

My journey as a student with Loyola Institute for Ministry (LIM) began with a chance encounter in Nairobi, between the then-Superior General of my congregation and Dr. Thomas Ryan of LIM. As I look back on my experience of studying Catholic social teaching, I can say that it was God's will that I became one of the participants in the course. My understanding and appreciation of CST has improved tremendously, and I felt a desire to share my newly acquired knowledge with others. This is because I realised that knowledge of this aspect of the Catholic faith would enable people to respond more concretely and with the eyes of faith to contemporary situations.

Inspired by CST, I collaborated with the Chikuni Women's Group to develop a project by local Zambian women to make charcoal from recycled waste products in response to unsustainable tree harvesting practices. This group of widows, whose members range from 35 to 68 years of age, meets once a week to share ideas and skills aimed at improving their livelihood. All eighteen of them are Catholics from the local parish. Since January 2019, the women's group has been coordinated by Sr. Edna Himoonde, a Religious Sister of the Holy Spirit and former Capacity Building Officer at the diocesan Development Office in Monze. When she moved to Chikuni, the group was inactive and had practically disbanded. With the help of officers from the Ministry of Community Development, she organised the group and has run a number of workshops ranging from money saving to income-generating activities in a bid to help women live independent and fulfilling lives.

It is with this group of women that I shared my knowledge as part of my studies in CST with the Loyola Institute for Ministry. I did this by conducting workshops with the women on CST and the UN Sustainable Development Goals (SDGs). Since the women already had consistent times for meeting, it was easy to arrange meetings with them. Furthermore, I felt that empowering women with knowledge about CST would benefit more people because of the influential role women play in both their families and communities. As an old African proverb states, "If you educate a man, you educate an individual, but if you educate a woman, you educate the entire nation."

In my first workshop with the women, I created a poster with CST themes and pictures. For each of the themes, I used an appropriate proverb which talked about that particular theme. For example, concerning the theme about the option for the poor, I used a Tonga proverb: *"Bazike bakaabana busenga"* (slaves shared their maize bran). The proverb teaches that no matter how poor a person is, he or she can still share the little they have with the person who has less and do it without complaining. I wanted participants to see that CST was related to their experiences and was not something far removed from their lives. The pictures and proverbs proved effective at overcoming the potential barrier posed by the limited educational background of the women. The use of pictures and proverbs helped them understand the content about CST without much difficulty. This was seen by the kind of remarks they made while the themes were presented to them. For example, after a presentation on caring for our common home, one participant commented, "If you kill your mother, who will take care of you?" She said this to refer to the earth which human beings are destroying by careless practices such as indiscriminate tree cutting. The participant's comment is reminiscent of Pope Francis's words in *Laudato Si'*: "To commit a crime against the natural world is a sin against ourselves and a sin against God" (no. 6).

In subsequent meetings, I put the women in small groups to give them an opportunity to brainstorm other appropriate proverbs for each CST theme. The women were able to come up with many related proverbs. For example, concerning the theme about the call to family, community, and participation, they mentioned the following Tonga proverb: *"Simweenda alikke kaamutola kalonga"* (the one who travelled alone was drowned in the stream). The teaching behind this theme is that we do not live and work in isolation. We need to interact with others, share what we have, and seek the advice of others. Similarly, on the theme about the life and dignity of the human person, one example given was *"mwami wakailomba nyeleti kumucete"* (the rich man sought a needle from a poor person). This teaches that nobody has everything he needs in life. Even the seemingly weak and vulnerable person has something valuable to offer to others.

Later, I introduced the UN SDGs to the women and by this time, their interest in CST was already raised. The UN SDGs were introduced to the participants after they had been exposed to knowledge about CST so that they begin to see that the Church does not work in isolation on social matters. As one Tonga proverb states, *"One finger cannot crush a louse."* The current global agenda makes the Church a significant potential partner in issues related to development.[1] Partnerships enable organisations to increase the likelihood of a project's success because each entity brings its perspectives and strengths that enrich the partnership, thereby enhancing the achievement of the targeted goal.

Later, as part of my Loyola course, I worked with the Women's Group to develop a project to put our understanding of CST into action. Together with the workshop participants, we chose the CST theme of caring for our common home, and this went hand in hand with advancing UN SDG goal number 7: affordable, sustainable, and clean energy for all. We decided to focus on environmental concerns in response to local need, because one of the biggest challenges experienced in the area is tree cutting, primarily for energy consumption. When I was a teacher-educator at Charles Lwanga Teacher Training College in Chikuni, I knew a number of student teachers whose parents used proceeds from charcoal sales to pay college tuition. During school holidays, students would help their parents in preparing charcoal so that when the new school term began, the needed money was available for their educational needs. The cycle of drought and poverty is likely to continue because many of the rural populations are ignorant of the repercussions of tree cutting.

While it is well-known that cutting down trees has negative effects on the environment, the practice is rampant in Zambia. Many households depend on either charcoal or firewood for home consumption of energy. The trees cut down are not replaced by planting new trees, resulting in widespread deforestation.[2] Continued cutting down of trees has also taken its toll on the climatic pattern of the area. Due to the persistent cutting down of trees, droughts are now a common occurrence. With the worsening drought over the years, the water level in dams used for hydro-power generation has significantly reduced, leading to power deficits. In 2019, this forced the state power utility ZESCO to announce increased rationing of power of up to 15 hours per day in most residential areas.[3]

---

[1] Katarzyna Cichos, Jarosław A. Sobkowiak, Radosław Zenderowski, Ryszard F. Sadowski, Beata Zbarachewicz, Stanisław Dziekoński, eds., *Sustainable Development Goals and the Catholic Church: Catholic Social Teaching and the UN's Agenda 2030* (London: Routledge, 2020).
[2] Southern African Regional Poverty Network, "Poverty Reduction Strategy Paper for Zambia," sarpn.org/CountryPovertyPapers/Zambia/Strategy/chapter3.pdf.
[3] Chris Mfula and Taonga Clifford Mitimingi, "Electricity Price in Zambia to Double after Importing Power from SA," *Business Day,* September 17, 2019, www.businesslive.co.za/bd/world/africa/2019-09-17-electricity-price-in-zambia-to-double-after-importing-power-from-sa.

Zambia's national electricity grid is mainly connected to homes and industries in towns, leaving many rural peasants with little choice but to engage in charcoal burning as a source of energy. Zambia's challenges are not unique, as one in ten people still lacks electricity, mostly in rural areas of the developing world.[4] High electricity tariffs have forced many of the townspeople to prefer charcoal to electricity as a form of energy. This exacerbates the practice of charcoal burning beyond those with no access to the grid. Unexplained and prolonged power outages have also made the sale of charcoal a lucrative business.

As a contribution to discouraging the practice of tree cutting, the Chikuni Women's Group is creating an alternative source of energy using recycled paper. With the help of the Women's Group coordinator, Sr. Edna Himoonde, who learned about this alternative source of energy during her days as the Human Capacity Officer at the diocesan Development Office in Monze, the group came up with a project about saving trees by making charcoal out of paper and corncob ash. The women collect used paper and cardboard boxes to make a special kind of charcoal which they use instead of the traditional charcoal made from harvested trees.

After collecting the paper, the women shred it into very small pieces and then soak it in water for over a week in order to make a thick paste. Later, corn stalks and empty corn cobs are burnt to make ash which is added to the thick mixture of paper and water. When the mixture is thoroughly stirred, the pulp is scooped into small balls which are left to dry in the sun. Once the balls are dry enough, they can be used as an alternative to traditional charcoal.

This alternative form of charcoal is helping members of the Women's group desist from tree cutting. It has also helped reduce littering in their households as well as the community where the women hail from, since every piece of paper is put to good use. Previously, uncollected heaps of paper posed a danger to the health of the community. Especially in the rainy season, heaps of garbage are a good breeding ground for diseases such as cholera, which has become a yearly feature in most crowded cities in Zambia. An article about cholera hot-spots in Zambia indicates that widespread cholera outbreaks in Zambia have occurred since 1977. The last major outbreak took place from October 2017 to June 2018, resulting in a total of 5,935 reported cases and 114 deaths.[5] This has led some opposition political parties

---

[4] United Nations Development Programme, "Goal 7: Affordable and Clean Energy," www.undp.org/sustainable-development-goals#affordable-and-clean-energy.

[5] World Health Organization, "WHO Supports the Cholera Vaccination Campaign in Zambia's Hot Spot Districts as the Country Accelerates its Efforts to Eliminate the Deadly Disease," June 22, 2021, www.afro.who.int/news/who-supports-cholera-vaccination-campaign-zambias-hot-spot-districts-country-accelerates-its.

to comment in jest that cholera in Zambia is treated like an annual traditional ceremony.[6]

The initiative of making charcoal out of used paper has attracted the attention of Non-Governmental Organizations (NGOs) involved in the preservation of the environment. In March 2021, the Chikuni Women's group was invited to a Field Day where they made a presentation about the initiative to communities from across different sectors of society. With this exposure, the women have now been invited to work in collaboration with the Provincial Forestry Office. However, due to Covid-19 restrictions, no follow up meetings have yet taken place.

Currently in Zambia, trees are cut down indiscriminately for charcoal and hundreds of bags are sold countrywide on a daily basis, thus posing a risk of deforestation. Inconsistencies in the rainfall pattern are already noticeable each passing year. Pope Francis's words at the inauguration of the *Laudato Si'* Action Platform cannot be more true: "From God's hands we have received a garden, we cannot leave a desert to our children."[7] The limited rainfall cannot support the adequate growth of many crops including the staple food, maize, and this has resulted into recurrent poor yields. With unpredictable rain patterns, many families have turned to charcoal burning for their livelihood.

It is quite clear that the issue about sustainable energy is intrinsically connected to justice and care for the environment. In the social encyclical *Caritas in Veritate*, Pope Benedict XVI implores all people of goodwill to be more conscious of the way they use energy. He also calls upon developed countries and companies not to hoard all forms of non-renewable energy at the expense of poorer nations: "The fact that some States, power groups, and companies hoard non-renewable energy resources represents a grave obstacle to development in poor countries. Those countries lack the economic means either to gain access to existing sources of non-renewable energy or to finance research into new alternatives" (no. 49).

In *Laudato Si'*, Pope Francis reminds humanity that the natural environment is a common good and the responsibility of everyone (no. 95). The Pope's message is very clear: "Everyone's talents and involvement are needed to redress the damage caused by human abuse of God's creation ... each according to his or her own culture, experience, involvements, and talents" (no. 14). With this appeal from the Pope comes the realization that the care for the environment cannot be

---

[6] "Health Minister Shouldn't Treat Cholera like an 'Annual Traditional Ceremony,'" *Zambian Eye*, October 12, 2017, zambianeye.com/health-minister-shouldnt-treat-cholera-like-an-annual-traditional-ceremony-upnd.

[7] "Pope Francis on *Laudato Si'* Platform: 'What World Will We Leave Our Children?'" *Vatican News*, May 25, 2021, www.vaticannews.va/en/pope/news/2021-05/pope-francis-videomessage-laudato-si-platform.html.

tackled by only a section of humanity but requires the collective efforts of all nations in order to achieve the desired result of having a world that supports the life of its current occupants and future generations. While the initiative of making charcoal out of paper and corn cob ash may not be at a large scale, it has opened the eyes of many to see that each person, in whatever little corner they are, can join the fight against deforestation. As Fr. Agbhonkhianmeghe Orobator, the former Jesuit Provincial of the Eastern African Province, encourages, initiatives are being made to inspire people towards change so that they in turn may be drivers of much-desired change.[8]

The government of the Republic of Zambia through the Department of Forestry continually educates members of the public about the negative effects of cutting down trees through means such as radio programs aired on various community radio stations. However, the practice has continued because charcoal is the cheapest form of energy available. The far-reaching implications for this seemingly cheap form of energy make it a very expensive undertaking in the long run.

There is still need to enact vigorous campaigns to deter people from engaging in tree cutting and charcoal burning. Continued education on tree planting is necessary so that people's consciences are formed to appreciate resources meant for the common good. As Florence Caffrey Bourg points out, "Our consciences are meant to seek goodness for all, not just ourselves."[9] If these ideas were constantly translated into action by every person, we would all be conscious about our use of the world's resources and, hopefully, the current trend of tree cutting would abate.

The only way the cutting down of trees for charcoal will be brought under control is to explore and invest in cheaper and common sources of energy such as the alternative charcoal made by the Chikuni Women's Group. For as long as electricity tariffs remain high and the use of alternative sources of energy is not adequately explored, the detrimental activity of cutting down trees for charcoal will be perpetuated. It is therefore important that such innovative ideas are supported and explored on a wider scale in order to preserve trees for posterity. As I learned through my collaboration with the Chikuni Women's Group, education in Catholic social teaching can inspire and empower people to act together for environmental protection.

---

[8] The Agenda with Steve Paikin, "Agbhonkhianmeghe Orobator: Good News for Africa," YouTube, www.youtube.com/watch?v=j3YwKQrs5oo.
[9] Florence Caffrey Bourg, *Spirituality, Morality, and Ethics* (New Orleans: Loyola Institute for Ministry, 2016), 100.

"I Am My Brother's/Sister's Keeper": A Perspective from Catholic Social Teaching
Lucy Kimaro, PhD

This essay focuses on Catholic social teaching in connection to my ministry as a teacher at Catholic University of Eastern Africa (CUEA) in Nairobi, Kenya. In my teaching, it has always been my effort not only to disseminate knowledge to learners but also help them see the value of human life by being good to others, as advocated by CST. Pope Benedict XVI states that the "dynamic of charity received and given is what gives rise to the Church's social teaching" (*Caritas in Veritate*, no. 5). The empowerment of young people in a Catholic institution, like CUEA, is to enable them to build a just society. This includes students recognizing and valuing all that helps humanity live at peace with God's creation.

At CUEA, our students are prepared as Christians to advocate for justice. I often encourage them to join university student clubs that help students engage in activities connected to Catholic social teaching, including environmental, pro-life, gender clubs, and many others. It is my duty to help students realize that as faithful Christians their responsibility includes the promotion of human dignity. It entails the protection of the quality of humanness whose value is worthy of great respect. Every person is created in the image and likeness of God (Genesis 1:26–27). Thomas Massaro states that "because all humans marvelously reflect the image of God, they are all entitled to be treated with greatest respect and dignity."[10] I personally remind my students that as Christians, their faith has meaning when they practice it as directed by Jesus in the Beatitudes. For instance, in our discussion about dialogue with people of other religions, I tell them that it is important to dialogue not only through debates, but also through actions. Good deeds can change attitudes and create a situation of trust. This can be done by demonstrating a true Christian faith, the fullness of gospel values in life.

A determination to do good to humanity from all cultures, religions, and races is that for which Catholic social teaching advocates. Our Christian faith calls us to live more fully "the realities of the gospel and the reign of God," which "requires not only knowledge" but a deep and well-developed spirituality and "baptismal commitment."[11] This essay describes activities in which my students and I have been involved to transform life. To make the world a better place, we are

---

[10] Thomas Massaro, *Living Justice: Catholic Social Teaching in Action* (London: Rowman & Littlefield, 2016), 83.

[11] Barbara J. Fleischer and Tracey Lamont, "Practical Theology and Ministry Praxis," in *Introduction to Practical Theology,* ed. B.J. Fleischer and T. Lamont (New Orleans: Loyola Institute for Ministry, 2020), 4.

involved in advocacy for poverty alleviation, environmental conservation, and peacebuilding. Christian faith entails praxis, that is, action which "flows from the vision and Spirit of Christ's work in the Universe, action soaked in waters of baptism" directed towards spiritual, social, and economic transformation.[12]

Poverty Alleviation and Solidarity

Reflecting on Church teaching related to the preferential option for the poor, Massaro states that "the Church is here interpreting its entire mission as one of service to those in dire need. Bringing the gospel to people in the fullest sense means caring simultaneously for their many needs, both spiritual and material."[13] The spirit is nourished better when the body is in good health. Thus, I have used several methods to mobilize our university community to support the material needs of students from poor backgrounds.

When I was the Deputy Dean of Students some years back, I worked with student leaders to raise funds to support students in need. With permission from the university, I visited some NGOs, banks, and institutions with student leaders to explain the special needs of some students. We carried with us the academic reports and family history of these students. We collected and contributed some money to help students clear their fee balance, buy food, or pay their lease. I also mobilized students and staff within the campus under the "*Elimisha Mwenzako*" initiative, which literally meant "educate your colleague," to collect money and help some students clear their fee balance. This initiative enabled students to contribute funds to support students in need. We prepared t-shirts and organized sport competitions that enabled us to raise a reasonable amount of money. In this case, students who had not been able to do exams in the previous semester because of the fee balance were helped. The first beneficiaries were six students who each received Kshs. 50,000 (equivalent to US $500).

The initiative to be in solidarity with the needy is a serious concern in the university which respects gospel values. Such effort is reflected in the *Compendium of the Social Doctrine of the Church*'s statement that "solidarity is an authentic moral virtue" and, here quoting John Paul II, "It is a firm and persevering determination to commit oneself to the common good, that is to say to the good of all and of each individual, because we are all really responsible for all" (no. 193). Acts of kindness and generosity require commitment to love the neighbor, as stated by Jesus: "If you wish to be perfect, go, sell what you have and give to the poor, and you will have treasure in heaven" (Matthew 19:21).

---

[12] Fleischer and Lamont, "Practical Theology and Ministry Praxis," 6.
[13] Massaro, *Living Justice*, 118.

A reflection from 1 Corinthians 13:1–4 motivated many students to show solidarity with their colleagues: "If I speak in human and angelic tongues, but do not have love, I am a resounding gong or a clashing cymbal. And if I have the gift of prophecy, and comprehend all mysteries and all knowledge, if I have all faith so as to move mountains but do not have love, I am nothing. ... Love is patient, love is kind." It is love for others that pushed many students to contribute money for their colleagues to clear their fees despite their own financial challenges. As a result, we got funds that supported a good number of students. We are happy that this was a very successful initiative; some students who received support are now teachers, lawyers, or business entrepreneurs. The majority of these former students of CUEA are now working and able to support their siblings and other people. Such activities and commitments of helping needy students helped the student leaders know the importance of promoting social justice within the campus and society.

In the spirit of solidarity, the students and staff members in St. Cecilia Choir at CUEA contributed money to support one of the choir members who was facing financial difficulties. The lockdowns and many other problems caused by the Covid-19 pandemic have caused unbelievable suffering to many people, including students. Even in such a situation, individuals are not left alone with their problems to suffer. The chairperson of St. Cecilia Choir made it clear to contributors, as the Swahili proverb says, "*kutoa ni moyo siyo utajiri*" which literally means "giving is heart not wealth." So, the choir members made a lot of effort to contribute Kshs 20,000 (equivalent to US $200). This amount helped the student meet basic needs, as he continues to appeal for more financial support inside and outside the university which will help him clear a fee balance. Beyond this example, there are many other financial contributions made in the spirit of solidarity for students or staff members who lost their dear ones and are in dire need of financial assistance. The contributors are always aware of the biblical warning that neglect of the poor is a dishonor before God. The poor or needy people are special in God's eyes, and that is why communities have a grave responsibility to care for them (Matthew 25:31–46).

Working with the poor demonstrates what John Paul II called "the Gospel of life" (*Evangelium Vitae*, no. 1), hence revealing the intrinsic value of every human being, for all humans are made in God's image. It is a way of acting that encourages the promotion of justice even when the situation is hostile. Failure to support social justice in the society of our time is an unfortunate matter. Echoing Paul VI, Pope Benedict XVI calls attention to "the scandal of glaring inequalities" (*Caritas in Veritate*, no. 22). The Church demonstrates that true justice demands that one be helped and given respect based on one's dignity as God's son or daughter.

In addition to fostering solidarity within the CUEA community, I have also been involved in student and staff activities, organizing several community service trips where we demonstrated love to neighbors beyond the university. Food items and clothes were among the things collected from students and staff for people in places stricken by famine due to long-time drought. Other places visited include areas where farmers were attacked and displaced by Somali Islamic extremists in the Eastern part of Kenya, and orphanages and elderly homes in different parts of Nairobi. All these activities promote "development, social well-being, the search for a satisfactory solution to the grave socio-economic problems besetting humanity" (*Caritas in Veritate*, no. 5).

One of the university's core values is witnessing to the gospel, so the university ensures that every person who has passed through the institution understands and promotes the dignity of the human person. These students and staff work hand-in-hand with the Church to alleviate poverty in society. Efforts for poverty alleviation and support for vulnerable people have been present within the Christian tradition from the very beginning. As Massaro states, "The ministry of Jesus, in both words and deeds, was deeply wrapped up with this commitment to the well-being of the least fortunate."[14] To be a Christian entails doing works that witness Jesus Christ. Education is only useful if it can help someone change and then use that knowledge to bring changes to the lives of other people. Doing good to others is an expression of our true Christian faith and moral vision. Our CUEA students are challenged to respond to challenges their brothers and sisters face, including vulnerable groups like elderly people, physically challenged people, and orphans.

A Duty to Care for Planet Earth

Taking responsibility to care for planet Earth is part and parcel of my teaching ministry and learning in a Catholic institution like our university. The planet is the mother of all that lives, hence, she needs a lot of care. Pope Francis in *Laudato Si'* advocates for the "care for nature and for the most vulnerable" (no. 64). It is an act of faith to protect and care for the environment. The care for the earth is a human duty towards nature, so it is an important part of Christian life; working towards a common good for humanity and the world as a whole.

As part of critical gospel reflection on our social and environmental situations, I participated in the Interfaith Youth Forum on Environment and Global Strike for Climate (September 20–21, 2019; Nairobi, Kenya). CUEA was one of the organizers of the event. Participants were challenged by the discussion of the threats faced by nature. The

---

[14] Massaro, *Living Justice*, 117.

talks of the day included encouraging various religious groups to respond to Pope Francis's encyclical *Laudato Si'* in taking serious initiatives to work for the care of our environment. All participants were made to understand that environmental protection is a duty for everyone. All should give priority to this noble initiative. Through this event, students learned to respect and preserve nature. It has been a custom to care for natural sites like rivers, forests, mountains, trees, land, and others. Yet in our time the human failure to conserve nature has caused drought, famine, and diseases, just to mention a few. So many problems are caused by human carelessness and greed, especially deforestation, burning trees because of charcoal, clearing large tracts of land for farming, and extraction of minerals. An African proverb warns against such bad human behaviors: "Do not finish the arrowroot, think of the future." People are to use the gifts of creation wisely, so as to yield ample food, clothing, health, and other benefits. We are given freedom to use nature for our survival but this should be with boundaries guided by God's moral law, revealed in Scripture.

Conclusion

In a nutshell, it is important to know that whatever small part we play, such as helping a person in need or working for the care of the environment, reflects our desire to help life flourish. This work is an effort which values life and respects and promotes God's work of creation. Hence, our Christian faith action in word and deed can be the source of hope and transformation not only for individuals but also community and society. This is that for which Catholic social teaching advocates: looking at the problem of our sisters and brothers as our own, as a challenge to love our neighbor. In my ministry of teaching at CUEA, I accompany students as they practice this solidarity and thereby grow in love.

Small Christian Communities as Opportunities for Teaching and Living CST
Sr. Jane Frances Mulongo

In this essay, I wish to highlight my experiences sharing Catholic social teaching with young people and adults in Small Christian Communities (SCCs) in Kenya. SCCs were officially adopted by the Association of Member Episcopal Conferences in Eastern Africa (AMECEA) in 1976. Before that, Bishops Fritz Lobinger and Oswald Hirmer promoted the idea of Basic Christian Communities to fellow bishops in South Africa, following a practice they observed in Latin America. These bishops founded the LUMKO Missiological Institute in South Africa, developed the Bible sharing concept, prepared training materials, and trained ministers. With time Basic Christian Communities became Small Christian Communities and found their way into AMECEA countries.

The Association of Member Episcopal Conferences in Eastern Africa (AMECEA) assembled in Malawi in 1979 to assess the progress made in building Small Christian Communities (SCCs) since their inception into the local churches in 1976. They agreed that SCCs are to remain a pastoral priority in the region.[15] Quoting Pope John Paul II about the Church being a "community of disciples and confessors ... a community aware of its life and activity" (*Redemptor Hominis,* no. 21), the AMECEA bishops explained that SCCs are local incarnations of the One, Holy, Catholic, and Apostolic Church.[16] This is because in SCCs, the Church is brought down to the daily life situations and concerns of the people. In SCCs the mystery of Christ is recognized as members participate in the three elements that characterize a truly local church, namely *koinonia* (the communion of faith, hope, and love among them), the *kerygma* ("the apostolic teaching" and gospel reading, reflecting, and sharing), and *diakonia* (self-giving service for the sake of others).[17] In SCCs, members receive sacraments in a familiar environment of fraternal love. SCCs are therefore good centers for Christian formation and missionary outreach. They are a sign of vitality within the Church, an instrument of formation and evangelization, and a solid starting point for a new society based on a "civilization of love" (*Redemptoris Missio,* no. 51).

In a parish, every Catholic family is expected to belong to a SCC, which takes the name of a saint. SCCs are divided in sizes of about 10–15 families. Members of SCCs are neighbors living in one geographical area. Membership is determined by one's faith in Jesus Christ with no age limit. Meetings of SCCs are centered on Gospel reading (often the next Sunday's gospel), reflecting, and sharing. SCCs meet once a week rotationally in each other's homes. All SCCs together form a parish population, under the leadership of a pastor.

In my ministry, I strive to connect inspired members of SCCs with Catholic social teaching. CST addresses social, political, and economic injustices. It advocates justice, generosity, and mercy founded in the love of God and condemns everything that dehumanizes human beings. It also highlights the role of state, religious leadership, and social organization in this matter. CST is a rich heritage faithfully preserved and developed through gradual responses to emerging needs of human co-existence. The *Compendium of the Social Doctrine of the Church* states that principles of CST are "an expression of Christian anthropology" (no. 9). In relation to the three elements that characterize a truly local church (SCC), CST falls under the *kerygma* (apostolic teaching), and it inspires *diakonia* (service).

---

[15] AMECEA Study Conference, "Conclusions of the Study Conference of the AMECEA Plenary 1979," *African Ecclesial Review* 21, no. 5 (1979): 265.
[16] AMECEA Study Conference, "Conclusions of the Study Conference," 265–66.
[17] AMECEA Study Conference, "Conclusions of the Study Conference," 266.

Reading the Signs of the Times

Church leadership carries the responsibility of reading "the signs of the times and of interpreting them in the light of the Gospel" (*Gaudium et Spes*, no. 4). This effort is necessary to understand and meet the needs of young people. It is difficult to find enough youth from the same neighborhood who can form a viable SCC. The young people in the same neighborhood vary in age, levels of education, and interest. Young people are not yet settled; they move in and out of their neighborhoods and churches for studies, work, and seeking employment at different times, which makes consistency at meetings difficult. Indeed, exponential changes in society have affected all. With erratic attendance and participation by the young and old, some consideration and flexibility has become necessary to enable the faithful to practice their faith.

In most Catholic parishes in Kenya today, young people have been categorized in three groups. Much younger ones (still in primary school) belong to the Pontifical Missionary Childhood movement (PMC). They learn catechism, participate in liturgical dances, and do small chores like picking up rubbish in the parish compound. Junior youth, about 13–17 years old, are a group that feels lost. These are seeking identity and have many questions requiring professional handling. Some parishes have advanced more than others in preparing ministers specifically for this category of youth. Senior youth are 18 years old and above. The upper limit for this category is ambiguous. Some can be 35 years old but because they are not married, they still attend youth meetings, while others are in their early twenties and married or are single mothers who still attend youth meetings because their friends are there and they have a desire to belong somewhere and be mentored.

St. Don Bosco Youth SCC

I ministered to senior youth in Mother of the Apostles Matunda Parish in the Catholic Diocese of Eldoret (Kenya). This came after listening to parish announcements for a month and noticing with concern that youth were not being called upon to do anything. This bothered me. I noticed many young people present at Mass on Sundays but they would just walk off after. I decided to ask the parish priest if he had a plan in place for the youth, the future of the Church. His response was brief: "There is an issue," he said. I sought his permission to meet the youth the following Sunday immediately after Mass and it was granted. The turnout was amazing! Thirty of them came to meet me at that short notice. This made me happy, as I saw hope and possibility. The youth acknowledged not participating in the existing Small Christian Communities because:

- There is frequent asking for money (contributions for this and that), but they as youth do not have money.

- Some adults in SCCs criticize young people's behavior when sharing, which youth dislike.
- The youth speak "Sheng" language (a mixture of English and Kiswahili) which adults do not appreciate and may not understand.
- The youth see SCCs as a meeting for the elderly women and children, so they tell themselves, "Not now, our time will come."
- Some youth feel shy expressing themselves before a crowd and in front of elders (a developmental and cultural challenge).
- The youth tend to compare themselves in terms of dress, speech, and style, so some feel shame when they judge themselves as not good enough.
- Some find SCC meetings boring and repetitive, so they prefer to keep themselves busy with smart phones and watching television instead.
- Some are students so often in school. When at home, parents want them to do house chores and other errands.
- Some just ignore the call. Though aware that SCCs exist, they are just disinterested.

While acknowledging these challenges, the youth also expressed these desires:

- The need to have a youth project supported by the parish.
- They are technologically informed so they would like their own SCC where they can meet online and express themselves freely even beyond geographical boundaries.
- They would like to animate liturgy on Sundays, though one quipped, "The youth are never available when given this opportunity."
- They would like Church leadership to address youth requests and needs.

What these youth revealed is a microcosm of the situation in some SCCs. The Seven Step method of Gospel sharing taught widely at the beginning is no longer conversant to all. Some SCCs replace gospel sharing with rosary recitation. Leadership is sometimes a challenge, and willing lay ministers need skills. There is need for ongoing formation in SCCs if we truly consider them a pastoral priority in the church.

The agreement to start a SCC for the youth was unanimous. Permission was granted by the parish priest. We agreed to meet physically every Sunday after Mass. The group became known as St. Don Bosco Youth SCC. We learned a basic Bible sharing method known as the "Seven Steps."[18] Some youth have smart phones so sending Scripture and reflection messages on WhatsApp and taking group pictures became fast, easy, and exciting.

---

[18] *The Pastoral Use of the Bible: Gospel Sharing Methods* (Delmenville, South Africa: Lumko Institute, 1991).

The writings of Fr. Joseph Healey provided a perfect solution for the needs of this SCC.[19] He suggests a different activity for each weekly meeting:

- 1st Sunday of the month: Bible sharing
- 2nd Sunday: a seminar on a relevant subject (such as CST)
- 3rd Sunday: some hours of recollection or retreat
- 4th Sunday: an outreach activity.

We adapted these suggestions. Each Sunday has some youth responsible for its activity, to think ahead and remind participants and facilitators about what to bring, the venue, and the time. On a Bible sharing Sunday, a youth will volunteer to host the next. So far parents have been cooperative in creating a good environment for their sons and daughters to meet with fellow youth in their homes and share the Gospel. They often extend hospitality by providing some food. These youth now know each other's homes and families. On Sundays when they have seminars or hours of recollection, parish or sub-parish premises are used. On the Sunday when they go for community outreach, they gather after Mass then move as a group to the identified person or home. On arrival, their spokesperson introduces the group and states the reason of their visit. Always those in need have received them with gratitude.

I can attest that this approach is working for the youth. Practical indicators include their increased sense of responsibility and belonging to the parish. Some have become good lectors. They are getting freer, happier, and more confident. They now count on each other for support. For example, when one is bereaved, they readily gather around him or her, contribute money, and assist with chores. Those with motorbikes lift others when going for meetings, matches, or Mass. They planted some trees in their homes as a response to CST related to care for creation, and their outreach to persons in need in the parish (in response to CST on a preferential option for the poor) is ongoing. They are officially recognized at the sub-parish and parish levels, and hence assigned duties such as animating liturgies, cleaning and decorating the church, and contributing towards church projects. I would recommend this same approach to other parish youth groups.

St. Francis of Assisi SCC

St. Francis of Assisi SCC is under Kimwanga Parish in the Catholic Diocese of Bungoma (Kenya). This is my home SCC. Out of my many meetings with them, I choose here to highlight two. Once I distributed papers with the seven themes of CST translated into Kiswahili and in

---

[19] Joseph Healey, "Promoting Small Christian Communities in Africa Through the Internet," *International Journal of African Catholicism* 2, no. 1 (2011): 1–28.

picture form.[20] I asked the members a question: what do you see in these pictures? They interacted with them and responded to the question. We discussed each theme. We identified benefits in each theme when justice prevails using our context. Members saw themselves easily in theme 4 on "option for the poor and vulnerable," followed by theme 2, "call to family, community, and participation." I guess it is because they are in families, and they understand their roles well. Parents explained their role of authority and their preferential care for their elderly parents/parents-in-laws and their sick family members. Women showed good understanding of their role as home makers and expressed amazing readiness to accept and forgive their husbands and children for the sake of peace in the home.

On another visit, I joined them in the evaluation of an exercise they had completed—the making of compost pits (an agricultural project). They had worked on each other's compost pits rotationally, just as they do when hosting their SCC for gospel sharing. They went as a group digging the pits and laying materials (as they had been taught) from one family to another till all families had compost pits for manure. In the evaluation, benefits of that exercise were surfaced as follows: participation by all, the fun of working together, the advantages of using manure for farming over buying fertilizers. We traced how they had lived CST in that project. By all participating there was solidarity/team work (theme 6 of CST). The fun of working together gave them recreation, and it also pointed to the dignity of work and their self-given right to work (themes 3 and 5 of CST). They had learnt that manure was cheaper, crops using manure were healthier, and soil would not lose its nutrients as it does when fertilizer is used, which was a form of taking care of creation (theme 7 of CST). In fact, they were delighted to know that in their ordinary tasks they were living CST. They said they would maintain that merry-go-round service to each other. This decision reflected the wisdom of the whole group.

Catholic Women Association

The Catholic Women Association at Mother of Apostles Matunda Parish in the Catholic Diocese of Eldoret had me as one of the guest speakers on International Women's Day (8th March, 2021). The theme of their day was "Mwanamke Bomba," meaning a powerful, industrious, peaceful, and homemaker kind of woman. We discussed the woman's role in creating peace in the family and community (theme 2 of CST). Women with long married life experiences in the group

---

[20] Translated from English by the author for Loyola University New Orleans with permission of Catholic Relief Services, "Mada Kuu Katika Mafunzo Jamii ya Kikatoliki." Available for adults: cnh.loyno.edu/sites/default/files/images/cst_poster_adult_swahili_loyola_final.pdf and children: cnh.loyno.edu/ sites/default/files/images/cst_poster_children_swahili_loyola_final.pdf.

were invited to share what worked for them. Many shared as the audience listened intently and nodded in agreement. Among the many practical ways that worked well, three stood out: taming the tongue in conversations and guarding against the poison of gossip, hard work, and hygiene. Mama Wamboi (a teacher and member of the group) taught us how to make liquid soap to assist women to sustain home cleanliness at low costs. This free counselling session was beneficial, and the women resolved to have more of them in the future. The willingness, combined effort of sharing knowledge, and respectful manner with which this was done demonstrated equity and shared leadership and made each member feel special on Women's Day.

Moving from peacemaking in the home, we looked at the role of the state in peacemaking. We recognized village elders and their role in settling disputes, and the local police station and its role in the community. I taught them that our country Kenya is a signatory of the United Nations (UN) Charter on World Peace and gave them a bit of history about the First and Second World Wars. Some of them were young girls during World War II and recalled how their male relatives were taken to go and fight. The women were familiar with lorries (trucks) labeled UN and UNHCR (United Nations High Commissioner for Refugees) because they see them on transit to Turkana and South Sudan. These lorries bring food, medicines, doctors, and social workers to people suffering from hunger due to drought and war. We talked about UN's effort to maintain peace in the world and sustain life. Some had relatives who serve as peacekeepers in the Kenyan Army. There was appreciation for the state's efforts in peacekeeping. We sang, danced, and played different games, which made the women very happy.

Analysis and Recommendations

In my encounters with the three groups above, I have learnt that there is a lot of good will among the old and young in our parishes. They all desire to belong and participate in the Church as members of SCCs and other association groups. They learned catechism but could do with more knowledge, especially on CST, and skills to empower them as lay leaders in the Church. An example is when we had our first day of recollection with youth. At the mention of prayer, some knelt down. Many of us understood from catechism that prayer is done on the knees, a posture to show humility, but one that may not provide complete relaxation when one is recollecting. So there is need to learn other praying postures.

The style of teaching youth today must not be the kind that makes them passive recipients, but rather one that make them active determinants of what they need to solve puzzles in their lived experiences. Youth challenges today are more complex. They need youth ministers who are knowledgeable, interested, and open yet confidential, or else we may only be responding to symptoms of deeper issues exhibited by young people.

I noticed that becoming still, quiet, and getting inside oneself is a challenge for the young and old. Feedback after sessions of recollection include: "I stole glances to see how others did it," "In the short span of silence many thoughts came to my mind," "I feel uneasy within myself in silence," "I slept," etc. These are indicators too of the need for ongoing formation for our Christians, such as lessons on distractions in prayer and examination of conscience, among others. We learned the Ignatian examen prayer to guide youth in their recollection, but ongoing supports are necessary.

Phones require discipline. We have used smart phones and computers to exchange Scripture passages and reflections and to capture meeting events. However, these gadgets have other features that bring in the whole world. There is need to filter media information by the recipient, and selectively read, watch, and listen to materials displayed. Addiction to the smart phone, indeed to modern technology, is a challenge for the young and old. As religious leaders, catechists, teachers, and parents we will keep teaching morals to the best of our ability but unless the whole society cooperates on this matter of media addiction, particularly the media and entertainment industries, efforts in moral formation may be regrettably futile.

Cultures have important influence on behavior. An assumption has been passed on over generations that "young people do not speak in front of their parents," another is that "children are to be seen not to be heard." These are limiting and need to be examined. Certainly, there was value attached to them (perhaps respect), but when we gather as church (people of God), the adult needs the child just as the child needs the adult. This area is yet another one that needs wise challenging without breaking the value of culture.

I have learned that teaching adults is different from teaching youth. The youth I dealt with liked whole class input more than smaller group discussions and reporting in the plenary. We all participate in rooting out the learning and what we take away. They observed the teacher and would give feedback or check out what they perceived in terms of the teacher's behavior, knowledge, and beliefs. They enjoy summarizing their understanding in some creative ways (skits, poem, music, dance, art). We agreed to be flexible (mixing language and reducing pace) to accommodate our different needs as learners.

Adults are leaders and teachers in their own right. From the two groups of adults discussed above and others not mentioned here, adults have varied and long-lived experiences. With a trigger, such as encouragement to speak, they come out with powerful wisdom. As a facilitator, I sometimes shelved what I had prepared when I sensed a lot of energy around what came from the audience. This is because that energy is revealing what the real need could be. Adults like practical lessons beneficial to them economically, to their children or related to their social roles. They enjoy the input more and participate in a lively manner when they can see themselves in what is being said. For example, once I was sharing the story of St. Jane Frances de Chantal (whose name I bear), and at the mention that she had six children, a senior member interjected, "I beat her, I had twelve." Her spontaneous response caused laughter and was an indicator that she was listening and engaging.

Most adults already know what they want so they will be specific and selective about what to attend to and what to leave out. Many have the wisdom to sift information and share only what is necessary. I have observed that adults have greater capacity to initiate change and adapt well to changing circumstances than youth. Adults are more in touch with their humanness and can own up their mistakes with ease. Adults like to understand the message and carry it in the head or heart rather than write notes. Adults as well as youth have developed good ownership of their groups, and their leaders are chosen by themselves democratically. Reminders are essential for all as they do forget. Time keeping for meetings is a challenge to all.

I conclude by saying that SCCs and other associations in the parish are living systems. I am hopeful that when the Church (as institution) prioritizes formation of the laity, synodality will be experienced and hopefully remain the style of operating henceforth. This will be a second Pentecost for the Church (as the People of God) and the world will surely become a better place because people will feel involved, heard, and healed. Perhaps dialogue and serious ongoing faith formation will attract more men to participate actively in SCCs rather than leave it to women and children as is common today. We are blessed as a Church with increased participation by the laity; they are so gifted and willing to serve. What they need most is encouragement, empowerment, direction, and good leadership from their parish priests and the Church. M

Charity Bbalo is a Religious Sister of the Holy Spirit from the Diocese of Monze, Zambia. She is currently the Deputy Principal at St. Joseph's Girls' Secondary School in Monze. She holds a Bachelor of Arts with Education (English and Religious Studies) from the University of Zambia and a Master of Philosophy degree in Multicultural and International Education from Oslo University College, Norway. She recently graduated from the Loyola Institute for Ministry at Loyola University New Orleans and is a resource person in Catholic social teaching and the UN Sustainable Development Goals (SDGs) in both her ministry and her religious congregation.

Lucy Raphael Kimaro, PhD, is an Associate Professor at the Catholic University of Eastern Africa, Department of Religious Studies, Nairobi, Kenya. She is a member of the Grail religious community, and she is originally from

Tanzania. Her education background includes University of Dar-es-Salaam (Tanzania), University of St. Michael's College (Toronto, Canada), Catholic University of Eastern Africa (Kenya), and Loyola University New Orleans (USA). Her interests are gender issues, women's issues, interreligious dialogue, comparative religions, care for the environment, and spirituality.

Jane Frances Mulongo comes from the Catholic Diocese of Bungoma, in western Kenya. She is a Loreto sister, a Catholic nun in the Institute of the Blessed Virgin Mary – Eastern Africa Province. Jane Frances is a teacher by profession with long teaching experience. She holds a master's degree in Educational Administration and Planning from the Catholic University of Eastern Africa (Kenya). She is currently an online student at Loyola University New Orleans (USA), pursuing a Master of Pastoral Studies. Sr. Jane Frances is the new director of LUMKO East Africa. LUMKO workshops bring together pastoral workers, formators, and leaders of Small Christian Communities (SCCs) to gain skills in pastoral leadership. Last, but not least, Jane Frances is passionate about life. She believes that nurturing life is her eternal duty, the reason and purpose of her being.

Book Reviews

Follow Your Conscience: The Catholic Church and the Spirit of the Sixties. By Peter Cajka. Chicago: University of Chicago Press, 2021. 199 pages. $45.

Conscience is a topic very much alive in the discourse of moral theology today. The recent history of this idea, however, may not be known to all moral theologians who employ the concept; thus, historian Peter Cajka's book *Follow Your Conscience* stands as an invaluable resource. Cajka's work is engaging and well-written, making it an enjoyable read. With an impressive amount of research relying upon primary sources, Cajka traces the way conscience was used by Catholics, with a focus on the 1960s and thus two specific areas: conscientious objection to war and artificial contraception.

The book begins with a discussion of how the Thomistic understanding of conscience was popularized and employed in the 1960s and ends noting how conscience is still used, particularly in health care. The middle chapters are not strictly chronological, but rather discuss war and contraception, modern psychology's boost to conscience, and the conscience lobby.

Cajka's work will be significant for those moral theologians writing on the topics of war, political theology, medical ethics, and sexual ethics. Cajka demonstrates that Catholics succeeded in getting conscience language into American parlance, but he also indicates the baggage that comes with conscience and its misuse. Those whose work hinges on conscience will take care to clarify the meaning, distinguish it from previous uses and consider the critiques of twentieth century conscience use, particularly those of John Paul II and Benedict XVI, as mentioned (184–85). Cajka's narrative demonstrates the convenience of conscience, employed almost as a trump card against state or church policy one dislikes.

The moral theologian could appreciate clearer conclusions about the biggest dangers and best uses of conscience, but Cajka does not provide easy answers for the reader, who might see that conscience can actually prevent the use of reason and argument, while diminishing attention to the common good. The history reminds moral theologians to reflect upon and question the starting points for scholarship, including influences such as the surrounding culture.

Cajka's book does a lot of work in just under 200 pages, yet several points would have been strengthened by more thorough explanations. For example, Cajka notes that Catholic conscience language was originally employed against the state for conscientious objection to war, and then against the Church in protest of *Humanae Vitae*'s contraception ban. However, it is not clear how or why this transition was so easily made (89). Clearly, the concept was popular, in concert with discrediting authority (122); the missing piece here likely has to do with the dissolution of the Catholic subculture described by William Portier and changes to parish boundaries detailed by John McGreevy. Thomas Aquinas may deserve credit for the initial source of conscience language (90), but the use of conscience against the Church's stance on contraception seems more likely a function of Catholics finding a home in broader American culture than fastidious adherence to scholastic theology.

One other debatable point is the role played by priests. Whether in Catholic moral theology or Catholic history, scholars often assume an underlying ecclesiology that tends toward identifying the Church primarily as institution, with bishops and priests viewed as constituting the Church. Such lingering clericalism diminishes the thinking and activity of the laity prior to the council, while crediting priests with changes in laity. Cajka's variation of this is to see priests as "liberators of conscience and subjectivity" (193).

This seems to give priests too much credit, or perhaps not enough. As Leslie Woodcock Tentler has shown in *Catholics and Contraception*, some of the laity were employing contraception prior to *Humanae Vitae*, especially as they anticipated a change to Church teaching. Moreover, Cajka does not present evidence suggesting that lay and clerical views on contraception contrasted sharply. Rather than crediting priests and conscience, we might ask if credit goes to the increasingly pro-contraception American culture in which Catholics were now fully immersed. Conversely, a contrasting possibility not considered by Cajka would be that American Catholics first obediently followed their clergy in opposing contraception and then obediently followed their clergy in opposing *Humanae Vitae*. Future investigation and use of conscience must thus consider the ecclesiological and cultural dynamics.

MARIA C. MORROW
Independent Scholar

Losing Our Dignity: How Secularized Medicine Is Undermining Fundamental Human Equality. By Charles C. Camosy. Hyde Park, NY: New City Press, 2021. 222 pages. $22.95.

Charles Camosy argues that the last half-century saw a shift to secularization and irreligion in the United States. This produced a new distinction between "human beings" and "persons" in medical ethics and practice. This innovation is a departure from the universal Western consensus established, imperfectly practiced, but nonetheless striven for in Christianity, Judaism, and Islam that each human person possessed dignity because each reflects God's image and likeness (44). Taking its place is a secular utilitarian consensus which defined a human being's worth on "personhood," measured according to one's ability to exercise autonomous will, self-awareness, rationality, the ability to produce goods and services for a consumer economy, the capacity to make moral choices, and the ability to communicate to others (12). Those who fell short of these measures are vulnerable to being marginalized and denied care. Camosy points to institutionalized dementia patients who died of Covid as a likely early example of victims of this marginalization (15).

His first chapter gives a historical sketch of the evolution of medical ethics in the West from its majority Christian origins to its secular state today. From the beginning, Christianity made the care for the sick a core ministry. This was decisive to the development of medicine in the West, including the Catholic invention of medical ethics (28). Beginning in 1970, philosophers developed the field of bioethics with an intentionally secular outlook. They successfully worked to marginalize and exclude from their scholarly fora moral theologians and bioethicists who employed theological arguments (29–30). Even concepts with religious roots such as "dignity" have come under suspicion and criticism (31). Camosy argues that medicine is practicing the impossible, a secularized understanding which reduces the patient to an autonomous consumer of the purely clinical practices of medical professionals. The latter exclude questions and considerations of the spiritual and moral good of the people they treat.

The negative impact of this shift to utilitarian ethics is detailed by Camosy with five chapters, each dedicated to a well-known medical controversy: Jahi McMath, Terri Schiavo, the baby in Roe vs. Wade, Alfie Evans, and patients suffering from dementia. Here, the author makes concrete his critique of contemporary medical practices. His examples demonstrate what happens when medicine treats vulnerable human beings as abstract objects.

Camosy concludes with a discussion of short and medium-term strategies to reverse this course of secularization. First, a call for persons of faith to actively resist societal practices which define personhood based on one's ability to contribute, produce, and consume. This begins with a reestablishment of extended family networks which produce better care for its sick and disabled members at home. This is coupled with a call to accompany those persons who must be housed in health institutions, in particular dementia patients. This call includes lobbying government for policies to incentivize home care, and finance better care in institutions which treat elderly and dementia patients (166).

Second, Camosy calls for dialogue between people of faith and those with secular outlooks concerned about the rights and well-being of the elderly and disabled, to develop a new consensus of human dignity both inside and outside the medical field. The last chapter illustrates what we ought to do in case these efforts fail. Christians are reminded of their history of forming intentional communities of care for the sick and vulnerable and called to become loci of resistance to a secular society seeking to marginalize and dispose of them.

Camosy directs his book to the widest possible audience. He should find a ready reception amongst persons of faith. However, would secular persons he calls to dialogue want to enter such a project? Those readers find themselves absent as allies in Camosy's critique of the secular medical outlook in chapter one, only to be acknowledged and appealed to in the penultimate chapter. Secular persons may interpret chapter one as a tacit accusation of their collaboration in the secular worldview Camosy argues later they critique. They may find his call to dialogue too little, too late.

RAMON LUZARRAGA
Saint Martin's University

Disciplined by Race: Theological Ethics and the Problem of Asian American Identity. By Ki Joo Choi. Eugene, OR: Wipf & Stock, 2019. Xxi + 216 pages. $26.00.

In his book *Disciplined by Race*, Ki Joo Choi presents a timely and instructive study of the racialization of those we call Asian American. Drawing on sources ranging from popular journalism and opinion essays, social science, literary studies, to Christian ethics, the volume fills an essential lacuna in the contemporary discourse of moral theology. It offers a comprehensive ethical analysis of the racialization of Asian Americans that is theologically grounded, practically relevant, and socially aware.

More significantly, Choi's book can be assigned in both graduate and undergraduate classes, and to diverse student populations for an effective pedagogical approach to moral theological education and general education. It is especially helpful if the classes focus on the subjects of social justice, solidarity, and inter-group relations. This book can help encourage Asian American students to think more self-critically about their experiences as Asian Americans and examine how that might inform their thinking on a variety of theological questions, especially as they intersect with questions of racial justice. Likewise, non-Asian students can be encouraged to be more aware of the racial dimensions of American life in regard to Asian Americans, which are often overlooked in higher education. In this pedagogical sense, Choi's book offers two elements that set it apart from similar writings: the ends of racial recognition and the implications for social ethics.

First, Choi does not simply repeat the prevailing question of whether racial recognition matters or not. Rather, he encourages the reader to recognize how race is also *central* to Asian American lives. This point is key to understanding what the entire book is about: can we discuss what racism is and how it operates in our society if we fail to grasp how Asian Americans are impacted? Plainly, if we do not recognize the reality of race or racism in Asian American communities, then we are marginalizing Asian Americans further, or perpetuating invisibility and ignoring lived realities. Hence, Chapter 1 raises the question of whether Asian Americans are in fact persons of color. Chapter 2 examines how the idea of cultural authenticity can obscure Asian American racialization, perpetuating the idea that their identities are only defined by cultural practices and traditions while, in truth, they are also *"disciplined"* by race. Throughout Chapter 3, Choi challenges the idea of hybridity—Asian Americans' identity constructed as Americans while holding to their Asian culture. He argues that Asian Americans are being discriminated against by being given a hybrid identity, for the skewed and false idea of their culture, and for taking action to protect this mixed identity. By engaging narrative analysis of Asian American fictions, Chapter 4 demonstrates how Asian American identity is disciplined by white racism.

Choi encourages us to think about what we overlook with respect to how racism operates in our society especially if we do not attend to Asian American experiences of racism. Racism is anti-blackness, without a doubt, but anti-blackness extends to Asian Americans in such a way that their "model minority" status is intended to perpetuate the ends of anti-blackness. The model minority trope is not just a stereotype but perpetuates the interests of white racism by dividing communities of color. This is in part why racism against Asian Americans is not just an Asian American issue but also everyone's issue; we cannot understand the depths, expanse, and subjugating dynamic of white racism in the US unless we also pay attention to how racism manifests itself in Asian American lives.

Second, Choi's book leads one to question: if Asian American experiences of racism help us see the dynamic of racism more completely and with greater nuance, what are the implications for social ethics and our constructive response to racial injustice? Chapter 5 provides initial reflections, outlining misguided conceptions of autonomy and self-love as detrimental to the growth of relationality. Autonomy should be interpreted as the desire to belong, as being independent allows one to become a more effective part of the group. The author sees radical self-love as a contrast to autonomy, stating that an imbalance in the amount of self-love one has can cause unhealthy relationships. The call to action is to grow connections with one's culture by being autonomous yet keeping a balance between independence and self-love.

Choi seeks to weed out ingrained racism and group think mentalities and restore relationality, specifically within Asian American homes and surrounding communities. He highlights the ingrained racist ideas that are a part of whiteness in society. His case studies demonstrate that Asian Americans need "whiteness" in order to feel a sense of belonging, conformity to the "model minority" established by white America (151–155). Yet these expectations eliminate connectedness and promote assimilation, or even a superiority complex. In the end, Choi concludes that we need to refuse the incentives of white racism. Seeing this requires a lot of disciplining of one's own self-delusion of susceptibility and making sure it is being practiced through the discipline of loving others (176).

With these two carefully investigated elements, Choi's book is helpful in guiding both student groups and general readers to think more deeply about what racism is and how it operates in our racialized society. Asian American experiences of race or racism are, in this respect, a part of the whole picture, which entails not only thinking about Asian Americans, but also about how racism rears its ugly head against individuals and communities.

DAVID KWON
Saint Mary's University of Minnesota

Faithful Economics: 25 Short Insights. By Daniel K. Finn. Minneapolis: Fortress, 2021. 203 pages. $19.00.

Daniel Finn's *Faithful Economics* is a short compilation of standalone essays, containing reworked material from pieces Finn published over the last 25 years. As such, it provides an excellent overview of Finn's work as a Catholic economist and moral theologian. The most common recurring theme in these essays seems to be the proper relationship between mainstream economics ("the majority position within professional economics in Europe and North America," 95–96) and Catholic social teaching. For Finn, mainstream economics offers a mixed legacy as far as its usefulness for moral analysis is concerned. The titles of two of the most helpful essays in the book say it all: "What You Should Learn from Economics" and "What You Should Not Learn from Economics." In these chapters, Finn outlines some helpful tools provided by mainstream economics (such as "public policy should rely on economic incentives," 99), as well as some ways in which Catholic social teaching, heterodox economics, and behavioral economics offer valid critiques of mainstream economics.

More specifically, Finn is concerned that many American Catholics have accommodated libertarian or Republican economic ideals which stand in sharp contrast to traditional Catholic economic principles. Again, the titles of the essays make Finn's position plain: "Nine Libertarian Heresies that Tempt Neoconservative Catholics to Stray from Catholic Social Thought" is a perfect example. Since this accommodation is often done out of a concern to vote for pro-life candidates, Finn also includes a short overview of an interesting study done by three Harvard economists which finds strong evidence that abortion is a strategic issue for the Republican party, and not one based in genuine moral conviction. The reverse is true for Republican economic policies, (comparatively) rhetorically soft-pedaled, but based in actual moral conviction (171). In both cases, moral conviction is measured by the policy priorities made during periods where Republicans exercise a legislative majority.

The book is extremely readable for a lay audience, and exceptionally well laid out. Each essay is only around 2500 words, begins with a short abstract, and ends with a short conclusion. A reader could easily get the substance of a chapter simply by breezing through these short paragraphs. Professors or students looking for a text by an expert on both Catholic social teaching and mainstream economic theory will find this book extremely user-friendly. It is not, however, a comprehensive primer on Catholic social teaching. Several topics extensively covered in Catholic social teaching are not at all covered in these essays.

The thing most conspicuously missing from Finn's analysis is any treatment of Catholic social teaching on labor organizing. "This book didn't cover the thing I wanted it to" is often the laziest critique an academic can make, but in this case, I think it is warranted. Time and again in this book, Finn shows admirable concern about the "moral ecology" of markets and wishes to take seriously the Church's teaching on "structures of sin." And yet, there is very little account in this book of the moral ecology of labor relations in the United States, or how a Christian is supposed to work toward justice within them. On two occasions, Finn suggests that "if we want to reduce the injustice of abuse of power in any organization ... we can call a meeting and ask everyone to name the restrictions and opportunities each of them faces" (124). In a time where the labor movement in the United States is becoming considerably more organized and militant (there was a massive strike wave in 2018 and another just this past October), and when Catholic universities and hospitals regularly retain the services of union-busting law firms (in violation of "Economic Justice for All"), Catholic workers and institutions desperately need guidance on policies that would allow workers to exercise their right to organize for just working conditions.

CHRIS GOODING
Marquette University

Paul, Politics, and New Creation: Reconsidering Paul and Empire. Najeeb T. Haddad. Lanham: Lexington/Fortress Academic, 2021. vii + 213 pages. $100.00

Najeeb Haddad's *Paul, Politics, and New Creation* represents a revised doctoral dissertation, dealing with an important and yet controversial topic, namely, Paul's relationship to the Roman Empire and the expression of that relationship in Paul's letters. Haddad's volume consists of five chapters. The first chapter pertains to Paul's relationship to the Roman Empire in general, taking a look at the state of the question. Haddad argues that many of the scholars who focus on Paul as subversive rely on a paucity of evidence to support this view. It is difficult to reconcile the content of his epistles with an anti-Rome-imperial agenda.

Haddad's study "is a critique of counter-imperial interpretations of Paul" (2). He argues that "Paul's relationship to the civic authority is much more nuanced than previously suggested" (2–3). Paul's language is often more cosmic than political, plus he does not condemn every aspect of the present age but finds some value in it as well. Haddad explains that "parallel language does not necessarily imply a particular meaning. In this context, parallel language does not suggest a Pauline counter-imperial agenda. Parallel language can, possibly, inform a specific situation, but one cannot come to conclusions without understanding linguistic and rhetorical contexts of the Pauline texts themselves." (24)

The second chapter looks at Paul's rhetoric. Haddad maintains that "Paul does not undermine the civic authority by incorporating any of the rhetorical devices associated with figured speech in these passages" (43). The third chapter examines the way Rome became autocratic. The fourth chapter is important because it takes a look at the "church" in Paul's understanding, in light of Greco-Roman assemblies, as well as in light of the Septuagint. It becomes clear that Paul's understanding is something new, beyond either what was found in Greece, Rome, or the Septuagint (110). The argument is that ancient Greco-Roman assemblies are more likely the background than the Septuagint. For Paul, it was about living peacefully with everyone, as they were centered on Jesus's message.

I would pose one challenge here, and that would be that I think the Septuagintal background might be more significant than this chapter concedes, especially because of the context of *ekklesia* in the Septuagint, its use as a translation of Hebrew *qahal*, and the importance of this Old Testament ritual or liturgical community to what Paul discusses, e.g., in 1 Corinthians. The fifth chapter on creation and the new creation was quite illuminating. For Paul, as the chapter makes clear, the *kosmos* is creation where sin reigns. Jesus, however, reshapes "the course of history" (140) in Paul's thought, and thus we have Jesus as new Adam initiating a new creation (165).

Haddad's conclusion is spot on and provides a good summary of the volume as a whole, as when he explains: "For Paul, you were either among those 'being saved' or those 'perishing'; you are either 'in Christ' or 'in Adam.' All things not 'in Christ' will eventually fade away leaving only the *new creation* in Christ. ... Though Paul wrote in a society heavily influenced by the Roman Empire ... the empire has remarkably little role in Paul's eschatological soteriology" (175).

Haddad's volume makes an important contribution to Pauline studies and would make a fine textbook for a course on Paul, or on politics and the Bible. Any scholar interested in this topic will have to contend with Haddad's volume, which is erudite, and yet any graduate student would find the book sufficiently engaging and accessible.

JEFFREY L. MORROW
Seton Hall University

The Fullness of Free Time: A Theological Account of Leisure and Recreation in the Moral Life. By Conor M. Kelly. Washington, DC: Georgetown University Press, 2020. ix + 249 pages. $159.95 hardcover, $39.95 paperback, $39.95 ebook.

Conor Kelly's erudite and accessible vision of free time joins the ongoing theological and philosophical conversation whose diverse voices include Marva Dawn (*Keeping the Sabbath Holy*), Courtney Goto (*The Grace of Playing*), James Evans, Jr. (*Playing: Christian Explorations of Daily Living*), David Miller (*God and Games*), and Robert Johnston (*The Christian at Play*). Kelly "seeks to provide a deeply theological vision for the fullness of free time and then explore how the resources of theological ethics, especially the Catholic understanding of solidarity, can help moral agents transform leisure and recreation for themselves and in their communities in order to make this goodness of free time more apparent and appealing" (xiv). He describes these two aspects of free time over eight chapters which culminate in a compelling conclusion emphasizing the moral obligation of free time and less freedom for personal gratification.

Kelly starts to convey the goodness of free time by describing the nature and purpose of leisure and recreation with two lenses:
1) Mihaly Csikszentmihalyi's definition of "flow" as an "optimal experience" of "[being] so involved in an activity that nothing else seems to matter" (9–10) and 2) Augustine's distinction between enjoyment and use. Leisure describes free time activities of flow enjoyed as intrinsic goods which preview heavenly rest. Recreation describes non-flow free time activities used as instrumental goods which refresh people for vocational service. These theoretical definitions materialize into ordinary life via everyday solidarity. This principle, which ethically orients free time toward relationality, also is the virtue ensuring everyone's access to the relational goodness of leisure and recreation, by reforming structures which restrict or abuse free time. In these ways, Kelly envisions free time as "a genuine opportunity for the greater integration of faith and life" (56).

In the second section, the principle and virtue of everyday solidarity puts leisure in the service of relationality and structural reforms. This ordering of leisure follows Aquinas's ordering of love, functioning as evaluation of one's time spent with God, self, and others. Since cultures of overwork and poverty block the enjoyment of leisure, Kelly draws from Catholic social teaching to ground calls for legally mandated living wages, vacation time, and parental leave "so that free time will be less of a luxury good and more of an everyday opportunity for moral growth and relational fulfillment for all" (83).

The principle and virtue of everyday solidarity also envisions the use of recreational pursuits in such a way that "moral agents can approach their free time with the kind of intentionality that will allow this area of life to support their full flourishing instead of becoming a passive way of killing time" (205). For example, everyday solidarity encourages television watching to become a communal discussion of its content. This coincides with reforms easing access to alternative relational recreation activities, so that television's dominance of free time does not deaden one's sense of interconnectedness and commitment to the common good. Similarly, everyday solidarity encourages uses of digital media as opportunities to honor human connection and practice genuine empathy, and advocates reforms of reduced access costs and increased public internet availability to address digital divides. Everyday solidarity envisions sports as avenues to cultivate relationships with fellow fans and compassion for the humanity of athletes, while proposed reforms address the unethical influence of profits for broadcasting events and building stadiums. Everyday solidarity also cultivates a sense of travel with biblically hospitable relationality that maximizes tourism's benefits for the host while minimizing the visitor's damage to the environment.

Overall, *The Fullness of Free Time* is an instructive resource for higher-level undergraduate classes in theology or ethics, and best suits graduate seminars of spirituality and Catholic social teaching. It offers opportunities for personal spiritual introspection and discernment, especially when read with other theological and philosophical articulations of the greater integration of faith and free time in Christian living.

G. D. JONES
Duquesne University

The Abuse of Conscience: A Century of Catholic Moral Theology. By Matthew Levering. Grand Rapids, MI: William B. Eerdmans, 2021. viii + 360 pages. $45.00.

Matthew Levering's *The Abuse of Conscience* joins the body of work in moral theology that examines, explores, and delineates intellectual strands, features, and thinkers in twentieth-century moral theology. Levering's stated aims are "to introduce the main paths taken by Catholic moral theology in the twentieth century and to expose the deficiencies of the dominant academic versions of conscience-centered Catholic moral theology" (1). He specifically traces two intellectual trajectories within moral theology. The first surveys how pre-conciliar "conscience centered morality of the manuals based upon law" transitions into "conscience centered morality in an existentialist, freedom focused framework." The second considers how pre-conciliar attempts to move away from manuals to a more scriptural, virtue framing of moral theology continues in some post-conciliar Thomistic moral theology. Levering provides a balanced assessment of most thinkers, even as his preference for the second trajectory is clearly stated. He writes, "The path forward today consists in integrating the best biblical and Thomistic insight with an existentialist emphasis on a personal encounter with the Lord Jesus Christ. Conscience will continue to have a significant role, but now within the virtue of prudence" (16).

Levering's diagnosis of the problem, retrieval of an alternative path, and a proposed way forward unfolds over four chapters examining conscience in relation to 1) the Bible, 2) the moral manuals, 3) the Thomists, and 4) German thought. After providing a thematic overview in each chapter, Levering spends time explicating the work of several representative thinkers. The ecumenical group of philosophers and theologians include, for example, George Tyrrell, Philippe Delhaye, Michael Cronin, Michel Labourdette, OP; Servais Pinckaers, OP; Heidegger, Bonhoeffer, Rahner, and Ratzinger.

Levering helpfully traces how early twentieth century attention to scripture was a pivot from the moral minimalism often attributed to the manuals. Chapter three picks up the shift away from the moral manuals. Levering evaluates the work of several Thomists chosen for their attention to conscience in the context of Aquinas's full ethics and the virtues, specifically prudence. He concludes that Thomists Labourdette (1950s) and Pinckaers (post-Vatican II) "provide a rich understanding of conscience within prudence and the Christian moral life as a whole" (124).

Levering's choice of manualists in chapter two was refreshing. Even as Levering finds much to appreciate in the manualists, he thinks the stress they placed on conscience and law ultimately "distort the shape of Christian ethics." Whereby, a "better path consists in apprehending the Decalogue, and the moral precepts taught in the New Testament within a virtue-centered framework, constituted by communion with Christ and the grace of the Holy Spirit. Conscience has its proper role within this framework" (82–83). Picking up the conscience-centered theme in chapter four, Levering traces how German philosophical and theological thought influenced approaches to conscience, resulting in recasting conscience's centrality in an existential, transcendental key.

Levering concludes his study with a brief look at ethicists James Keenan, SJ, and Reinhard Hütter. Each reader will need to determine if the Fuchs-Rahner-Keenan vision of conscience is problematic and the Labourdette-Pinckaers-Hütter approach the solution. This reviewer sees value in elements of both approaches, with neither being sufficient in its entirety or on its own.

Every author makes choices, and Levering's review and sketching of twentieth century moral theology is masterful. Yet Levering's lack of sustained engagement with writings by women moral theologians (e.g., Anne E. Patrick, Linda Hogan) is notable. All 26 scholars plus the two in the conclusion are men. Likewise, the book's structure meant that the work of post-Vatican II biblical ethicists William Spohn and Lucas Chan, SJ, or Dominican biblical scholar Barbara Reid were not evaluated. This reviewer would look forward to a future work by Levering engaging these and other scholars.

The ninety-two pages of footnotes (almost a third of the book) provide additional insights and extensive commentary about each chapter or scholar, along with Levering's own analysis and positions. The thirty-six-page bibliography is a wonderful gift for researchers. All told, this book adds value to any theological library. It is most suited for PhD students, researchers, faculty, and libraries. Faculty could use it for lecture preparation regarding different intellectual strands and thinkers within twentieth century moral theology.

KATHRYN LILLA COX
University of San Diego

The Good Kill: Just War and Moral Injury. By Marc LiVecche. Oxford, UK: Oxford University Press, 2021. xvii + 235 pages. $61.50.

Western military forces acknowledge that character and ethical decision-making are among the most important components of training for soldiers. There are foundational laws to learn around rules of engagement, such as who and what are legitimate targets, but the kind of complex ethical dilemmas soldiers can face entails that a simple outline of rules is not sufficient preparation. Moreover, soldiers themselves can carry the wounds of moral injury when they have done or witnessed things that transgress their moral values or they have felt betrayed by commanders. Ethical challenges are only deepening with the increase of terrorism, urban warfare, non-state actors, use of children and non-uniformed combatants, artificial intelligence (AI) and autonomous weapons systems (AWS), and cyber and space battlespheres. These factors underline the critical importance of equipping soldiers, of all ranks, with moral courage and ethical foundations.

"When is it ever moral for soldiers to kill?" is Marc LiVecche's central question in *The Good Kill.* LiVecche, a research fellow and ethics teacher at the Stockdale Center for Ethical Leadership at the US Naval Academy, developed his dissertation into this book while a visiting scholar at Oxford University. Previously he had taught history and ethics at the site of the Auschwitz-Birkenau concentration camp in Poland, an experience he says rendered him unfit for pacifism.

LiVecche suggests that pacifism's objection to the use of force could be morally injurious if it leads to one's neighbor suffering injustice. LiVecche argues that convictions of a modified Just War theory are what will best equip soldiers to practice ethical combat behavior and avoid the wounds of moral injury. In one sense moral injury is a sign a person involved in perpetrating evil does have a conscience. Yet even killing an enemy in justified combat can leave a moral wound and, research shows, increase the chance of suicidal ideation. Grief and guilt can also emerge from what might be arguably morally defensible actions—as with accidental killing or a tactical need to kill a child (when used as shields or to trigger IEDs).

A pastoral response to moral injury includes therapeutic treatments but also liturgical space for seeking forgiveness and reconciliation. A strategic military response is to help prevent soldiers being exposed to moral injury. In modern warfare, avoiding moral challenges is unrealistic. LiVecche grapples with a Christian ideal of pacifism and ethical responsibility of showing both love and justice towards one's neighbor. He explains it is appropriate not to want to kill another person made in the image of God, and yet be willing to kill if necessary to stop the wellbeing of others being encroached. Love for neighbors may morally lead to using military force to hold back the unjust actions of others, in order to defend the common good and promote human flourishing.

LiVecche acknowledges an appeal to "love one's enemy" is a conceptual stretch, but exercising the "golden rule"—doing unto others what you would want them to do to you—is a helpful loving framework that respects the dignity of the other. This upholds just war principles of proportionality and discrimination, and conventions against cruel weapons and torture. Deeply understanding and applying this moral framework is what he suggests will best keep soldiers from unethical behavior and safeguard their mental health following armed conflict.

A unique contribution of the book is suggesting how to view an enemy soldier. To dehumanize and transgress the dignity of any person is problematic; seeing them as "comrades in arms" or essentially decent human beings has helped. However, this is increasingly difficult when an enemy does not follow the same rules of warfare or other military engagement. LiVecche helpfully suggests viewing the opposing force as made up of "enemy-neighbors." He advocates the posture of not aiming to kill but merely stop the enemy and view oneself as a mournful warrior who kills with regret. To carry guilt when a soldier kills morally is not necessary, but it is appropriate to know the weight of the action and acknowledge it as regrettable. This is necessary psychological and spiritual preparation for ethical combat behavior and avoiding moral injury.

This calls for psychological and spiritual preparation in moral courage and analysis before, during, and after deployment. LiVecche raises critical just war frameworks that add moral protection for the soul in preparation for military engagement, but also points towards the importance of understanding community and reconciliation space for homecoming and post-traumatic growth.

LiVecche artfully links contemporary psychology with ancient philosophical and theological wisdom, mixed with the testimony of veterans and insights of military ethicists. He navigates the reader through pacifism, just war theory, and the realism of "killing is wrong, but in war it is necessary," pointing to the ethical left and right of the arc that guides when it is justifiable. *The Good Kill: Just War and Moral Injury* thus upholds a high ideal of ethical behavior and morality, yet with a realistic understanding of how to navigate the moral bruising of what soldiers are required to do. Because of its unique approach to the topic of moral injury, this work is especially helpful for soldiers and military instructors and others who work with the armed forces, as well as chaplains, veteran welfare workers, and military ethicists and theologians who study armed conflict.

DARREN CRONSHAW
Australian College of Ministries, Sydney College of Divinity

Aquinas and the Infused Moral Virtues. By Angela McKay Knobel. Notre Dame, IN: University of Notre Dame Press, 2021. xi + 214 pages. $65.00.

Thomistic moral theologians have long puzzled over the question of how the virtues we acquire through the exercise of our natural capacities for action relate to those infused in us by God, through which our activity is reoriented to the end of supernatural beatitude. Are the former simply replaced by the latter when one enters a state of grace, or is there a role for both kinds of virtue in the moral life of the Christian? In *Aquinas and the Infused Moral Virtues*, Angela McKay Knobel seeks to carve out a space between these two opposing positions, arguing that while the "cultivation of the infused virtues is the only coherent goal of the Christian moral life" (150), the acquired virtues nevertheless persist in those transformed by grace as residual dispositions inclining them to act in a manner proportionate to their natural fulfillment (2). Although such dispositions no longer function as primary principles of action, Knobel suggests that they are "what we end up cultivating when we fall short of the goal of the Christian moral life" (2).

Knobel takes as her starting point Aquinas's theory of human nature and its capacities, contending that this theory "provides the bedrock not just for his account of natural virtue, but also for his account of supernatural virtue" (4). Despite assuming a fundamental correspondence between the two, Knobel primarily highlights the ways in which they differ, appealing often throughout her study to Aquinas's claim that infused virtue is only possessed *quasi imperfecta*. Knobel takes this claim to mean that, while acquired virtue enables one to reason from naturally known principles to a correct conclusion about what is to be done and to act accordingly, infused virtue confers no similar ability (68). She argues that this is because "reason is impaired in its ability to recognize what acts are proportionate to supernatural beatitude," such that even after we receive the infused virtues "we still need the help and guidance of the Holy Spirit" (68). Thus, whereas an ethic of acquired virtue is "centered around the notions of self-perfection and self-sufficiency," an ethic of infused virtue is necessarily "an ethic of humility and dependence" (178).

Knobel's understanding of this asymmetry between acquired and infused virtue informs her analysis at almost every level and provides the key to understanding her own distinctive solution to the problem of how the two are related. Knobel refrains from saying, as William Mattison does, that our acquired virtues are somehow transformed into infused virtues when we receive grace. To her mind, the difference between the two is so radical that, were this the case, it would not be clear "how anything at all persists through the transformation" (166).

Thus, intending to preserve the integrity of human agency, Knobel instead emphasizes the ways previously acquired virtues continue to influence our behavior even after our natural capacities have been transformed by grace. In this respect, Knobel's solution seeks to reflect more accurately the reality that Christians "not only remain capable of seeing the world in a light other than that of faith, but ... frequently act in accord with that lesser vision" (155). Despite the fact that the infused virtues are bestowed all at once upon the reception of grace, Knobel stresses that it takes time for them to become firmly established in us, such that "our first steps in the life of grace are likely to be hesitant and uncertain" (152).

This important insight finds further expression in Knobel's discussion of the Holy Spirit's involvement in graced human action. Regarding this topic, Knobel claims not simply that "we should always seek the Holy Spirit's guidance," but, more pessimistically, that we should "always distrust the dictates of our own reason" (72). Knobel's point, of course, is that even after reason is transformed by grace, it will continue to be habituated in ways that impede its ability to order our actions to a supernatural end. However, by pitting the guidance of the Holy Spirit against the activity of reason as she does, Knobel risks undermining the integrity of human agency in an entirely different way than the transformation view. Although she states explicitly that the Holy Spirit "does not act or choose for us" (73), her comments elsewhere seem to position this divine guidance in a competitive relationship with the exercise of our rational faculties. As she puts it in the concluding chapter, "Insofar as we fail to seek out divine guidance and are content to rely on our own reason, we will fall short of living the life made possible by grace" (171). Granted, Knobel acknowledges that "the most one can do, having prayed sincerely for guidance, is to act in the manner one's conscience dictates" (171). But why should these two activities be opposed, as if the Holy Spirit's prompting were present in one but not the other? After all, who is to say that the Holy Spirit cannot guide us precisely in and through our rational processes of moral deliberation?

This minor criticism notwithstanding, Knobel's book is a fine study of Aquinas's theory of virtue that will be essential reading not only for scholars working in the field of Thomistic ethics, but for any moral theologian interested in reflecting on the dynamics of graced human action.

NICHOLAS OGLE
University of Notre Dame

Crossing Wires: Making Sense of Technology, Transhumanism, & Christian Identity. By Joel Oesch. Eugene, OR: Wipf & Stock, 2020. xv + 153 pages. $22.00.

In *Crossing Wires,* Joel Oesch seeks to provide readers with "a primer on the world of digital technologies and the transhumanist philosophy that carries them forward, both with its possibilities and its consequences" (xi). He argues that a poignant and discerning response to transhumanism is needed. The book is framed around the question "What makes humans, human?" (xiii) It is written in a conversational and homiletic style and intended to be read with others, in a Bible study group or a Christian community.

Oesch perceives transhumanism as a threat to the biblical understanding of human nature. What he proposes is a Christian solution that counters the risk of heresy it poses. Beginning with a critical introduction of transhumanism in Chapter 1, Oesch raises an urgent warning: "The explicit goal of transhumanism is to change humanity into something else!" (2) He presents transhumanism as replacing the body with the mind and aiming to make humans into superhumans characterized by super-longevity, super-intelligence, and super-wellbeing. According to Oesch, what transhumanism propagates is a secular philosophy fundamentally incompatible with Christian theology. Chapter 2 establishes the link between current technologies related to online social networks and the transhumanist future. Oesch judges that "social networks are the gateway drug to transhumanism" (31) and stresses that physical proximity is essential to human experience. In Chapter 3, Oesch locates transhumanism within the "Myth of Progress." He proposes "a strong view of sin" (47) and the way of the cross to counter the threat of transhumanism.

Chapter 4 to Chapter 6 focus on critiquing the transhumanist understanding of body and freedom by quoting from Charles Taylor, John Paul II, Martin Luther, and Dietrich Bonhoeffer. Oesch begins with the definition of freedom as "the ability to make choices without restraint" (52). By referring to the movement of bodyhacking and the potential for digital sex, Oesch cautions against the transhumanist threat to the human body, sexuality, and gender, stating that it will "leave us with a loss of marital fidelity and long-term blessing of children while chasing unlimited forms of sexual pleasure divorced from procreation and commitment" (72). He emphasizes that the Christian understanding of embodiment, especially regarding sexuality, is a gift. In Chapter 6, Oesch revisits the definition of freedom in light of the changing nature of politics and civil life as it relates to community. He concludes that the Christian understanding of freedom is less about autonomy but is bound to liberation, sharing, and submission.

Moving from the challenges transhumanism presents to human sexuality and political communities, Chapter 7 argues that transhumanism threatens the *telos* of daily Christian living structured as work, play, and rest. Oesch reminds his readers that "the key here is understanding human nature" (105). He deems that transhumanism's total denial of the Christian truth regarding the existence of an irreducible human nature poses a threat to the future of education and work and disconnects human flourishing from value.

Oesch constructs his Christian theological understanding of human nature in the last two chapters. He is convinced that such proper understanding in light of Scripture will "lead us to a position in which we can freely use technologies without becoming slaves to them" (114). Oesch judges that while transhumanism promises that "a human being was destined to become a god" (126), Christians should look to "the resurrection of Jesus to make humans, human again" (126). He articulates "a picture of Christian anthropology" (130) characterized by the uniqueness of human identity. Oesch's theology is built on what he calls "three pillars" of human qualities: vocation, embodiment, and church-community. They coincide with "a creedal format where ... each one [is linked] to a person of the Trinity" (130).

While Oesch raises many important issues in *Crossing Wires* regarding the Digital Age, his discussion on human nature and the transhumanist threat lacks scholarly rigor. Though Oesch stresses a biblical foundation for proper understandings of human nature, body, sexuality, gender, and freedom, there seems to be no engagement with recent discussions in biblical studies, theological anthropology, feminist theology and ethics, and gender studies. The book might serve as a conversation starter in lower-level undergraduate classes.

SIMEIQI HE
Drew University

Brown Church: Five Centuries of Latina/o Social Justice, Theology, and Identity. By Robert Chao Romero. Downers Grove, IL: InterVarsity, 2020. ix + 235 pages. $20.99.

In *Brown Church: Five Centuries of Latina/o Social Justice, Theology, and Identity*, Robert Chao Romero offers a historical-theological account of the long history of Latina/o experiences throughout the modern era. Chao Romero's primary concern is to unite two areas of studies he considers disconnected: Chicana/o Studies and theology. Therefore, he combines the broader history of Latinas/os in Latin America and the United States with the religious and theological contributions members of the community have made to Latina/o religion and culture. Such enterprise introduces the reader to the concept of

"Brown Church" and "Brown Theology," which Romero views as often overlooked, if not altogether ignored, aspects in theological discussions, as they represent the long struggle for equality and racial and social justice in Latin America and the United States.

In eight chapters, not including the introduction and conclusion, Chao Romero weaves together a narrative that includes both local and broader pursuits of social justice. Each chapter discusses a certain moment in Latina/o history he then connects to an important historical figure and response to the social and racial communities faced at given times. To connect Chicana/o Studies with theology, Romero discusses *El Plan Espiritual del Aztlán*, the 1969 Chicana/o movement's manifesto. Afterward, he presents what he calls *El Plan Espiritual del Galilee* as Jesus's word of the Good News rooted in discipleship and restoration. Based on this framework, Romero introduces historical events and figures to outline Latina/o people's long-standing contributions to equality and justice of the past five centuries. Readers will learn about key figures in the Latina/o community such as Bartolomé de Las Casas, Garcilaso de la Vege el Inca, Guaman Poma, Sor Juana Inés de la Cruz, Padre Antonio José Martínez, César Chávez (the author consistently uses this spelling with accent marks in his work), and Saint Oscar Romero.

Methodologically, the author does not offer an extensive historical analysis of Latina/o studies. Instead, he presents snapshots of events allowing him to weave a tapestry of how the Latina/o community became a "Brown Church." It is important to note that Chao Romero does not have a denomination in mind to which he attributes the term. Instead, his project is ecumenical in scope, allowing him to explore, for example, the connection between Catholic liberation theology and the *Misión Integral* of the evangelical branch of Latin American religion. Chao Romero's commitment to dialogue and his critical examination of religion's oppressive and liberating roles for the community may be one of the book's greatest assets.

Despite the book's important insights, I see two missed opportunities in Chao Romero's work. First, Chao Romero promises that he seeks "to engage the study of Latina/o spirituality utilizing the critical race theory (CRT) framework of community cultural wealth" (10). Unfortunately, he does not follow through with his promise. Although he mentions CRT occasionally in some of his chapters, it remains unclear how his research benefitted from such a theoretical framework. Secondly, it is striking that Chao Romero seems to exclude LGBTQ+ social justice advocates from his work. For example, scholars such as Gloria Anzaldúa who identified as a queer scholar in Chicana/o studies has frequently debated gender oppression in her works. One must raise the question of whether there is room for LGBTQ+ people in Romero's "Brown Church."

Lastly, a brief word on terminology: in the spirit of self-naming, Chao Romero chooses to use the term "Latina/o" in his book to identify the individuals and communities discussed in his book. A brief section on why he chooses such terminology would have been a helpful addition to *Brown Church*, since other scholars and communities use terms such as Latin@, LatinaXo, Latinx, or Latine to identify themselves. It also remains unclear whether he distinguishes between different groups as Latinas/os or whether he uses it as a universal term for anyone of Latin descent.

Overall, readers familiar or unfamiliar with Latina/o history and theology will find great value in *Brown Church*. It serves as a concise and easily accessible survey of key events in Latin American US history and theology and their communities' struggle for equality, justice, and identity. Readers will gather important historical-theological information and a list of established and up-and-coming scholars in Latina/o theology, which invites us to inquire further into this important field of study. This book would also serve as a valuable contribution in undergraduate and graduate classrooms alike.

JENS MUELLER
St. Joseph's College of Marian University

Articles available to view
or download at:

jmt.scholasticahq.com

The Journal of moral Theology is Sponsored by:
Mount St. Mary's University

The School of Arts, Humanities, and Social Sciences
Saint Vincent College

www.ingramcontent.com/pod-product-compliance
Lightning Source LLC
Chambersburg PA
CBHW062045220426
43662CB00010B/1662